ALONG THE COTSWOLD WAYS

By the same author

ALONG THE CHILTERN WAYS

ALONG THE COTSWOLD WAYS

G. R. Crosher

CASSELL
LONDON

CASSELL & COMPANY LIMITED
35 Red Lion Square, London WC1R 4SG
and at Sydney, Auckland, Toronto, Johannesburg
an affiliate of
Macmillan Publishing Co., Inc.
New York

First published 1976
1st edition, 2nd impression June 1977

ISBN 0 304 29462 4

Printed in Great Britain by
Fletcher & Son Ltd, Norwich

Contents

Illustrations

Illustrations

Between pages 114 and 115

All the photographs were specially taken for this book by W. R. Crosher

To
MADELINE and WILFRID
who in different ways
helped a lot

Along the Cotswold Ways

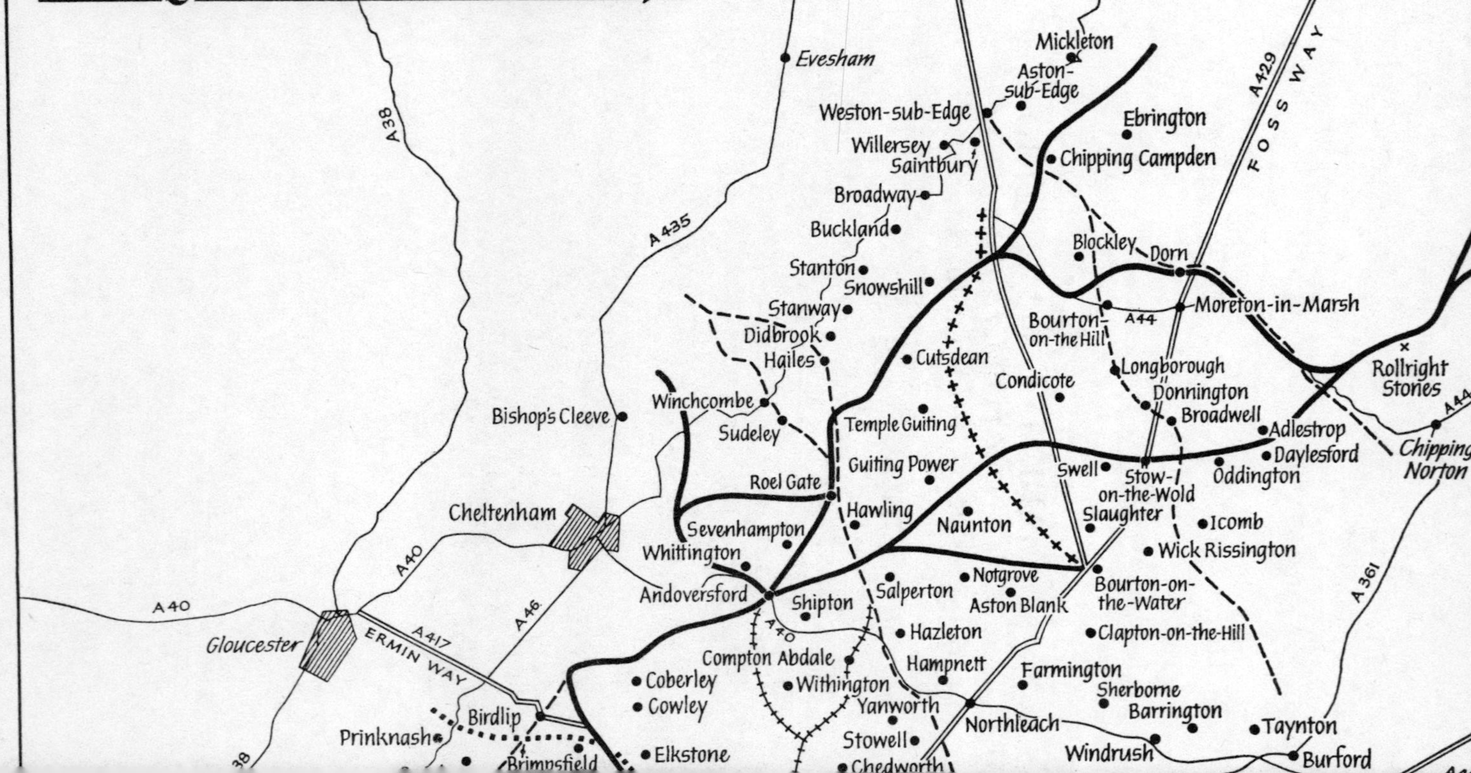

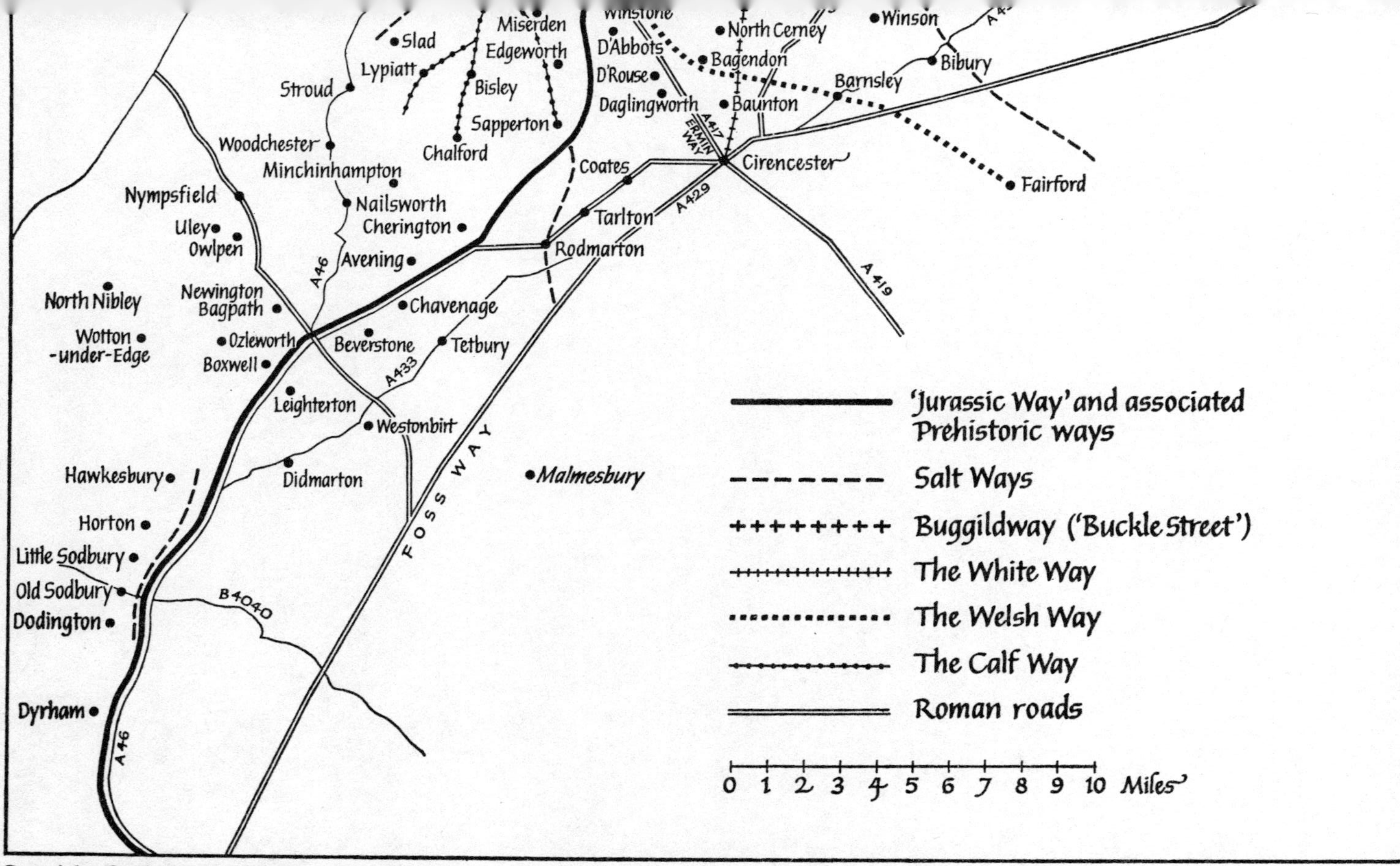
Winstone
Miserden
Edgeworth
Slad
Lypiatt
Stroud
Bisley
Sapperton
Chalford
Woodchester
Minchinhampton
Nailsworth
Cherington
Nympsfield
Uley
Owlpen
Avening
A46
North Nibley
Newington Bagpath
Chavenage
Wotton -under-Edge
Ozleworth
Beverstone
Tetbury
Boxwell
A433
Leighterton
Westonbirt
Hawkesbury
Didmarton
Malmesbury
Horton
Little Sodbury
Old Sodbury
Dodington
B4040
Dyrham
A46
FOSS WAY
D'Abbots
D'Rouse
Daglingworth
North Cerney
Bagendon
Baunton
A417
ERMIN WAY
Coates
Tarlton
Rodmarton
Cirencester
A429
Winson
Bibury
Barnsley
Fairford
A419
'Jurassic Way' and associated Prehistoric ways
Salt Ways
Buggildway ('Buckle Street')
The White Way
The Welsh Way
The Calf Way
Roman roads
0 1 2 3 4 5 6 7 8 9 10 Miles

Author's Note

The Ordnance Survey maps (1 : 50,000 series), which cover the ground slightly differently from those of the old one-inch series, require seven sheets to include all the places visited in this book. Sheets 151 and 163 cover most of Cotswold; lesser areas are to be found on the surrounding sheets: 150, 162, 164, 172 and 173.

Though this book includes many ways by which the varying parts of Cotswold may be visited, those wishing for a footpath route may be interested in the map of 'The Cotswold Way', published by the Ramblers' Association and available in most local bookshops. It follows only occasionally that part of the Prehistoric Way sometimes labelled 'The Cotswold Ridgeway'; it is more a series of linking and signposted footpaths comprising a walk of about 100 miles keeping mainly to the Edge.

ONE

Towards the Beginning

There are many ways by which the visitor can approach the Cotswolds. He can, if intent only on the show-pieces and little inclined to be critical, plan a route linking the well-known tourist attractions ... and so at the end of a day have gathered a few, often crowded impressions and little else. Or he can, if not in such a hurry and wishing to see a little more than the immediately obvious, turn aside along some inviting lane and meander ... which will often provide refreshingly different views of the hills and almost certainly will lead him to some of the more or less featured villages. Or, by choosing in advance a centre—the towns have a selection of hotels and some villages have inns with accommodation—he can venture on a more detailed series of routes, along the river valleys perhaps, linking a succession of 'beauty spots' (which the experienced visitor will visit out of season). Or, if seeking a more intimate approach, he can leave the car altogether and take to footpath or bridle-way....

Of course, those who decide to travel leisurely will see most; and for today's visitor there remains in Cotswold very much more than shots for his camera and items for the 'Olde England' calendars. When travelling anywhere in England one is passing through a landscape which has grown through thousands of years—and this is, perhaps, clearer on Cotswold than almost anywhere else. To give some coherence to what may easily become a random confusion of impressions, to gain some understanding of what is to be seen, the visitor needs a mental outline—not so much a route on a map but, rather, an itinerary of the changes brought by time. It need not be detailed; indeed, a wider though slighter understanding may help the visitor to see more than will be caught by those knowledgeable only in, for example, Iron Age fortifications or the architectural fashions of the eighteenth century. Detailed but limited knowledge may hamper the less erudite of us.

To find a satisfying approach to such a region as Cotswold it is probably advisable initially to look away from the more photogenic places (which can, of course, be visited en route) and seek a starting point nearer the source of the long process by which nature's hill-scape has been changed to its present appearance. Such a starting point will not be among the trim fields of a valley, still less among the antique shops and cafés of a recognised tourist attraction. The story, as far back as we can reasonably go, began on the hills themselves. It is there we must start, approaching Cotswold from a distance in both time and space.

One such starting point may be found a few miles east of the valley in which lies Moreton-in-Marsh, at the Rollright Stones standing high on the boundary between Oxfordshire and Warwickshire. The Stones, which comprise a circle, a cluster of slabs which once formed a burial chamber, and a monolith of unguessable significance, are worth visiting for themselves—and, more incidentally, for the view of the fields tilting down to form valleys that contribute to the middle Thames. Though as yet the ancient monument has attracted little detailed investigation, the works can be approximately dated: the stone circle is accorded to the Bronze Age—that is, its stones were dragged from the surrounding hillsides and set in their present upright positions rather more than four thousand years ago; the burial chamber, clearly Neolithic, is several centuries older, while the monolith was probably erected between these two periods, for early peoples, it seems, often added to sites hallowed by their predecessors. So much the visitor may gather from a brief pause on a family outing . . . though perhaps high summer is not the best time for a visit. A November afternoon with mist creeping up from the lowland or an April dusk when the shadows are blurring will make the surrounding and regrettably necessary fences less obtrusive than the clusters of sombre pines and larches; the visitor may then recall that, like many a prehistoric site, the Rollright Stones have gathered legends—which, even if they sound all but ridiculous to our twentieth-century ears, can hint of ancient mystery. The curious about such matters will find details in the writings of Sir Arthur Evans, a great collector of folk-tales. At some remote but unspecified period a king and his troops (including some knights who at the time were plotting against their royal master) were met at Rollright by a witch who, apparently to demonstrate her occult skills rather than from military necessity, turned them all to stone: His Royal Highness into the rearing monolith still known as the King

Stone, his troops into the circle of the King's Men, the Whispering Knights into the burial chamber. Indeed, the legend-addict can add more, for the King Stone is one of those monoliths which goes down to a stream to drink when it hears the clock strike midnight, while anyone thinking to move the Whispering Knights for some useful purpose—to form a bridge, for example—should know that the stones will persist in dangerously fidgeting until they are replaced. Those for whom such legends have no appeal but who can, even so, imagine that the Bronze-agers were capable of constructing an elaborate astronomical calendar, can find support for their hopes in Alexander Thom's *Megalithic Sites in Britain.* In short, the Rollright Stones, like many another ancient monument, offer their visitors interpretations to suit differing tastes.

More to the present purpose than legends, theories or even the Stones themselves is the lane which passes by them. At a glance it appears unremarkable; it is not unlike many another lane hereabouts, adequately metalled and confined between stone walls. But its course lengthways along the ridge marks it out as among the earliest of routes and, as such, one of the first human contributions to the landscape. Millennia before the fields now sloping down from it were fashioned from forest, centuries before the first of the Stones was set up, men, women and children had worn that ridge-following route. It had become, as it was to remain for four thousand years and more, one of the major approaches to Cotswold.

That lane, so deceptively ordinary, is part of one of the major arteries of prehistoric Britain. It is what the late Dr O. G. S. Crawford called a 'natural road' in his *Archaeology in the Field,* an absorbing book even for those not skilled or energetic enough to take literally to the field to participate in unravelling the distant past. Crawford classified roads as 'made' and 'natural'; the former are, of course, those which, like the Roman roads and the motorways, have been deliberately constructed and are, even the Roman ones, recent in archaeological reckoning. The 'natural roads', said Crawford,

> are not made or designed but grew in response to the need of going from one place to another. They were natural tracks before the human race came into existence. They were formed by animals and led from pasture-grounds to drinking-places. . . . The formation of animal tracks does not cease when man comes upon the scene; they are merely diverted to human needs. The

> caravan or small party of mules carrying merchandise, food, fuel, or building materials from one settlement to another, or from the wood or quarry to the village, will choose that route which combines directness with the avoidance of natural obstacles. River-crossings and bogs are avoided; valleys that must be crossed will be crossed at their narrowest points; the heads of valleys will often not be crossed but circumvented, for it is better to go a little further round than have to descend and climb again. The best route between two places was not, we may be sure, discovered at once; it was the result of a long process of trial and error during which difficult passages were gradually eliminated and short cuts discovered. A natural track is therefore a product of evolution, of accumulated acts of artificial selection, chiefly performed by human beings but to which animals have, I am sure, made many contributions.... The chief natural tracks are ridgeways which are found not only in Britain but all over the world.

The 'natural road' that uses the ridge on which stand the Rollright Stones is not, however, a mere fragment of lane leading from one long-forgotten somewhere to another; it was—and in many parts still is—one of England's highways in both senses of the word. For fifty centuries at the least it has linked the West Country to the Northeast. Its course can be followed by road, track or footpath from Somerset to the Humber. Of its animal originators we can know nothing; but certainly from the New Stone Age—that is, from the time when man was changing from hunter to incipient farmer, a change whose immense potentialities are still unexhausted—it has served travellers of all periods, and stretches of it have recently been accorded '(T)' after their number on the road-signs.

To approach Cotswold by such a route would, surely, be to start as near the beginning of human time as possible. But before doing so, we should perhaps take a quick glance at the route in its entirety in order to appreciate a little of its wider significance. From the southern shore of the Humber (some authorities believe that the route went even further north after that prehistorically formidable obstacle had been ferried), it runs southwards along the ridge of Lincoln Edge and so avoids the low-lying, formerly marsh-and-forest land on either side. Its users did not have to negotiate a ford for thirty miles, the first one being that across the Witham at Lincoln. From there the route continued along the ridge slightly west of south until a second crossing of the Witham above Grantham.

Thereafter the Way kept to the raised ground between the streams flowing eastwards to the Fens and those draining northwesterly into the Trent until across the Welland it reached the northeastern end of the low ridge linking Rockingham, Naseby and Daventry. From there a curving course, first west, then more southerly, enabled it to keep above the headstreams of the Warwickshire Avon to its north and those of the Thames tributaries draining towards Oxford, until it could climb the eastern end of the 25-mile-long ridge that begins with Edge Hill and ends beyond the Rollright Stones. West of Rollright the Evenlode valley intrudes; a later route, probably of Iron Age usage, crossed to Stow-on-the-Wold and made more directly for the Cotswold Edge. But the Neolithic people more probably took a drier route by curving north of where Moreton-in-Marsh now stands and so gained Cotswold Edge on Broadway Hill. From there a slightly sinuous course of lane and track and road now follows the rim of the hills and approximates to the Way's route for most of twenty miles. Near Birdlip, the steep-sided valley of the Frome—the only river to rise on the eastern slope of Cotswold and force its way through to the west—necessitated a southerly curve until, after ten miles, a miniature plateau enabled the Way to reach the Edge again. Southwards it continued, following the rim of the escarpment until reaching Lansdown Hill from where it dropped down to the Bath Avon. One more river to cross, and the route is heading for the ridges of the Southwest. All told, more than two hundred miles of easy going for man and beast.

Such is the ancient Way. Perhaps because it traverses so much of England it has never attracted a single, familiar name. Even the sixty or so miles of it along Cotswold have been known, at least from early medieval times, by a variety of names: the 'Ridgeway' in sundry spellings; the 'Portway' (where it led towards a 'port' or market); the 'Wildenewaye', the road used by those living in open country; or, for a length near Moreton-in-Marsh, intriguingly but inexplicably as the 'Lodreswei', the robbers' way. Latterly it has been dubbed the Cotswold Ridgeway—which, in view of its extent, is too limiting and too local a name. Archaeologists, no doubt finding such variety untidy, have called its entirety the Jurassic Way.

That name is not one to make for popular appeal. It is too learned and specialised to link readily in the mind with such similarly ancient Ways as Berkshire's Ridgeway, the Icknield Way (which may recall the British tribe of the Iceni) or the Pilgrims' Way (which was millennia-old before medieval pilgrims trudged or rode along the chalk hills from Winchester to Canterbury). Yet the name 'Jurassic Way' has one advantage: it draws attention to the Way's geological origin. It follows the line of the Jurassic formation—or, to be more exact, the Edge formed when, in times so remote as to baffle the imagination, the originally level and sea-laid layers of limestone, after being heaved up to form a plateau, sank into the hollow down which the Thames was to flow, and so left as a ridge the rim of its northwest-facing escarpment. This in its more northerly lengths was worn down by the immense glaciers of the last Ice Age while its weaker points were widened into valleys by the huge quantities of water released as the ice-sheets gradually melted. Further south, the almost cliff-like scarp of Cotswold escaped the ice though not the erosion of the huge lake which, trapped between ice and escarpment, covered much of the West Midlands and helped to fashion the Severn valley. Through all those changes, the uppermost layers of the Jurassic series, the limestones, contrived to keep their essential character, forming a tilting plateau and becoming after the final disappearance of the ice so thinly soiled that little but grasses and scrub would grow ... the 200-mile-long strip of comparatively open country which, when man first appeared in Britain, provided easy going across a land then largely covered by forest and marsh.

The name 'Jurassic Way' may also remind us of the stone, sea-laid and composed of minute, fish-roe-like granules, named oolite from the Greek *oön*, egg, and *lithos*, stone. It is one of the best of building materials. Soft enough when quarried to shape and carve, the limestone hardens on exposure and mellows to all shades from creamy grey to deep buff. Hewn in blocks it makes excellent walls; left out to the frost it will split into layers thin enough for roofing; fragments can, in skilled hands, be used for lesser buildings and in-filling or, unmortared, for dry-stone walls to fields. As many an ecclesiastical building—from humble village churches to Lincoln Cathedral—demonstrates, it will withstand the weather's ravages through six or seven centuries; as many a house shows—whether 400 years old or modern—it can create homes at once serviceable and quietly dignified that fit both the windswept hills and the greener valleys. It has been used for a hundred purposes from pig-sties to castles, from privies to façades, from prehistoric tombs to bus-shelters, from grimacing gargoyles to soaring spires. It has won renown in a multitude of photographs, but for today's visitor it has done far more than provide picturesque 'corners'. In the hands of those who from long practice learnt how to use it and passed on their understanding through forty generations, the stone has caught and held the needs and aspirations, the beliefs and achievements—and the fears and follies, too, at times—of countless people who have contributed to the making of this part of England.

The ancient Way forms perhaps the best approach to Cotswold. Its often lofty going, besides giving frequent panoramas of the surrounding country, ever reminds the traveller of Cotswold's beginnings. But, though keeping rigidly to it would, no doubt, be stimulating to the archaeologically inclined, for the less specialised of us such a route would miss much. As will be seen later, from the Way lead many lesser routes, some almost as ancient as the Way itself, some more recent, and all having much to show the visitor. Collectively they can give an impression of much that has since Neolithic times made Cotswold.

Before setting out, however, a last word—of warning or help, according to taste. When using the ancient Ways and their comparatively more recent additions, it is advisable not to be too literal in interpreting the present road, 'green lane' or footpath as the original route. Crawford's 'natural roads' must have been a series of wide, grassy tracks crossing an expansive, unrestricted landscape; and even the medieval additions were only rarely defined between stone walls. Though later we shall have to look into the causes of their present tidy widths, it is enough for the moment to know that the Ways are still approximately traceable and that, since they have survived in varying conditions, they offer variety of going. Indeed, with a little imagination, the traveller, if he feels a need to escape from his car for a spell, will not infrequently find a path or bridleway going approximately parallel to the metalled portions of the Way's course. If he chooses to regard these as traces of former variations to the Way it would be impossible to prove that he is stretching historical accuracy beyond the probable. And often, such variations—as also some of the still unmetalled stretches—will lead by out-of-the-way hamlets and farmsteads that the motorist knows nothing of and into regions still quietly rural. With a 1 : 50,000 Ordnance Survey map, a little forethought and, perhaps, an obliging friend or spouse to drive to the walk's end, it is often possible to choose one's going to suit one's mood.

Whatever the method of travelling, what the visitor gets out of it will largely depend upon what he brings to it. Some outline knowledge of the ways of living and the changes to them that have made the present is a necessary beginning—but only a beginning for, to gain much from what he sees, the visitor must use his own understanding and, at times, his imagination. In the following pages will be found some of the material for such a beginning. Inevitably it is far from complete for truly there is not a building or an acre which does not have something to tell the passer-by if he can read it.

TWO

The Makers of the Ways

The New Stone-agers took their first steps along the route of the ancient Way some 6,000 years ago, give or take a half-millennium according to the authority quoted. No doubt before their time those beings whom for convenience we classify as Palaeolithic and Mesolithic trod the hills on hunting expeditions and seed-and-root searches; but the tracks they made would have been fragments of path only incidentally linked, not a continuous route heading purposefully across 200 miles. Such early peoples are, therefore, outside the scope of this book. Though it is no doubt reprehensible to dismiss the thousands of generations of them in a mere paragraph, it must be accepted that the Old Stone-agers, in spite of all the time they had, left nothing for today's visitors to see—except, for the keen-sighted and knowledgeable, the always present possibility of discovering some rudimentary stone tool.

In truth our knowledge of the ways of living of the Neolithic peoples is sketchy at best. We know that some time before 3500 B.C. they had established themselves on the uplands of southern Britain. We know, too, that they were acquainted with the twin discoveries on which are based what we assume to be civilisation: that food plants can be grown from seeds and that several species of animal, formerly hunted, can be bred in comparative captivity. Though their very limited equipment allowed them to cultivate only the thin-soiled and easily cleared uplands, these discoveries made them less dependent than their hunting and gathering predecessors had been on the food supply that nature provides when left to itself. We know, too, that they had invented an adaptable means of keeping warm by making incipient textiles from their animals' wool, and that by transforming hitherto useless clay into useful pots they had devised a means of storing surplus food (not to mention helping in such chores as fetching water). Their known dwelling sites have yielded evidence that they continued to hunt, but we may hazard that that pursuit (which was to survive as a secondary food-source for the next 5,000 years) became gradually less important as they learnt more about crop-growing and animal husbandry.

For today's sightseers, the New Stone-agers have left the first recognisable human impress on the landscape. Probably necessity caused them to make circular banks of earth with 'causewayed' entrances. These are the remains of what are believed to have been pounds in which their cattle were at times driven, possibly for the autumn slaughtering—like their successors for the next fifty centuries they found winter fodder a problem and had to kill off much of their stock and store the meat against the lean months of winter and early spring. Unfortunately for us, the sites they chose for these pounds were often suitable for the more elaborate 'forts' of some of their successors, and so many have been in part overlaid by larger, more defensive earthworks. Other circular banks, and long parallel banks, too, are assumed to have been of religious significance—but these, too, appear to have often been altered by later peoples. The New Stone-agers' more recognisable and more significant contributions to today's sights have been, at least until comparatively recently, less altered: the large, long mounds of earth they raised over their dead, the so-called long barrows. Cotswold is rich in these and when we come to examine the Ways they will be considered in some detail. It is enough for the moment to note that they represent a considerable amount of work, and so imply that Neolithic people, however primitively they lived, were capable of organising themselves for collective action and must have been moved by deeply-held religious beliefs.

The source of their 'monuments' as of their agriculture is at present a matter of dispute among the experts. It used to be held that both—and much else that contributed to man's change from savage hunter to primitive farmer—were spread from a single source in the Middle East, a theory that assumed early man elsewhere to have been lacking in originality. Recently radio-carbon dating and its ally, tree-ring calibration—the curious will find that Colin Renfrew's *Before Civilization* explains how science has come to the aid of archaeology—by questioning the formerly accepted time-scale have hinted that some of the New Stone-agers' discoveries may have been less limited in their origins and so open the encouraging possibility that human inventiveness may be more wide-spread than was once thought.

The Neolithic way of life brought the first of the Ways into being. The stone, mainly but not only flint, needed for tools was not to be found conveniently near every grazing ground. Some regions were plentifully supplied, others had little; so people travelled to obtain such an essential. We may assume that primitive trading grew up, though it must have been based on exchange or ceremonial giving. We know that certain valued kinds of stone were often carried considerable distances: axes made of Cornish greenstone, of Pembrokeshire dolerite, and of Borrowdale Ash from the Lake District have turned up in Neolithic contexts well over a hundred miles from their places of origin. We know, too, that specially useful flints were mined in considerable quantities from at least 3000 B.C., in Sussex, Wiltshire, the Chilterns and most impressively at Grime's Graves near Weeting, Norfolk. Travelling being then and for long afterwards hampered by the expanses of forest and marsh that covered the lowlands, Neolithic trade routes followed the hill-ridges, the long lines marked on the maps of Prehistoric Britain. But those must have been only the major routes; as will be considered later, the siting of many of the long barrows close to lesser ridge-following ways implies that the Neolithic areas of habitation were threaded by paths. Cotswold has many such secondary ways.

Nowadays emphasis on the idea that the New Stone-agers were conquered and replaced by peoples knowing metallurgy and so possessing more efficient weapons has been softened. Certainly from a century or two either side of 2300 B.C., first people with new pottery forms (and so often called Beaker people though they also knew copper and tin) and, later, more readily classifiable Bronze-agers arrived ... though whether they ousted or worked with the Neolithic peoples is at present uncertain. From about 2100 B.C. one group, centred on Wessex, appears to have been dominant, and their grave-goods, far richer than those of their predecessors, imply not only wealth but trade-routes reaching as far as the eastern Mediterranean, Spain and the Baltic countries. Cotswold would seem to have been on the fringe of their territory.

Bronze-agers' handiwork is fairly readily found in museums. Their main contributions to the landscape are the stone circle and the round barrow. Later people often took over and added to sites sacred to their predecessors, and evidence suggests that some stone circles may date from the late Neolithic—the great complex at Avebury and the first Stonehenge are cases. More originally Bronze Age are the round barrows—but somehow they register less with the sightseer. There are, of course, many more of them than there are long barrows and, usually covering a single interment, they are often much slighter in appearance (and many on Cotswold, as elsewhere, have during the past decades been rendered more insignificant by ploughing). For the expert there are several different patterns and therefore more possibilities to discuss. For the rest of us they are too plentiful and scarcely impressive enough for more than a passing glance—though their siting, often along upland routes, should tell us that the Bronze-agers also used the ancient Ways.

As also did their successors, probably initially people of Bronze Age stock who had acquired a knowledge of the more complicated business of iron-smelting, but later—a century or two before the Romans—appeared more aggressive types known collectively as Belgae. The Iron-agers' major show-pieces are the so-called hill forts. It seems that the earliest and simplest ones were probably more in the nature of village-protecting surrounds; but, as Cotswold's examples show both by their still-substantial ramparts and by their siting where a steep hillslope gave additional protection, they appear to have become progressively more military. The viewer can hardly escape the conclusion that there must have been quite a lot of inter-tribal warfare, and excavation has confirmed it. In spite of probably being the most warlike of the Iron-agers, the Belgae abandoned the limited and more easily defended hill forts for what the archaeologists call 'oppida': rudimentary towns each surrounded by a largish cultivable area and protected in part by natural defences, in part by straightish ditches and banks (once topped with wooden walls) across the more vulnerable approaches. Cotswold has a remarkable example at Bagendon and probably another at Minchinhampton, plus several lengths of ditch-and-bank apparently constructed across routes in use during the half-century before the Roman arrival.

Like their predecessors, the Iron-agers must have used the existing Ways. Many of their forts capping spurs of the Edge are close to the Jurassic Way. Their need for iron (and for other metals, as well as coal) brought into use tracks leading to their sources of supply. An example is the ancient route which branches off the Neolithic Way near Sapperton and, after fording the Frome, follows a lesser ridge through the hill country east and north of Painswick. Across the lowest practicable Severn crossing it reaches Welsh gold and the iron of the Forest of Dean. Further north, from the neighbourhood of Andoversford, a meeting-place of ancient Ways, another route made a short cut fairly directly to the Iron Age fort inside which Stow-on-the-Wold was built and met the original, more meandering Way again on the ridge where stand the Rollright Stones. (And the line is continued by another Iron Age short cut through Banbury to Hunsbury fort guarding the Nene crossing to Northampton and so providing a shorter route for the transport of iron across half England.) The Cotswold length of this Iron Age route is less insistent on avoiding valleys than the earlier Way, and so may imply wider use of horses and wagons in late Iron Age times.

Such early Ways were created by passing feet and hooves. The Romans, as everyone knows, made roads. They surveyed the route, employed natives to dig the necessary wide ditch or raise the necessary embankment, and then laid layers of graduated and rammed stone to end up with a level surface. The purpose of a Roman road was military. That the great Foss Way carves a line across England approximating at a lower level to the prehistoric Way is incidental. For the Romans the almost continuous ridge formed not a natural route for man and beast but a temporary frontier between the already conquered South and East and the yet-to-be-won North and West; to move troops speedily from a quiet sector to a threatened point demanded a continuous smooth road. As the Roman legions pressed westwards they needed roads reaching beyond this frontier, and so laid the so-called Ermin Way from Cirencester to Gloucester, Ryknild Street into the West Midlands, and a lesser unnamed road, perhaps a Roman adaptation of an earlier way, from a settlement on the Foss Way near Easton Grey through Frocester to the Severn crossing between Arlingham and Newnham.

Similarly the Romans sited military camps (which when the frontier was moved westwards became more peaceably inclined settlements), within easy range of earlier and still potentially defensible forts. From the 'Roman Settlement' mapped close to Bourton-on-the-Water, for example, an eye could be kept on the Iron Age forts at Salmonsbury and Stow, while Cirencester, originally the base for the Second Legion, was close to the Belgic oppidum at Bagendon and an earlier fort near Coates. By about A.D. 65 when Gloucester had replaced Cirencester as the military centre of the region and had become the base from which a decade later the restless Silures of South Wales were subdued, no doubt the roads saw increasing civilian traffic. By A.D. 75 the frontier had been moved to Caerleon-on-Usk, and Cirencester was developing its trading potentialities and becoming the local administrative centre before eventually becoming the capital of 'Britannia Prima', one of the four provinces of Roman Britain. No doubt the Cotsallers had long returned to their essential occupation of food production—even more necessary as Roman taxes had to be paid—though most of another century was to pass before retired Roman officials or Romanised British leaders began to build themselves villas in the valleys of Cotswold.

Even today's travellers can scarcely escape the essentially military character of the Roman road system. In truth the roads are not quite so aggressively straight on the ground as they appear on the map; and yet their persistent directness with only an occasional concession to the country through which they pass still tells us that they are the products of conquest, not of growth. And even now scarcely a village breaks the rigid going—as if the later, village-building Angles and Saxons had little time for the soft life which had sprung from commerce, though truly they were probably more concerned that the paved roads might encourage raiding Britons or provide warpaths for the often quarrelsome little kingdoms that for the first three centuries of Anglo-Saxon England shared the country.

The obviousness of Roman roads should not, however, be allowed to leave the impression that the inhabitants of Roman Britain, both native and imported, became suddenly indifferent to the earlier Ways. One has only to plot on a map the known villa sites to realise that access to them must have often been by way of pre-Roman paths—unless we are to assume that potential villa-owners deliberately wandered into almost virgin territory and there set their slaves to work. The villa was essentially a farm-plus-production-centre needing reasonable access to the local market for its profits. And yet, except for one close to Cirencester and another east of Stow, none of the twenty-two Cotswold villas is sited within a mile of a Roman road, and many are much further from one. The famous Chedworth villa, for example, is fully two winding miles from the Foss Way, but barely a mile from a track, now known as the White Way, which must have been in use when the nearby Neolithic barrow was raised; the much larger but less tourist-attracting villa at Woodchester is three very hilly miles from the nearest road accorded to the Romans—and that somewhat uncertainly—but less than a mile from a ridge-following route that passes three long barrows and curls around one of the most impressive of Cotswold's Iron Age forts. And perhaps of even more significance, the three Roman market centres on Cotswold (as distinct from military-originated towns) are sited off the roads—that near Andoversford, though at a meeting-place of earlier routes, being six miles from the nearest. All of which suggests that the traveller who, impressed by things Roman, feels a thrill when driving along a Roman Road, need seldom feel let down if he turns aside occasionally along one or other earlier Way; he will, it seems, often be following not the legionaries but the more peaceably inclined merchants, villa-owners, slaves and Britons.

The many lesser lanes that thread their winding, up-and-down ways from one Cotswold village to another are products of the centuries following the Romans. It seems that on Cotswold the end of Roman Britain was delayed a century beyond the date of A.D. 421 given in our school history books. Little incipient Anglo-Saxon kingdoms had been established for two or three generations to the south and the east before what must have been an uneasy time of diminishing Roman-originated security and comfort abruptly ended in A.D. 577, at which time, as the *Anglo-Saxon Chronicle* tells, the West Saxons under 'Cuthine and Ceawlin fought against the Britons and killed three kings, Conmail, Condidan and Farinmail at a place called Deorham; and they captured from them three cities, Gloucester, Cirencester and Bath'. The three British kings and the three captured towns imply that some time during the century following the withdrawal of the Legions and of the Roman administration, the Cotswold region had been divided into small units. 'Deorham' is identified with Dyrham, six miles north of Bath and close under the Edge. There can be little doubt that the men of Wessex approached along the prehistoric Way from the south while the Britons used the Way from the north. A half-century later, in a battle at Cirencester, Wessex was defeated by Mercia and much of Cotswold thereafter became Mercian though its eastern slopes appear to have remained part of Wessex. Accurate defining of Anglo-Saxon kingdoms is a tricky business, but the names of Rodmarton and Didmarton southwest of Cirencester, and of Marshfield on a line with them near Bath, each have a syllable deriving from 'Mearc', a march or boundary. Though none is recorded before the Domesday Book, it would seem likely that it was during the conflicts between Mercia and Wessex in the seventh and eighth centuries that each received its informative name.

It was during the Anglo-Saxon centuries that the settlement

pattern we know became established. No doubt former assumptions about groups of Anglo-Saxon churls tramping out into almost untouched lowland forest to begin the laborious work of creating the villages and fields of England is an exaggeration. There can no longer be much doubt that where the Anglo-Saxons found usable land—upland cleared from Neolithic times onwards and still used by Britons, deserted villa lands which the natural forest had not yet reclaimed—they seized it. H. P. R. Finberg's researches into the ancestry of Withington—to be found in *Gloucestershire Studies*—have shown that the Anglo-Saxon parish boundary largely coincides with that of a Roman villa; the recording of nearby Chedworth as a village as early as A.D. 862 suggests that its villa land, too, may have been kept in almost continuous cultivation, as also perhaps was that of Woodchester's villa whose Anglo-Saxon village is first mentioned early in the eighth century. Even so, much of the transformation of the wooded valleys and of the Vale below the Edge into productive farmland must have been undertaken by Anglo-Saxon settlers (and their British slaves, too), and the lanes that now link them must have been first trodden by them.

Their settlements are for the most part under the Edge or in the valleys among the hills, and are usually sited where the layer of clayey fullers' earth checked the seepage through the upper limestone and so caused springs to issue. Prehistoric Way and Roman road alike tend to bypass them. Initially their villages may have been largely self-supporting; but by the eighth century it is clear that the uplands, which had formed the grazing grounds of their predecessors, were maintaining comparatively large flocks of sheep, and wool, which was for the next eight centuries to bring work to Cotswold and riches to some of its leading figures, was becoming increasingly important. It may be that the Anglo-Saxons were reviving a trade interrupted by their ancestors' arrival. The pre-Roman people of Bagendon, we know, wove cloth on a scale that suggests meeting more than local needs. It seems likely that the villa-owners kept large flocks and went in for cloth production—though, unexpectedly, most authorities seem reluctant to confirm the probability. Though Anglo-Saxon wool production tends to be overlooked, we have indisputable evidence of both manufacture and export of finished clothing in the letter in which Charlemagne complained to Offa the Great of Mercia about 'the size of the cloaks, that you may order them to be such as used to come to us in former times'. Unfortunately the origin of the offending garments is not given, though Cotswold was then part of Offa's enlarged kingdom. We are on more certain ground when the Domesday Book listed, for the Conqueror's fiscal benefit, the names of the settlements that had been founded during the preceding five centuries. Three Shiptons (sheep-tons) are recorded on Cotswold, and a Sheepscombe; Yanworth was the 'lamb-enclosure', and Sherborne the 'clear stream' used for washing the sheep. When early medieval field-names are added, half the villages on Cotswold have their sheep hill, rams' close or slait (originally 'slaeget', a sheep pasture); many have their wool-house and some their woad hill. By then Cotswold had become a major supplier of the weavers of Flanders and Italy, and renowned throughout Europe for the quality of its fleeces.

Meanwhile the Normans had arrived. Their military works on Cotswold are fewer than might be expected. The original Beverstone castle may have been Norman; the oldest work now visible is thirteenth-century while Sudeley near Winchcombe was not begun until early in the 1400s. Castles at Cirencester and Tetbury were destroyed by Stephen and not rebuilt. Otherwise there are only a few earthen mottes on which early castles were constructed, originally of wood, protected by moats which in limestone country can never have held water. The three examples in the upper Frome valley are so unobtrusively sited as to tempt one—in the absence as yet of detailed investigation—to think of those adulterine castles raised in Stephen's reign when, Bristol being held by the king's opponents, Cotswold probably saw over-much of the violence and plundering committed by the lawless while 'Christ slept, and all His saints'. Perhaps in this category should be placed a large mound in a copse just south of the junction of the A 417 and the A 436, as yet uninvestigated and undated.

Much more noteworthy is the Norman ecclesiastical contribution to Cotswold. A few churches, notably Bibury and Coln Rogers, show that the Anglo-Saxons built churches in the local stone; nearly half Cotswold's churches are at least in part Norman workmanship—and when built among the hovels that then comprised a village must have impressed the English with the architectural superiority of their conquerors.

The Normans and the people of medieval England generally must have used the Ways already in being. Some stretches have attracted the name of Salt Way or Salt Path from the trade, based in part on the mines of the Droitwich neighbourhood and in part on the extraction of salt from the sea, which enabled the autumn-slaughtered meat to be preserved through the winter. Many more of the Ways must have been in effect sheep ways and wool ways though—perhaps because the sheep were so common hereabouts—none has been named after this all-important source of wealth. For from the eleventh century the landowners of Cotswold, mostly monastic, derived a major part of their income from wool-production ... at least until about 1350.

The slow-growing prosperity of the 1100s and 1200s produced an increase in population which required that land hitherto uncultivated should be brought under the plough. Villages increased the sizes of their common fields and planted new hamlets on former waste. Besides adding its contribution to such expansion of existing settlements, the wool trade added two new towns: Stow-on-the-Wold, where the Iron Age Way crossed the Foss Way, grew from an insignificant hamlet; Northleach was deliberately planned and built where the Foss Way was crossed by two earlier routes. Both were built essentially as markets—Stow for sheep, Northleach for wool. The increasing wealth is also reflected in many Cotswold churches. The earlier small, dark Norman buildings were in part remodelled and given larger windows and more embellishments during the century and a half before, in 1349, the first nation-wide and hideously destructive visitation of the Black Death brought church-building to an abrupt stop. As can be readily seen by today's visitor, few Cotswold churches do not show some of their thirteenth- and early fourteenth-century improvements in slim lancet windows and gracefully traceried 'Decorated' ones, while at times almost the whole surviving building is of then-new work. From that period, too, date the earliest domestic stone buildings, mainly originally granges (monastic farm-houses), residences of the higher clergy, and tithe barns in which the villagers' compulsory contribution to the Church was stored prior to sale. Many such buildings survived the Reformation to become today's manorhouses—though, befitting their lay owners' desire to keep abreast of modern trends, they have often acquired Renaissance features or perhaps a Stuart or a Georgian wing. The barns were, until the last fifty years or so, too valuable to the farmer to be adapted to serve non-agricultural needs and so often still stand as they were built, hugely timbered and massively walled.

In fact, before 1349 the forward march had begun to stumble. It is probable that a succession of poor harvests early in the 1300s, their effects exaggerated by the demands of militarily-inclined kings, had begun a decline; the Black Death had, it seems, accelerated a process already shaping. We know that increasingly from about 1320 landowners took to letting their lands to their tenants in order to secure a steadier income from money rents. This change coincided with the withdrawal of foreign wool-buyers, often Italians who had acted both as gatherers of papal dues and as wool-merchants, and who had added to their profits by often buying the wool-crop several years in advance—a practice which brought trouble to both large-scale producer and buyer as the decline set in. These wool-merchants also suffered as financial backers of Edward III's war against France, the opening campaigns of what we know as the Hundred Years' War. Even so, wool production did not decline as speedily. It seems that the serfs who could often rent the land for which they had formerly worked—and their lords' demesne, too, in many instances—enlarged their modest flocks, while into the place of the foreign wool-factors stepped English middlemen such as the Grevels of Chipping Campden, the Forteys and the Busshes of Northleach, and the Tames of Fairford, the families whose brasses still adorn the churches they rebuilt in their home-towns and which are, even today, monuments to both their wealth and their piety.

The wool-merchants' business activities must have involved the sorting and grading of the wool after purchase ... and from that it was only a small step to becoming involved in the dependent cloth-making which, from Edward III's time, had been encouraged by the government. As the trade has left several items of industrial archaeology in the Cotswold area, perhaps a brief outline of the major processes required to turn raw wool into saleable cloth may be helpful.

Sheep do not conveniently grow wool of consistent quality all over their bodies, so the first matter is breaking the fleeces and separating the long strands from the short, the coarse from the fine. Scouring is then necessary to remove the natural grease (in medieval times boiling in stale urine was found effective), and the wool has then to be dried—in the open air or in specially warmed and ventilated drying sheds. Dyeing followed if multi-coloured cloth was required, though until well into the eighteenth century undyed cloth and cloth dyed 'in the piece' provided by far the greater part of Cotswold's production. Carding to disentangle the strands by means of spikes set into cards then followed. The wool was then spun into thread or yarn, initially by spindle and distaff, and from early medieval times on simple hand-operated spinning wheels.

The thread had to be wound in 'chains', recognised lengths for easy handling. Weaving followed, but except with very fine thread produced a mesh too open for use as cloth. To make the cloth compact, to cause its fibres to 'felt', was the purpose of fulling. This originally meant treading or 'walking' the cloth after it had been soaped or treated with clayey fullers' earth to speed the felting. By early medieval times fulling mills had been built in which a series of fulling stocks—gigantic wooden hammers each weighing over a hundredweight and powered by a water-driven shaft—rose and fell alternately on to the cloth in the 'stock pit' below; twelve hours' fulling was required to turn new-woven fabric into the famous Cotswold broadcloth. The cloth had then to be dried and after dyeing—a very skilled process—dried again. Then the nap had to be raised by means of teasels, the spiky heads of a specially-grown, large thistle. The 'fluffiness' resulting had to be sheared off—the shears used were long and heavy, and required expert handling—to leave the cloth, after rolling, smooth and ready for market.

In medieval times and through the Tudor period most of these processes were done individually in the home. The Cotswold Ways and lanes must have been busy with packhorse and donkey carrying their loads of part-finished material on its various stages of production—wool to spinners, woven cloth to the fullers, the nearly-finished cloth to the shearers, and so on. Carding was a recognised children's occupation, spinning was left mainly to the women, especially the unmarried. Until the seventeenth century the industry was essentially cottage-based or, more accurately, village-based, and the only process requiring more than could be undertaken in home or outbuilding was fulling. The building and equipping of the necessary mill was a costly business. On Cotswold as elsewhere the first fulling mills were built by the monastic owners of the great sheep runs: the Knights Templars had one working at Temple Guiting as early as 1182; Winchcombe abbey had two at about the same time. The rise of the cloth-making industry—which was to provide Britain's main export from about 1450 until after the Stuart century—brought little change in methods of production; its development depended much more on organisation of the collection and redistribution of the part-finished cloth. The organising fell into the merchants' hands; they saw that the wool and the results of the various individual occupations were sent on their ways to the next worker, that the piece-work pay was forthcoming, and at times supplied such necessary equipment as looms and dyes by a system not unlike hire purchase, the worker having instalments deducted from his earnings. By the time the first Stuart king gained the throne, fulling mills and dyeing sheds had become a feature of many a Cotswold valley and most suitably-sited villages had their weavers' cottages. Even such a remote village as Owlpen could boast thirteen weavers in 1608 while Newington Bagpath, which must have been almost inaccessible in bad weather, had a mill as well as the weavers' cottages which still stand there.

The impression today's traveller gets is that the trade must have brought much well-being to the villages and small towns. It seems to have fostered, and been fostered by, a growing spread of wealth—many farmers, large and small, and many craftsmen, too, sharing in an upsurge of prosperity. During the period from about 1560 to 1620—the 'Great Rebuilding' as Dr W. G. Hoskins calls it in his *Making of the English Landscape*—over much of southern England the medieval wood-and-thatch hovels were replaced by stone houses and cottages (though the latter were in fact not labourers' homes but those of craftsmen). Cotswold certainly shared in this activity—as almost every village shows in its older houses. But in the wool trade there were also considerable economic ups and downs. By the 1620s there was extensive unemployment and some disorder arising in part from the diminishing demand for broadcloth and the increasing popularity of the 'New Draperies', worsteds and other lighter fabrics for which Cotswold wool was unsuitable. Called upon to help, the government attempted to reorganise the industry and to regulate the quality of the cloth—which offended the workers—before trying to replace the export of undyed cloth by home-dyed—which lost valuable Continental markets. As the breach between King and Parliament widened, governmental interference tended to make the trade favour Parliament, a trend which was encouraged when, on the outbreak of the Civil War, Charles ordered his cavalry commander, Prince Rupert, to commandeer 'great quantities of cloth canvas and lacharame' from the Cotswold centres 'for supplying ye gt necessities our souldiers have of suits'.

Meanwhile the first changes in manufacturing methods had been prompted by the need to maintain production. More efficient spinning wheels—of the type we first met in the fairy-story illustrations—had replaced the crude medieval ones, and being operated by the spinster's foot, they did away with the need for an assistant. Gig mills had been built in which nap-raising was speeded by circular, water-powered drums into which the teasels were fitted. The eighteenth century brought more inventions: the 'flying shuttle' to replace the assistant who had been needed to return the shuttle to the weaver when cloth wider than a man's reach was being woven; the 'spinning jenny'; a carding machine to take over the work formerly done by children; a lawn-mower-like 'cross-cutter' to replace the hand-shearers; and finally and inevitably the power loom. Such developments necessitated the transfer of the many processes from the scattered villages into buildings grouped around the all-important mill. They necessitated, too, capital. By 1757 Josiah Tucker, dean of Gloucester and known to many mill-owning families, could write: 'One Person, with a great Stock and large Credit, buys the Wool, pays for the Spinning, Weaving, Milling, Dyeing, Shearing, Dressing, etc. That is, he is Master of the whole Manufacture from first to last, and probably employs a thousand Persons under him.' The 'gentleman clothier' had arrived, and new, larger mills were being built beside the more constant streams and fine houses on the hills above.

The increasing mechanisation, cutting down labour, brought much unrest among the workers who had known the semi-independence of the cottage industry; in fact their earnings were probably no less, but as machines replaced hands the risks of unemployment increased while concentration of the industry in the valleys around Stroud brought impoverishment to many an outlying village. Nor did the changes bring lasting production. From the 1820s and 1830s overseas competition increasingly intruded and also that of the Yorkshire woollen industry based on steam power. The mid-nineteenth century saw increasing closure of unprofitable mills, many bankruptcies and growing unemployment. There had been more than 160 mills in 1820; by 1900 only twenty were still producing cloth.

Through all this period the Ways remained the Ways. Only the most serviceable of them were suitable for carts and wagons; for the most part the traffic was of packhorses for which, as the trade grew, more and more narrow steep lanes zigzagged past workers' cottage-rows on the way up the valley-sides to the major routes. The needs of the trade prompted attempts at road improvement and some sections of the modern roads owe their present course to the turn-pike trusts. Even small Minchinhampton, striving to retain its productivity, undertook no less than five road-improvement schemes and hoped to gain more business by advertising its efforts not only in the local and the London newspapers but also in the

St James Chronicle of Dublin. Cotswold roads, however, remained notoriously inadequate; limestone, though ideal for building and sculpture, powders under constant traffic, making thick dust in summer, slippery mud in wet weather. The transport needs of Cotswold's main industry were not to be met until the canal age, when the Stroudwater was linked to both the Severn and, via the famous tunnel, the Thames. A half-century later came the first of the railways which, by diverting traffic along the few routes that ventured to cross Cotswold, left the earlier Ways mere local roads ... until from the early 1900s the car began to reclaim them.

Meanwhile, from about 1750 onwards the landscape crossed by the Ways was undergoing a change. The wide, unbounded uplands which from before the Conquest had provided almost continuous sheep runs, were increasingly divided into fields defined by stone walls. As elsewhere, from early Tudor times individual landowners had urged, persuaded or compelled their tenants to accept some remodelling of the old and wasteful medieval open-field system. From about 1750 the process, encouraged by both a growing population and the need to maintain food production during the wars with France, became more wide-spread by way of private Parliamentary Acts. Scarcely a year passed without a Cotswold parish being enclosed. By the time of Waterloo almost all the former open sheep country had been turned into the fields we know, and the ancient Ways had lost their original easy meandering between confining walls. Since then a century-and-a-half's mellowing has made the appearance acceptable—indeed to many of today's travellers Cotswold must appear always to have been a land of walled fields. But to the people of the time of change, particularly to the poorer villagers who could not afford to enclose the fragments of land allotted to them and so had to sell them to their richer neighbours and who also often lost their grazing rights when former commons became fields—the changes were for them drastic, at times disastrous. For the most part they remained inarticulate, but found spokesmen to oppose both the damage to their way of living and to the appearance of the landscape. Such a champion was Cobbett, that forceful Radical who always had one eye on the virtues of Old England. In 1821, riding from Cirencester to Gloucester past walls not yet weathered into grey and fields as yet unimproved by modern fertilising and deep ploughing, he found 'anything so ugly I have never seen before. The stone which, on the other side of Cirencester, lay a good way under ground, here lies very near the surface. The plough is constantly bringing it up, and thus, in general, come the means of making the walls that serve as fences. Anything quite so cheerless as this I do not recollect to have seen.' The turnips, he added, 'are not a *fiftieth* part' of a crop he had seen elsewhere in his travels: 'thirty acres here ... have less *food* upon them than I saw the other day upon half an acre'. One wonders what old Cobbett would think of our cherishing the landscape he so detested, and of our paying what he would have considered a fortune to live in (after modernising) the stone cottages of the labourers he tried to champion. One wonders, too, what he would think of the thousands and thousands of us who along ancient Way, Roman road, turn-pike modification, A-roads, B-roads, and motorway, contribute to an industry he would have found utterly incomprehensible: tourism which is now one of Cotswold's major money-bringers. Would he, one wonders, have considered us little better than the visitors he saw at Cheltenham—'the lame and the lazy, the gourmandising and guzzling, the bilious and the nervous' —whom he willingly turned his back on to go 'between stone walls, over a country little better than that from Cirencester to Burlip-hill ... a very poor, dull, and uninteresting country all the way to Oxford'?

Such a question is unfair, both to us and to Cobbett. He came to Cotswold to criticise what he saw as a retrograde step, and to prophesy the consequences; and, as is usual with prophets, he was both gloomy and wrong. We visit Cotswold for very different reasons and in a very different frame of mind. If, like Cobbett, we find what we look for, we shall enjoy our visits much more than he did his. We will be looking for the very varied attractions of Cotswold which his eye, intent on finding faults, far too often overlooked.

It is time we were on our way.

THREE

The Ways of the North Cotswolds

After passing the Rollright Stones, the prehistoric Way leads southwestwards, climbing gently. A half-mile on, just after the turning to Long Compton, a lesser lane bears right while the straighter one continues down into the valley of the Evenlode across which stands Stow-on-the-Wold. As has been mentioned, that route, though often referred to as part of the Cotswold Way and in use in the Iron Age, appears to have been a shortening of the original Way. For that it is necessary to look a little further north and take the lesser lane that branches to the right a half-mile southwest of the Rollright Stones.

At the first abrupt turn of this lane the Way continues appropriately as a bridle-path between two little valleys to make for Salter's Well Farm whose name tells that medieval salt-carriers used earlier tracks. This particular stretch making for the slight ridge between the headstreams of the north-flowing Stour and those of the south-flowing Evenlode, was just the route people of early times would have taken. It can even now be approximately followed. Westwards from Salter's Well Farm it is mapped as a footpath until its line is taken up by the A 44 for a mile to the cumbersome Four Shire Stone (where, since the county boundaries have been adjusted, only three shires meet); but the plough having nearly erased it, its course is more readily followed by field walls than by footprints. Just beyond the Four Shire Stone the line is continued as a track—it has clearly suffered much modification—around what was a wartime airfield and is now the Fire Service Technical College. Then as a lane it crosses the Foss Way a mile north of Moreton-in-Marsh to reach the hamlet of Dorn.

Now a few farms and, behind one, a medieval chapel long desecrated, Dorn was not always so slight. A 'Roman Settlement' is shown on the map and this, though not yet excavated, has yielded over two hundred Roman coins, two sculptured heads and many other fragments. Dorn is believed to be the site of a Roman market centre; the name is of British origin—probably from 'Doru', a gap or gateway (through the hills?)—which suggests that it survived inhabited into Anglo-Saxon times. Though near the Foss Way, the township actually stood a quarter-mile along a by-lane which implies that the lane was in use before the Romans arrived. All told, it looks as if the prehistoric Way took this route rather than cross the Evenlode to Stow or tackle the marshy land which gave Moreton-in-Marsh its name ... for, despite what television quiz-masters and others tell us, the suffix 'Marsh' is not a corruption of 'March' meaning a boundary. In the Place-name Society's authoritative four-volume work, *Place Names of Gloucestershire*, A. H. Smith states that not only does Moreton mean 'farmstead in the moor or marshland', but the area about the present town was known into the seventeenth century as Henmarsh, the marshland frequented by (moor)hens. The driest route from Rollright's ridge to Cotswold was along the low rise on which Dorn stands, approximating to the lane which continues to climb past Batsford towards a swelling on the skyline which was, before the plough began to level it, a Neolithic long barrow.

Clearly, on the ridge above Batsford the Enclosure Commissioners or some later tidy-minded roadmakers have been at work. An early route would have been more curving ... but like the present lane, it would have avoided the hollow in which Blockley lies, and skirted the combe filled by Bourton Woods, before picking up the ridge along which the Moreton–Broadway road, the A 44, heads for the rim of the Cotswold escarpment. Even though that road has long been civilised by stone walls and tarmac, it is still a ridge route ... which, besides suggesting a prehistoric origin, can in some weathers enable the traveller to glimpse what the hills have meant to former Cotsallers and so appreciate why landowners grew windbreaks of trees along either side of the road. For it must be said firmly that Cotswold knows more seasons than the late summer so often seen in coloured photographs. Cotswold has a spring which can be delightful with bluebells, cowslips, star-speckled wild garlic, and the first fresh shoots of its countless trees ... though often a south-westerly is sending cloud-shadows racing across the open country and bringing sudden, chill showers. Cotswold has a late autumn, too, when mellow sunlight can find hints of gold in the buffs and creams of the stone and enrich the reddish browns of the newly ploughed fields ... or can bring rain-storms sweeping in from the Atlantic blurring all to grey. And, compared with the adjacent lowlands, its winters can be bleak. The village of Snowshill high up on the Edge owes its name to being where the snow lay longest for, as an old and bitter saying has it, on Cotswold 'winter never dies in her dam's belly'.

If the weather is not distracting on this first stretch of Cotswold and the traveller has a philosophical turn of mind, he might like to reflect on the chance by which some individuals of the past have been long remembered and others, probably no less worthy, have been forgotten. For the word Cotswold derives not only from the Anglo-Saxon word for 'high, open land'; its first syllable remembers one Cod (the 'o' is long to rhyme with 'rode') who before the eighth century had also named Cutsdean five miles to the southwest, a nearby and now-lost hamlet of Codswell, and Codes-byrig, 'Cod's fortified place', which stood in Lower Swell near Stow-on-the-Wold. Why from among his many contemporaries he should have achieved the distinction of naming the whole upland is beyond our knowing. We may, if we choose, guess that in the days of the Anglo-Saxon arrival he fought nobly against the Britons—though, as custom regarded individual efforts on, and rewards from, the battle-field as belonging to the royal or tribal leader, his valour would not have been credited to him in folktale or chronicle. Or was he perhaps 'oath-worthy' so that all with whom he dealt—his thanely equals in the hundred moot, his churls in the village gathering—knew his word could be relied on and his justice fair? Or he could have been a model family-man who rarely beat his wife, delighted to dandle his latest offspring, and dutifully arranged suitable marriages for his daughters. Or he may owe his unusual distinction to all those qualities and more, to having been the kind of leader who, in the bucolic and very human society of his time, was summed up in the finest epitaph a man could earn: 'a good neighbour'.

This stretch of the ancient Way must have reached Broadway Hill before curving southwestwards along the Edge. There near—or from within?—the Fox Inn we can look over the combe down which the modern road twists through a multitude of beeches to reach the expanse of the Avon vale. On a clear day the great field pattern stretches out to Worcester in the Severn valley and on to the Clee Hills and the beginnings of Wales, while northeastwards the tower of Chipping Campden church and a few grey roofs peer through the trees of a valley tilting towards the end of Cotswold.

Perhaps, however, Broadway Hill should be visited not on a summer's day but when a March gale is chasing cloud-shadows across the hills or at an April dusk chill enough to remind that winter has barely gone. For it was on a spring day in 1661 that the spot came into persisting public notice when 'on Broadway-hill in sight of Campden' was erected the gibbet on which were hanged widowed Joan Perry and her sons, John and Richard, for a murder they could not have committed and so began a mystery which has ever since baffled those who like their happenings to have orderly, intelligible explanations.

Often entitled 'The Campden Wonder', the story has prompted several authors to weave a novel—or in John Masefield's case, a play—to provide it with a plausible denouement. More interesting is Sir George Clark's meticulous and detailed book which deals with the actual events. For those who have not come across the mystery a brief summary may indicate why it has remained tantalising for so long. It tells that on an August afternoon in 1660 William Harrison, elderly steward to the dowager Lady Campden, set out to collect rents in Ebrington and Charingworth, a few miles east of Campden, and failed to return home at nightfall. Concerned, Mrs Harrison sent their servant, John Perry, to search for him and when, by next daybreak, he too had not come back, the Harrisons' son Edward joined in. He met John Perry returning from Ebrington alone. Resuming the search together, they found 'in the Highway between Ebrington and Campden, near unto a great Furz-brake' William Harrison's hat, (collar)band, and comb, 'the Hat and Comb being hacked and cut, the Band bloody.... The news thereof, coming to Campden, so alarmed the Town, that Men, Women, and Children hasted thence, in Multitudes, to search for Mr Harrison's supposed dead Body, but all in vain.' John Perry was questioned and, though his somewhat rambling account of his search was corroborated in part by witnesses, he was detained. A week later he asked to be brought again before the J.P.—probably Sir Thomas Overbury the younger who later wrote a full account of the mystery. Perry then told a different story: his brother Richard and his mother Joan Perry had often urged him to tell them 'when his Master went to receive his Lady's Rents' so that they might 'way lay and rob him'; on the evening in question Richard, aided by the mother, had murdered Harrison and thrown his body 'into the Great Sink by Wallington's Mill'. Though a search found nothing, all three were charged with the murder. The first judge before whom they appeared was troubled by the persisting absence of the corpse. A second judge decided that the case was proved. Joan Perry, John and Richard, were hanged on Broadway Hill ... and two years later William Harrison returned to Chipping Campden unharmed and apparently unconcerned.

If that was all, there would perhaps be less to wonder about in 'The Campden Wonder'. Unlike contemporaries, we can bring in psychology to explain John Perry's strange and crucial admission—and, indeed, Sir George Clark's book, *The Campden Wonder*, ends with a chapter offering such an explanation. Also unlike contemporaries, we cannot be satisfied that Joan Perry was a witch who had wafted Harrison away for a couple of years. For, to us, the crux of the 'Wonder' is not so much John Perry's mental disorders, horrible though their consequences were, but the story by which William Harrison explained his two-year absence. Had he returned vague about what had happened we could assume prolonged amnesia; but Harrison's story is anything but vague. He was, he says, attacked by three mounted strangers who were so little interested in the £23 rent money he had collected that they thrust into his pockets so much of their own cash that its weight 'sorely bruised' him. Then they forced him to ride half across England with them in order to sell him as a slave—and this was a man described as already 'old and infirm' and whose market value, incidentally, his attackers had decreased by wounding him. He was, he says, shipped to 'near Smyrna' and sold as a slave. For nearly two years he worked for an unnamed surgeon of 'eighty-seven years of age' who shortly before he died gave him a 'silver Bowl, double gilt'. This bowl enabled Harrison to persuade a seaman to ship him to Portugal where a gentleman 'born near Wisbech in Lincolnshire' procured for him a passage to Dover 'from whence I made Shift to get to London', and so home to Campden. But nowhere in Harrison's story are there any statements which could then have been checked. He names none of the persons he met, he is persistently imprecise about places—they are always 'near' somewhere else—and nowhere does he show any sign of uncertainty which might hint if not of mental derangement at least of senility. It is all straightforward, coherent and quite unbelievable ... and so leaves the suspicion that Harrison had intended to disappear on that August afternoon in 1660, and that the 'Hacked and Cut' hat and the 'bloody' collarband were intended to be found. And nowhere in his story does Harrison show any concern that his absence had caused the deaths of three innocent people ... or four if we accept a note which a contemporary added on a blank page of his printed copy of 'The True and perfect account of the Examination, Confession, Trial, Condemnation, and Execution of Joan Perry, and her two sons, John and Richard Perry, for the supposed Murder of William Harrison, Gent....' published in 1676:

> John Perry hung in chains on the same gallows. Richard and Joan Perry were after execution taken down and buried under the gallows.... After Harrison's return John was taken down and buried and Harrison's wife soon after (being a snotty covetous presbyterian) hung herself in her own house.

Not perhaps the story to recall while picnicking on Broadway Hill on a summer's day and admiring the view. But as the dusk thickens and the wind blows chill, we might feel more inclined to remember the three unmarked graves thereabouts. We might also find ourselves wondering what William Harrison thought during the sixteen or so years he lived after his return to Campden when business took him in that direction and, as he hurried home, he had to pass the gibbet that would still have been standing 'on Broadway-hill in sight of Campden'.

On reaching Broadway Hill the prehistoric Way must have curved around the head of the valley of the little River Dickler, and so begun its journey along Cotswold Edge. But before following it southwards there are places in this northern part of the hills which need to be looked at. One of the two salt ways which crossed the region would serve as a route, though neither is named on the map.

The significance of salt ways will be considered later when the best known of them is followed across Cotswold. For the present we need only to glance at the minor ones hereabouts. One, as has been noticed, linked Campden via Dorn and Salter's Well Farm with the Way passing the Rollright Stones using part of the ancient route. The other appears to have branched off a mile or so south of Campden to pass Stow-on-the-Wold and follow the high ground between the Windrush and the Evenlode, probably eventually reaching the middle Thames. It named a 'Saltforde' in Wick Rissington in the fourteenth century, and a 'Saltuuelle' in Icomb before the Conquest. Either village would make a good starting-place.

Though both are indisputably Cotswold, Wick Rissington and Icomb are very different. Wick Rissington spreads its houses and cottages leisurely around a large green below the sharp rise of its hill; Icomb is a neighbourly little place of brief streets where three hollows meet. Wick's great house is a steep mile away up on the hill; originally eighteenth-century, it was obviously sited for the view and can never have been part of the village. Icomb Place, though now screened by evergreens, has ended the village street since it was built about 1420 by Sir John Blaket. Though restored early this century, it has retained one of its medieval courtyards, a contemporary gateway with the original windows—'fifteenth-century Perpendicular' to the architecturally-minded from the vertical stone tracery then in vogue—and its embattled parapets, there being in 1420 a need for an appearance of defensibility.

The village churches, though rebuilt about the same time, are also rather dissimilar, and both are remarkable. Each dates from the thirteenth century—that is, from the time when the ponderous, round-arched, massively-pillared Norman style had given way to the gentler, pointed-arched Gothic. The first expressions of this style, known to ecclesiologists as 'Early English' though it was Continent-wide, allowed buildings to be lighter in fact and appearance, the weight of their structure depending more on balancing the thrusts between their parts than on mere bulk of wall and pillar. This innovation is often associated with the contemporaneous Cistercians whose austere outlook disfavoured the rich mouldings and the carvings that had increasingly embellished the heavy lines of the Norman; the new 'Early English' relied for its visual appeal on proportion, on its simply-moulded arches and on the slim grace of its lancet windows. It was the style which created Rievaulx Abbey and Salisbury Cathedral before Henry VIII's religious policy brought the ruin of the one and heavy-handed restoration left the other a chill reminder of what had been. In Icomb's scarcely-touched chancel can be seen, in small village scale, the original grace and inspiration.

An additional attraction of this little church is the transept built or remodelled as a chapel about 1420. In it is the fine tomb of Sir John Blaket. His effigy in full armour has suffered less than many of its age, and shows him in the fashion and appearance of his early manhood. Medieval belief assumed that on resurrection the dead would appear as of thirty-three years old, the age of Christ at His Crucifixion and Resurrection. The effigy was not intended as a portrait: an idealised Christian knight was what the sculptor would have been paid to produce.

Below the effigy, carved figures of the Trinity, angels, a saint, a knight and lady have unusually survived. Just above it a minute contemporary window allows a view from outside, a feature whose purpose is difficult to assert. It is wrongly placed to have been one of those 'low side-windows' about which experts on old churches used to argue and may have been intended to provide a sight of the altar from the churchyard. Could Sir John have possessed a sacred relic, long since lost, which had been placed on his effigy and so visible to those who peered in?

The chancel of Wick Rissington church is in the same style, but it was built a little later, about 1265. Most noticeable in the east windows can be seen the beginning of the development from the first Gothic simplicity. Above each pair of lancet windows is a lozenge-shaped window, the sides slightly curved; it is as if the originally-minded mason was experimenting with grouping his windows so that each pair formed in effect a single, larger window, the space immediately above which could become an upper extension ... the idea that was during the next eighty years to be developed into the elaborate and often exquisite tracery of the 'Decorated'. At the time of its rebuilding, Wick Rissington's little church was very, very modern.

Musical visitors may find a bonus in the organ at Wick Rissington; it was that on which Cheltenham-born Gustav Holst played during his first professional engagement, as organist and choirmaster. He was then only nineteen; his 'Cotswolds' Symphony was still eight years ahead and his better known *The Planets* more than twenty years away.

Motorists may assume that the A 424 keeping to the crest between Wick Rissington and Icomb follows the line of this eastern salt way. Walkers can guess that it became the track leading over Icomb Hill past an unfinished Iron Age fort to reach the hamlet of Maugersbury, the parent settlement to Stow-on-the-Wold. In almost unpronounceable spelling Maugersbury's name was recorded three centuries before King Aethelred II established a 'stow', a place for religious gathering, on the hill above in honour of the murdered and canonised King Edward of the East Angles. Maugersbury has become a cluster of neat stone farms and houses, some of Stuart date, about an Elizabethan manorhouse, and a curious building, semi-circular in plan, known as The Crescent. This was a cottage-row built by the Chamberlayne squire of about 1800 for his workers, and included centrally a Sunday School for their children, a communal oven, furnace and coal-store. Each family was given an acre of land and a pig. Not untypically, the building was sited down a by-lane out of view of the manorhouse windows; it has been converted into a single house—and that is not untypical, too.

Stow-on-the-Wold would be more appropriately visited when on the Iron Age route across Cotswold; and it seems likely that this eastern salt way skirted the town. It named a now-lost 'saltstraet' in Broadwell, a mainly eighteenth-century village around a good green. Donnington, a little to the northwest, also had its 'salt strete' as early as the eighth century, no doubt linking it with Longborough across the 'Saltemor' mentioned in a document of 1277 (and for today's walker there is a little used bridle-path which may approximate to its route). But unless the traveller takes a two-mile loop to the west he risks missing what, for many a thirsty but companionable local, is the attraction of the neighbourhood. In a lane just off the A 424 and at the lower end of a long, artificial and purposeful lake stands a group of eighteenth- and nineteenth-century buildings comprising a rural 'industrial complex' of mills, bakehouse and malthouse: Donnington Brewery, which has evaded being taken over and is still run by the Arkell family who founded it there in 1827 and are still contributing, most efficiently and tastily, to the refreshment of the north Cotswolds through seventeen local houses. The secluded setting and the fine stone buildings (unfortunately necessity has replaced their stone roofs with Welsh slate) might suggest even to a convinced teetotaller that beer cannot be as offensive as he may have assumed ... at least not Donnington's produced from locally grown barley with the assistance of power from the traditional mill-wheels.

Longborough, a mile to the north, owes its name not to its layout but to the Neolithic barrow, or what is left of it, up beside the main road. With its sloping triangular green set about with trim houses companionably close together, Longborough enjoys views across the low land watered by the infant Evenlode to the ridge on which stand the Rollright Stones. For the visitor a good view-point is the garden or the bar of the Coach and Horses, which serves mainly the locals and so has not been modernised (which often means improbably antiquated) for the tourists. The church at the lower end of the green is also worth a call. Originally Norman—the south doorway has its first capitals—it was in 1325 appropriated to Hailes abbey ... which meant that though the incumbent may have been deprived of much of his tithes, the abbey undertook to maintain the fabric of the chancel with its good east window and the unusual canopied bellcote above it. About the same time the beautiful south transept was added probably by the family of the knight whose effigy lies inside. Much of the work is of about 1330 when the almost austere 'Early English' of Icomb's chancel and Wick Rissington's had become softened. The former lancet windows, grouped in twos and threes, have lost their slim individuality as the space above them has been fashioned into flowing tracery and so been transformed into what was later and appropriately called the Decorated style. The most graceful achievement of the medieval Gothic, it was to grow in confidence until, in 1349, the Black Death brought it to a cruel and abrupt end.

For those interested in such matters, the two tombs now in the south transept show interesting contrasts. The effigy of the fourteenth-century knight lies on a table tomb, its only ornament having been the figures which once graced the sides. Near him Sir William and Lady Leigh lie also with hands in prayer in medieval recumbency, but his armour and her gown are of about 1630. More significantly, the darkly pillared canopy above them is unmistakably of classical inspiration, while one boy among the little 'weepers' below reads a book, a touch unlikely in the medieval centuries. The Renaissance, encouraging book-learning and admiration of Roman architecture (but also contributing to the break with Rome), has intervened between the two monuments.

A footpath leading from a few steps north of the Coach and Horses and passing below Sezincote almost hidden by fine trees would seem the line of this eastern salt way. Sezincote, though looking and sounding un-English, was Cheisnecott, the 'gravel cottage', in the Domesday Book, and a manor. Now it is a few cottages and outbuildings grouped around the House—and that is an unexpected one. Appreciation will depend on whether the visitor is likely to consider an easternness comparable with Brighton Pavilion suited to a Cotswold setting ... for Sezincote House, which charmed the Prince Regent when he visited it in 1807, is believed to have inspired (if that is the word) Brighton's distinctive work.

Sezincote was designed by Samuel Pepys Cockerell for his brother, Sir Charles Cockerell, who had made a fortune in the

East India Company and wished both to enjoy his wealth and to demonstrate what it could do in the way of a country house. In the orangy local stone, the house appears a compromise between the Cockerell brothers' Indian interests and the contemporary ideas of a gentleman's house, plus a few concessions to the English climate. Its large round-headed windows, neo-classical in proportion, are embellished with decoration of Eastern origin, its onion-shaped dome rises between chimney-stacks that despite attempts to give them hints of the Orient persist in being chimney-stacks, its low-pitched roofs end not in traditional finials or classical figures but in diminutive minarets. Now that the fine cedars of its park have grown to maturity, the house is perhaps acceptable, though the visitor may be reluctant to go as far as David Verey in his *Buildings of Gloucestershire* and call it a 'happy example of early nineteenth-century picturesque composition' or join in Edith Brill's hopes, expressed in her delightful and personal *Portrait of the Cotswolds*, that 'the Cotswolds have a way of absorbing eccentricities and that a house not in the vernacular could have its place'. Sezincote's oddity seems still to express its originator's determination to show at all costs that he was no ordinary country gentleman—which may make us suspect that Sir Charles, in spite of his great wealth, may have needed such a house as Sezincote to mask his ordinariness.

A mile north of Sezincote, the footpath way reaches Bourton-on-the-Hill climbing up the A 44 on the way from Moreton-in-Marsh to the Cotswold Edge. Its houses and cottages cling to its steep street with a purposefulness often found on Cotswold. At the top where the street bends stands the Horse and Groom, with a quietly dignified exterior befitting its eighteenth-century construction—it still has 'shell lights' to two of its windows—though inside modern notions of the decorative value of unstained wood are rather insistent. Visitors can look over their pint through the window of bar or lounge down the mixture of cottages and houses, close together as if supporting one another on the slope, that forms Bourton's street.

Bourton church, halfway up or down the hill, was Norman; its prim exterior tells that it has been remodelled several times. It has, however, one rare though fairly recent curiosity: its Standard Winchester Bushel and Peck measures. The medieval notions of measurement having been sketchy and various, the law demanded in 1587 that each parish should have such measures, and once they must have been common; but Victorian church-refurbishers too often disposed of such irreligious items. Bourton-on-the-Hill is one of the few places where a local curiosity-collector of about 1870 returned the parish possessions.

Bourton House at the bottom of the street was built about 1580, but most of what is visible if the gate in the high wall happens to be open is about two centuries younger and so boasts Ionic pilasters and a classical appearance. The original brewhouse and stables, now apparently adapted to living quarters, remain from the first House, and there is a large handsome barn dated 1570, all in the local warm buff stone.

Bourton Manorhouse was the home of the two Sir Thomas Overburys, uncle and nephew, in the seventeenth century. Both were associated with murders: the nephew, as has been told, recorded 'The Campden Wonder', the uncle was more directly and disastrously associated as the victim of an earlier part-passionate, part-political crime. The story was in its day very sensational. Sir Thomas, 'something of a poet and something more of a courtier', added distinction to James I's court; but when the royal favourite, Robert Carr, earl of Somerset, succumbed to the charms of the young, impetuous and recently married Frances Howard, countess of Essex, and the essential divorces came to be assumed, Sir Thomas Overbury's religious views caused him to protest vigorously ... so vigorously that Frances persuaded Carr to persuade the king to send Overbury to the Tower. There Carr and Frances supplied him with a wide variety of sweetmeats to relieve the tedium of the Tower fare and, since they contained a wide variety of poisons, to relieve him also of his life. Sir Thomas took three years to die, after which Carr and Frances obtained their respective divorces with royal approval and their ostentatious wedding was attended by His Majesty. But at court it was not always easy to retain royal favour against the envy and persistence of rivals; and soon Carr's enemies had become acquainted with the poison-supplying apothecary and were uncovering the murder. Carr, Frances, and four accomplices were arrested, charged, and found guilty. The four accomplices were hanged, but Carr and his Frances only suffered five years in the Tower ... which unjust denouement is perhaps rendered a little less unacceptable by the fact that, during their imprisonment, infatuation had turned into bitter hatred and though they came out to live in the same house (under restraint), Carr and Frances insisted on having their rooms as far apart as they possibly could.

Although no record tells of this eastern salt way's association with Blockley, two miles north of Bourton-on-the-Hill, it must have gone there. During the centuries before Chipping Campden and Moreton-in-Marsh grew to share the business of the north Cotswolds and while many a future parish had only a 'field chapel' without a graveyard, Blockley church had provided the last resting-place for a wide area. This may account for the raised floor of what was in the eighteenth century the Rushout family chapel; it is told that when being reconstructed, the lower part of the chapel—or was it a crypt serving as a charnel house?—was found to contain the remains of some two thousand skeletons. Confirming the extensive use of Blockley's burial facilities is the name of Porch House—its gables and four-centre-arched doorway with early Renaissance surround suggest a Tudor rebuilding—which is said to have provided overnight shelter for coffins brought from outlying parts of the large parish.

Blockley church, befitting the place's former importance, is large and well towered in rather orangy stone, but inside it is a little gaunt. Some traces of Norman work survive, but the building has suffered unsympathetic restoration and is now more interesting for its details. These include an early chained Bible from the days when books were very costly and, for those who find social significance in monumental fashions, quite a varied collection. Besides two late medieval brasses to priests, there are two monuments of Stuart date with kneeling figures—submissive medieval recumbency was then being abandoned for an assumed more personal approach to God. There follows in date an eighteenth-century series of noncommittal busts of the Rushout lords and ladies of the manor, all shown improbably in their early adulthood, and finally a mourning figure of 1800 drooping over an urn and hinting of the meaningful Victorian efforts to come.

Blockley village consists of fragments of streets and house-rows of the last three centuries—including some early twentieth-century suburban and some better, more fitting later ones—rather than a coherent place grown up about a recognisable centre. It seems to keep starting and stopping as it clambers across and about its little valleys.

Blockley has had an up-and-down history, too. An early reference tells of a dispute there about land between the abbey of Worcester who held the manor and that sinister character, Eadric Streona of Mercia, whose shadow makes even murkier the amply dark reign of Aethelred II (Ethelred the Unready to us though to his contemporaries 'unraed' meant nearer 'unwise'). The authors of the *Anglo-Saxon Chronicle* blame Eadric rather than the king for the succession of misfortunes; he appears to have habitually given Aethelred dubious advice and then, when disaster threatened, to have sided with the invading Danish Canute. Not surprisingly, the chroniclers add responsibility for sundry political murders. It seems, however, that Canute took his measure. Having acquired the kingdom, he used Eadric briefly to assert his authority in the Midlands, and then had him murdered. All told, one of the more repulsive characters in an unedifying period—though it seems that Eadric did not return the land at Blockley he had seized from the abbey of Worcester. When, seventy years later, the Domesday Book was compiled, it was still in lay possession.

Not an auspicious beginning, and thereafter Blockley thrived only patchily. It apparently gained little from the wool which brought wealth and work to nearby Chipping Campden. Blockley's hills provided grazing for some 2,000 of the bishop of Worcester's sheep; in 1384 William Grevel, the leading wool-merchant of Campden, bought the entire shearing but Blockley appears not to have benefited, as Grevel no doubt did, from the resale abroad. With the decline of the wool trade Blockley must have struggled along providing its necessities from more general agriculture. It appears to have been still struggling two hundred years later in the Rushouts' time as lords of the manor; Elizabeth (née Rushout), dowager countess of Northampton who died in 1730, was moved to alleviate the local poverty a little by a bequest by which loaves of bread were left for the poor in their church seats every other Sunday, a practice discontinued only in the 1920s. Not until the late eighteenth century was Blockley stirred by compensating industrial activity. Mills powered by the little streams were built to prepare silk for the ribbon-making factories of Coventry; by 1850 there were six of them employing about a hundred workers apiece, and the cottages which now stand in random rows had been built. But Free Trade came in, a lowering of tariffs allowed French silks into the country, and both Coventry and Blockley silk-workers suffered. By 1875 only two mills were still working, though a few other, very modest businesses had been set up including a small collar-making concern and two family firms of piano-makers. With such help Blockley struggled on though hampered by transport difficulties—its derelict station is two miles to the north

—until with the twentieth century came the bus and the car and opportunities to find work beyond its green valleys. Architecturally speaking, Blockley has not come out of its history as a show-place and few visitors stand about clicking their cameras. But for those seeking more than the obviously photogenic it has the character imposed by its varying fortunes.

Near by, and much more photographed Chipping Camden looks as if it has always been a more fortunate place. It had acquired a market by 1180 and so the prefix 'Chipping' from the Anglo-Saxon 'cepíng', a market. It came to thrive on wool, having as its leading townsman during the last half of the fourteenth century William Grevel, 'the flower of the wool merchants of all England' as is said on his tomb in the church. Remarkably his tall-windowed house has survived to grace what for tourists is one of the most fascinating of High Streets (though to get a contemporary measure of Grevel's wealth when looking at his house, the sightseer should imagine the street being composed mainly of timber-and-mud hovels). Grevel brought employment to many of Campden's four hundred or so inhabitants, but his business methods may have been more profitable than scrupulous, for on a tax-roll of 1380 is a note that he and his son John had been pardoned 'for all unjust and excessive weighings and purchase of wool contrary to the statute'. By then the Grevels had begun their climb up the social scale. John's son was to attain a knighthood, his grandson Thomas was to marry an heiress of the earls of Warwick and to become Sir Fulke Greville —the grandfather of the Sír Fulke who was patron to Shakespeare and Ben Jonson. Meanwhile, as a visit to Campden church shows, other families had come to occupy the Grevels' place in Campden and the wool trade: William and Alice Welley, John Lethenard, three-times married William Gibbys, wool-families, have their tombs in the church which, after William Grevel's time, they helped to rebuild ... though another wool-merchant, Robert Calf, is not remembered there but in Campden's Woolstaplers' Hall which he built and, more humbly, in the name of Calf's Lane.

When the wool trade deserted Campden for more industrialised Stroud, we might expect the town to have declined. William Camden, the historian contemporary of Shakespeare, found once-prosperous Winchcombe 'a poor beggarly town' and larger Cirencester had 'scarce the fourth part within the wall inhabited'. By contrast Campden was, he wrote, 'well peopled and of good resort'. It owed its survival to its newly acquired lord of the manor, Sir

Baptist Hicks, of a Gloucestershire family of mercers-become-landowners and from 1628 Viscount Campden of Campden. He it was who about 1613 built a splendid new manorhouse—which his grandson preferred to burn down rather than surrender to the Parliamentarians, so that little now remains but the lodges and the gateway. Perhaps Sir Baptist encouraged a new industry in Campden, the making of sacks and rope from locally grown hemp. He certainly gave the town its much-photographed Market Hall and the distinguished row of almshouses in Church Street (which cost him the then-considerable sum of £1,300). The appearance of many of the houses in the town suggests building during Sir Baptist's lifetime. He and his lady lie in Campden church under a splendid Renaissance canopy. By their time effigies may be assumed to try for a likeness—which may occasionally raise a visitor's eyebrow. He looks composed enough, but she . . . ? It is often said that a successful man must have a determined woman behind him.

Sir Baptist's successor and eldest daughter, Viscountess Juliana, whose bailiff contributed so much to the mystery of 'The Campden Wonder', is said to have been a generous and helpful lady of the manor. Was she in part responsible for Campden's avoiding Charles I's demand of £20 towards his ill-fated Ship Money? The town never paid. It was then suffering an outbreak of plague which, according to the churchwardens' records, had been caused by 'an infected dead dog, which was thrown amongst growing hemp, and infected those which gathered the hemp a month after'. (Among their accounts are also items which show the varied matters churchwardens had to deal with: the cost of sending a woman to London to be cured of the King's Evil; gifts to 'a woman ready to die', a condition she apparently accepted for some years; the fees of a bonesetter of Broadway and the costs of the men who held the patient; gifts to three boys 'that were appointed to go to the Isle of Providence' and so formed, possibly unwillingly, Campden's contribution to the early settlement of New England.)

By the early 1800s Campden had acquired some silk mills and at least one flax mill—a row of cottages is still named 'Twine Cottages' —which must have helped the humbler townspeople. Regular employment had by then become very necessary, for in 1799 the common fields which had sustained the place for perhaps a thousand years were enclosed; those lesser landholders who had relied on their few acres and their grazing rights for much of their food would have found themselves ousted as they were obliged to sell the land they could not afford to hedge or fence. But as elsewhere such small industries dwindled as competition from larger manufactories grew, and Campden suffered the nineteenth-century decline of so much of rural England ... until it was rescued by its own attractive appearance.

About the turn of this century it caught the eye of a group of craftsmen inspired by the ideas of William Morris and his abhorrence of what he regarded as the soullessness of the Industrial Revolution. His disciple in Campden was C. R. Ashbee who in 1906 expressed his hopes in his *Craftsmanship in Competitive Industry*, and founded a Guild of Handicrafts 'to do good work, and to do it in such a way as to conduce to the welfare of the workmen'. In a former silk mill and some nearby empty cottages, Ashbee gathered his guild members to begin the revival of Campden as a centre for all kinds of craft from the restoration of old buildings to bookbinding and jewellery-making. Enthusiasm was not, however, to overcome mass production and the public's readiness to accept the more-or-less adequate. The Guild's products, of fine design and immaculate workmanship, proved too costly for all but a few discerning and moneyed admirers. Yet Ashbee's efforts were not wholly lost. He and his fellow workers had drawn attention to Campden, and their activities led to the foundation of the Campden Trust to restore and preserve the buildings. Since then others have come who, being often foremost in their craft, have contributed to the town's reputation and well-being and, above all, have attracted visitors and so encouraged Campden's present industry: tourism. That may, at summer weekends, seem an artificial and irritating occupation, and one wonders what the locals thought when many of their newer homes—so carefully suitable, of course, that the estate won a prize for design—had to be tucked discreetly away from the perfection of their High Street. But tourism depends on maintaining appearances as well as profits.

Campden church whose immaculate tower rises above the little streets at the far end of the High Street is an almost unavoidable sight for visitors, though perhaps not all join in the praise that it is expected to justify. So thoroughly remodelled between about 1460 and 1510 that little trace of the earlier building can be found, it is substantially a 'wool church' built in what ecclesiologists call the 'Perpendicular Gothic' ... and that combination implies both its achievement and its limitations.

Technically this last phase of medieval building came near to gaining the full benefit of the Gothic style introduced three centuries earlier. The pointed arch, capable of spanning varying widths without loss of strength, opened possibilities of distributing the thrusts from one part of the building to another while the invention of the flying buttress enabled the thrusts—from the main roof, for example—to be carried over outer parts such as aisles to foundations outside the main supporting arcade. Such a realisation opened the way not only to much thinner walls and slimmer pillars but to windows so large that they could fill in the spaces in what was almost a stone frame.

In fact no building utilising the full possibilities of the style was ever built, but the underlying method demanded some understanding of its principles and so created the need for a more controlled, less individual approach. Building became increasingly a matter not for local craftsmen (who had at times indulged their own fancies) but for experts; the Master Mason (often architect to us) had come into his own, and his own was via his assistants and apprentices to give a sameness and a rigidity to fifteenth-century work throughout the country. The aspiration that had produced the first Gothic and the individuality that had spread through the 'Decorated' had to go. In their place was a structure of near-mechanical perfection which seemed to require by way of decoration patterns based on verticals in wall panelling and most noticeably in window tracery. The viewer does not have to be told a second time that the work is dubbed 'Perpendicular'.

The new style was also economical. Research has revealed Master Masons ordering standardised units of stonework from workshops specialising in architectural items, implying something near to mass production. It is not surprising that the style is sometimes called 'businessman's Gothic', and that even the most pious of wool merchants used it extensively when he rebuilt his home-town church to the glory of God and of his own family.

As may be seen in the Cotswolds and elsewhere, these 'wool churches' at times achieve a loftiness and a dignity beyond the run of small-town and village churches; Northleach's is enchanting but it owes much to its details. And when, as at Fairford, the glass has survived almost in entirety—and to be fair to their designers, the windows were not intended to be filled with the poor glass they often now frame—the light inside is so softened that the church seems to hold ancient mystery. But sometimes the very spaciousness of a 'Perp' church, the great achievement of its designer, gives a feeling of emptiness, almost of aridity. Then the visitor may perhaps recall the time of its building. It was the century following the repeated visitations of the Black Death when men, taught to accept that God rewarded the obedient and punished the wrongdoer, struggled to understand how He could have sent a pestilence which struck indiscriminately and on a scale which, in many a town and village, killed hideously a third of the population within two or three weeks. It was the century which saw rival popes struggling for the headship of the Church which, to counteract the inevitable weakening of its authority, demanded and at times cruelly enforced unquestioning acceptance of its teaching. It was the century during which England and France—and hordes of mercenaries from half Europe—were embroiled in a seemingly endless war that had begun as a belated feudal adventure and ended with a growing awareness of national identity, an awareness that was to shatter the unity of Christendom. It was not a time when those who built for the Church or the rich of their home-towns were encouraged to express their individuality—except occasionally those who carved the wooden animals and the stone grotesques or painted the Doom on the wall when they seem at times to have expressed, perhaps unconsciously, their tortured fears. And significantly 'Perpendicular Gothic' was an English invention. Formerly, England's craftsmen had found inspiration in architectural ideas that were common to Christendom. Now, often paid by those whose wealth depended on international trade and who therefore looked to and at times financed governments which would favour English interests, they built in a peculiarly national style.

Chipping Campden, so obviously a tourist attraction, tends to overshadow other places in its neighbourhood. Two miles to the northeast is Ebrington (to some locals still 'Yabberton'), on the hilly fringe of what was Henmarsh and appropriately some of its cottage rows are thatched. The church, set on the end of a little ridge giving views of the hills above Blockley and Campden, has gathered something from every century since it was built about 1100. Perhaps most striking is the tomb of Sir John Fortesque, author of legal treatises and Lord Chief Justice during the middle years of the Wars of the Roses, an uncomfortable time for one holding such a position. Sir John supported the Lancastrians. When the Yorkist Edward IV triumphed at Tewkesbury in 1471, Sir John suffered from the contemporary custom of charging losing opponents with a variety of treasons; but because of his age the attainder was reversed and Sir John was allowed to live out his last years at Ebrington where he died in 1484 at over ninety—an achievement at a time when nature, unassisted by violent politics, tended to assure a comparatively short expectancy of life. Sir John's effigy shows him in his finery as Lord Chief Justice; the painted stone has been a little obviously touched up.

Northwest are Hidcote House—Stuart and remarkably unaltered—and Kiftsgate House, the gardens of both of which are opened to the public during the summer and attract visitors to the neighbourhood. Less visited but no less interesting in their differing ways are the villages that lie under the Edge between the most northerly fragment of Cotswold, fort-capped Meon Hill, and photogenic Broadway.

Mickleton, the most northerly, is a place to wander round because its interest is more individual than collective. Lying where the hills end and the Vale spreads out it has, as one might expect, a mixture of houses: some of stone, some timber-and-stone, some plastered, some thatched. The manorhouse, originally Stuart, was until recently a school and, according to an informative resident, suffered in consequence; it stands neglected and empty behind its high wall. Nearby is Medford House built about 1695. Classical notions had by then filtered to Cotswold. They demanded that at least externally a house should show a formal appearance, and so symmetry had to replace the earlier haphazardness (often the product of internal needs and growth). Also, as at Medford House, a porticoed entrance was a required distinction and commonplace eaves had to be hidden behind a cornice (here topped with vases). Yet traditional stone-mullioned windows were retained as if the architect—or was he only the local master-builder?—could not bring himself completely to break with the earlier style. On the fringes of Mickleton are much more recent houses in reconstituted stone though one wonders if some of them needed to have such aggressively angular roofs. Perhaps when trees have grown up about them they will look more in keeping . . . which cannot be expected from the brick-and-slate houses that intrude here and there. They may be a hundred years old but they show no intention of mellowing.

For those who like their history to be deeper than governmental activities and economic repercussions, Mickleton is one of those places where an illuminating item of local history has been recorded. It concerns the enclosure of its ancient common fields—

but in 1616, long before Enclosure Acts and government-appointed Commissioners. Mickleton's enclosure took place when the lord of the manor had to persuade his tenants to share out the village land—and in many cases of which we have details persuasion resulted in allocating inadequate portions of land or in undisguised eviction and the destruction of village homes. Not so at Mickleton. Its squire, apparently much less grasping and autocratic than most of his contemporaries, called meetings of his tenants to discuss how the common fields and the village waste should be shared, and all —except one—agreed with the forty-seven acres allowed for each yardland (the medieval unit). But just to allot the agreed area in large plots, it was soon realised, would result in some tenants receiving better land than others, so each yardland was reassessed at thirty acres while the remaining seventeen to each were more fairly distributed. All, except one, neighbourly agreed. It was then realised that Mickleton's poor, who had eked out their livelihoods by grazing their few animals on the waste, would suffer by the new arrangements. So the squire persuaded his tenants to give up an acre or two each which was collectively to be retained as common, and himself granted leases at very low rents to the more needy, made gifts to them of money, food and clothing, and instituted a charity for the aged poor. This last item was probably intended to quiet the one dissenting voice; for the only opponent was the vicar. He maintained that enclosure, by allowing landholders to convert former arable land into pasture, would seriously deplete his tithe of grain; and the glebe (land long before set aside for clergy maintenance) would, he insisted, remain glebe—which would allow him to claim the produce from what had been church land whoever came to hold it. Though offered compensation of eight acres of arable, twenty of meadow, and an additional right to the hay of twelve other plots, the vicar remained unsatisfied ... and even after the squire had promised him an extra £10 a year in cash, he insisted on taking the matter to court. There many of the tenants witnessed that all except the vicar were well satisfied: the poor had their rights preserved and their charity, the lord could look forward to greater profits from his compact and more manageable demesne and the tenants had their shares (many of which, by the squire's generosity, had been converted from mere copyhold for life into estates of inheritance). The vicar lost his case; but those of us who like to glimpse social history being made must be grateful to him for being so awkward a neighbour as to cause Mickleton's affairs to be recorded in the State Papers of the time.

Southwards from Mickleton there is the road or for the walker a series of footpaths linking the five villages which lie under the woods clambering up to the Edge. Above, along the crest, a lane follows a route that must in Iron Age times have linked the ancient Way with Meon Hill fort; the lower ways would seem to have come into being when the Anglo-Saxons established the villages.

Aston-sub-Edge has a row of good cottages on a by-road along its stream and one of the most delightful of manorhouses. In honey-coloured stone, its many gables are still topped with ball-finials while at one side is a half-timbered portion from an even earlier house. The whole must look much as it did when Prince Rupert, King Charles I's nephew—and later his commander against Parliament—visited the house in the days before civil war was thought of.

Rupert's host at Aston-sub-Edge was another notable royalist, Endymion Porter, part poet, part patron of the arts, and the occasion of the prince's visit was the 'Cotswold Olympicks', a rustic tournament which had been revived in 1605 by Robert Dover, a Warwickshire solicitor. To make the occasion more than usually memorable, Porter gave Dover 'some of the king's old clothes, with a hat and a feather and ruff, purposely to grace him'. Held on the crest of what is now Dover's Hill above Weston-sub-Edge, the games included skittles, leaping, the quintain, wrestling, cudgel-playing, coursing and shin-kicking ... which despite their crudity as sports had earned King James's approval so that such poets of the day as Michael Drayton and Thomas Heywood wrote verses in their honour and Ben Jonson composed an 'epigram to my Joviall Good Friend, Mr Robert Dover' which ended:

> But I can tell thee, Dover, how thy Games
> Renew the Glories of our blessed James ...
> How they advance true love and neighbourhood,
> And doe both Church and Common wealth the good
> In spite of Hipocrites, who are the worst
> Of Subjects; Let such envie till they burst!

Except for a break under the Commonwealth, the meetings were kept up annually until 1851 when they were ended because, according to some authorities, they had become 'too rough', according to others enclosure of the common land had limited space. The site, with its view over the Vale of Evesham, is now owned by the National Trust and recently the games have been revived, though perhaps not with all the original vigour. (According to Miss Edith Brill, in shin-kicking 'the two contestants had iron plates on the toes of their boots and, holding each other by the shoulder with out-stretched arms, kicked at each other's shins until one was obliged to give in.' Revival of that particular sport seems unlikely.)

The strip of country southwestwards was once famous for its orchards. Plums were grown for plum jerkum, a local beverage of considerable liveliness, and little Saintbury once had its cherry fair. Weston-sub-Edge's lanes still twist and turn among remaining orchards to link a mixture of houses, some old, some new, the most noteworthy being Latimers, gabled, tall-chimneyed and Tudor.

Saintbury's houses and farms, all except one attractive, climb up from its cross on the main road to its church set finely high on a brief levelling of the wooded escarpment. From the churchyard one looks over the grey roofs and the many trees of the village to Bredon Hill standing up out of the Vale, and to the Malverns, backed on a clear day by the greyly distant Welsh mountains. There can hardly be another church with such a view, and for the architecturally inclined or the merely curious, a look inside is interesting. It is mostly fourteenth-century, though its 'Decorated' work is restrained. The Norman doorway with, above it, a Saxon 'mass dial' must have come from an earlier church. In the base of the tower, which formed the south transept and is now the bell-chamber, stands a curious octagonal stone table whose origin and purpose are uncertain. It is claimed to have been an altar in use in pre-Christian time—which would make it incredibly well preserved. David Verey in the Gloucestershire volume of the *Buildings of England* series assumes it to have been a dole table on which gifts of charity bread were placed for distribution among the local poor, which suggests a date roughly contemporary with the oldest of the initials carved on it. Or it may have once stood outside the church as a table about which lepers gathered to eat food left by the charitable. The leprous were often compelled to spend much of their time walking from place to place and Saintbury's lane linked the usable portion of Roman Ryknild Street with the ancient and lonely Ways that cross on Broadway Hill.

Willersey, between Saintbury and Broadway, has a long green with the houses, dating from about 1650, set well back from the road, and another neat street leading to the church. Because next door to much-visited Broadway, Willersey tends to be overlooked ... which means it is less cluttered with parked cars during holiday times, has few notices for cafés or antiques, and gives the impression that its houses are homes. An Australian friend, recommended the Cotswolds as a tourists' 'must', spent a fortnight conscientiously visiting all the better known spots, came on Willersey by accident and judged it the pleasantest village he had seen.

From Willersey to Broadway is barely two miles along the A 46. The walker's path is better, and the motorist might prefer to take the lane which meets the A 44 a mile northwest of Broadway. At Broadway it is not the new housing towards Willersey that brings the cameras out and the customers into the hotels, cafés and 'antiques'. It is the street which makes it, in Pevsner's words, 'the show village of England' where 'Tudor, Stuart and Georgian are happily mixed'. It is almost improbably good, and the occupants of the street—mainly outsiders, one suspects—have for the past several decades kept up Broadway's tourist-attracting charms. One wonders, however, how much longer they will be able to do so. Already the Old Coach and Horses has given way to 'new development'—in the Cotswold style of course. By the time that has begun to mellow and merge into the street will other buildings have begun to be 'developed'?

The famous street is, in fact, a main-road off-shoot of the village which started in a combe a mile to the south, at Bury End. There is the original Broadway, with its church unusually dedicated to Eadburgha, granddaughter to Alfred the Great. At first glance the church looks fifteenth-century; but step inside and one sees immediately Norman pillars and arches showing the first attempts at the Gothic point. For the first five hundred years of its history, Broadway's centre was thereabouts; and still a few old cottages stand along the lane which passes what were the village mill and, though remodelled since the 1300s, the grange of the manor-owning abbots of Pershore.

Beyond the church the lane goes on to climb to Snowshill ('Snawsl' to some locals), a cluster of trim houses where the road twists to negotiate the last quarter-mile of the hill. The manor-house, dating from about 1500, was part of Catherine Parr's dowry —some of the house she knew remains—was added to in the early 1700s, and so is now a mixture of early Tudor and early Georgian, and one of the most delightful of Cotswold houses. Now owned by the National Trust, it is also visited for its 'Magpie Museum', the collection of Charles Wade, 'scholar, architect and artist-craftsman', who owned and thoroughly restored the house in the 1920s. There is a varied collection of byegones ranging from eighteenth-century musical instruments to Cromwellian armour, from lace-working and wool-weaving equipment to such means of transport as hobby-horses and penny-farthings ... something, indeed, for everyone.

The lane through Snowshill was not, however, the original road up from Bury End. Until into the 1500s twisting Conygree Lane opposite the church (and now in part the drive to Dor Knap) was, incredibly, the main road from Oxford to Worcester. It led, of course, to the meeting-place of the prehistoric Ways on Broadway Hill.

FOUR

Ryknild Street and Buggildway

From Broadway Hill where the prehistoric Way coming from south of east must have curved southwesterly to follow the Edge, and another route in use in the Iron Age if not before led northwards to the fort on Meon Hill above Mickleton, two other ways went more directly southwards.

The more easterly of these is the Roman Ryknild Street. Once running from a township on the Foss Way near Bourton-on-the-Water through Alcester and Derby to York, it is below the Edge a minor but direct road which has borrowed the name of Buckle Street. Between Weston-sub-Edge and Saintbury it reaches the escarpment as a green lane, known formerly and bluntly as 'Dirty Lane', and then it climbs boldly through fine beechwoods to attain the crest ... only, except to very expert eyes, to disappear. One would have thought that even in Anglo-Saxon times such a road providing an easy way from the hill routes across still forested and still marshy lowland would have remained in frequent use; but either the locals, circa A.D. 700, had other ideas and other needs or some subsequent landowner has high-handedly ploughed it up.

For those who like to trace the Cotswold length of Ryknild (on foot of necessity and with an O.S. map in hand), the boundary between the parishes of Chipping Campden and Saintbury, following field walls, indicates the missing mile and a half. Along the A 44 southeast of Broadway Hill, Ryknild reappears as an unsignposted but not too overgrown bridle-path branching south from near an isolated bungalow. Here the raised Roman road, the 'agger', is clearer (excavation has revealed the stone slabs still in situ) with the walkers' path beside it. After crossing the Snowshill lane it becomes more defined, a track known as 'Switchback' to Spring Hill —after which it again loses itself except, here and there, for a slight ridging of the ground. A mile and a half further, at the hamlet of Hinchwick, it reappears as the lane approaching Condicote from

The Prehistoric Way skirting High Cotswold

COTSWOLD COUNTRY

From near Roman Ryknild Street, above Saintbury

Withington in the Coln valley

COTSWOLD VILLAGES

Hazleton on its hill

'he High Street, Chipping Campden

COTSWOLD STREETS

'illage street, Whittington

Farm under the hills, Roel near Guiting Power

COTSWOLD FARMS

Hill-top farm by its essential pond, Hawkesbury Upton

ross, green and church, Condicote

COTSWOLD HAMLETS

amlet by its brook, Lower Hilcott

Manorhouse and church, Owlpen

NEIGHBOURS

Manorhouse and tithe barn, Syde

Norman tower, thirteenth-century nave, Ozleworth

COTSWOLD CHURCHES

Fourteenth-century 'Decorated' transept, xteenth-century spire, Minchinhampton

Fifteenth-century church, Northleach

COTSWOLD 'WOOL CHURCH'

the north. As if determined to ignore Roman handiwork, that village has placed itself on a winding loop-road—and, being perhaps the pleasantest of Cotswold's upland villages, is worth the slight detour. Good, working, honest-looking farms stand around a walled green; to one side, almost hidden by trees is the small, mainly Norman church, plain except for an amateur-looking head under the piscina in the chancel, and with its walls leaning as if they have tired after standing most of nine hundred years. Southwards, as if in belated acknowledgement of Ryknild's existence, the village has allowed the name 'Condicote Lane' to be applied to two unmetalled and little-frequented miles of Roman origin. After the Stow–Bristol road, though Ryknild must have reached to the Foss Way, its course is now untraceable.

In the valley of the little River Eye near the southern end of Ryknild are two of Cotswold's more featured villages: Upper and Lower Slaughter. Apparently a single manor in the Domesday Book, they had been separated into two parishes before 1200, for each has a church possessing, among later remodelling, Norman work. Upper Slaughter appears to have had a castle, too, on the out-jutting ground east of the church and half-circled by the river, though nothing in the way of masonry is left.

Both Slaughters are well known from their photographs. Water adds charm to a view, and the little Eye, by reflecting the many trees and the trim, grey houses which are often linked to the road by foot-bridge, certainly has contributed to the look of both villages ... though it contributed more rurally before its banks were confined by stone walls and the stream-side strips of grass became lawns. The most noteworthy house in Upper Slaughter is its manor-house, mainly sixteenth-century with later additions and, like the smaller houses, all very carefully preserved. Lower Slaughter, too, has a good gabled manorhouse a half-century or so younger, and now a hotel. The village also has its mill of about 1820 and unfortunately in brick though it has been left its mill-wheel. Both villages tend to appear less charming at summer weekends; they are too small to cope with the streams of visitors. A better time is early spring or well into the autumn ... though too wet a day might remind that the name Slaughter comes from 'sloh', a slough or mire—rather an insult to the sparkling Eye. At any season the sentimental might prefer the less convincing alternative derivation from 'slah-treow', a sloe tree.

Like the Slaughters, Bourton-on-the-Water owes much to its

Narcissus habit of admiring its own reflection in the river Windrush. Its tree-shaded river-side green and its graceful bridges have been subjects of countless photographs ... and for today's visitors there are such additional attractions as a small zoo, a 'butterfly museum', an aquariun, a model village, and a working mill, with the inevitable cafés, tea-shops, gift shops, et cetera. Since tourism is nowadays one of the major industries of Cotswold, one must expect such a place ... though a visitor arriving at the height of the holiday season and allergic to the more vivid forms of sign might be forgiven for wondering if Bourton is not risking destroying the charms that have brought the car-loads and the coach-loads. He may, however, notice that many of the houses are pleasant, and the church, though largely remodelled in 1784 and again between 1875 and 1890 and so several centuries younger than its more sentimental visitors may assume, is less pretentious Victorian Gothic than many (except for the Georgian tower and the chancel which is genuine fourteenth-century—though its original restfulness has been lost by the much later and rather overpowering painted ceiling).

Less visited is the original Bourton, Salmonsbury Camp lying where the Windrush and the Dickler join, an unexpectedly low situation for what began as an early Iron Age fort. The curious will not find it easily. A lane parallel to the Rissington road follows the fort's bank across the rather dejected land east of Bourton until a 'Danger: keep out' notice brings a stop. Excavations in 1860 discovered nearly 150 iron bars of the type that were used as currency about the time of Julius Caesar's visit. Another archaeological dig in 1931 added the foundations of a dwelling, circular with mud-and-wattle walls and a thatched roof, and a scarcely less primitive Anglo-Saxon hut, a reminder that the fort owes its name of Salmonsbury not to the fish in the nearby rivers but to 'suhl-man', the Anglo-Saxon for ploughman.

Similarly linking Broadway Hill with the neighbourhood of Bourton-on-the-Water is another, slightly more curving route: Buggildway or, as known since the seventeenth century, Buckle Street. It starts off as the minor road signposted 'Snowshill' and appears to have taken over a mile or so of the prehistoric Way (depending on how we assume that route's curving to change from the ridge now used by the A 44 to follow the Edge). Buggildway's course along the Cotswold crest begins with an almost Romanly direct half-mile and, as if some later landowner wished to acknowledge that it was no ordinary lane, a pair of stone gate-posts (but no longer any gates) gives it a distinguished send-off.

Though keeping to the Edge, Buggildway at first goes slightly below the summit, so the views are of the wide fieldscape tilting southeastwards. Those who wish again to admire the huge expanse of the Vale with the bulge of Bredon Hill in the middle distance will have to go the few paces to triple-turreted Broadway Tower, raised in 1800 by an earl of Coventry so that, it is said, he might see it from Spring Hill a mile and a half to the southeast. Not until Buggildway curves round the wood that clings to the combe-sides above Bury End will the traveller glimpse the wider view; and shortly afterwards the route edges more southerly and goes across High Cotswold.

It is a lofty and often lonely Way, for the most part a motorable lane and for a few miles about the Stow–Stanway road of B-road surfacing. Quarries towards its southern end, most overgrown, one still producing the wherewithal for reconstituted stone, tell of a former usage; but its directness and its keeping to the ridge suggest an origin earlier than the Anglo-Saxon lady Burghild who had given it its name by at least A.D. 709—and one wonders what she would think of her once distinguished name being corrupted into such an everyday object as a buckle. It passes several round barrows, some rendered slight by ploughing, one of the group once known as Salters' Pool Barrows standing up well on the sky-line, while above Lower Slaughter it runs close to the large, tree-clad tumulus known as Wagborough Bush. Incidentally a route from which an expansive view of green and reddish-brown field reaches out first to one side then to the other, Buggildway suggests a pre-Roman link between the meeting-place on Broadway Hill and the Iron Age fort near Bourton-on-the-Water, and a pause along it may still give a feeling of ancient remoteness.

The villages as usual lie off the Way, in the valley of the Windrush. That river rises a little south of Snowshill, at least during the wetter months; during the summer it is often hardly liquid enough to justify the name of Ford to one of its highest hamlets. Before reaching Ford, however, it has trickled below Cutsdean, a village owing its name to the Anglo-Saxon leader who, as has been noted, is everlastingly remembered in the name Cotswold.

Built high, Cutsdean fits such a beginning—even though the books all but ignore it and Verey in his *Buildings of Gloucestershire* finds space for only five lines about its church which, apart from its 'probably fourteenth-century tower', is 'without interest'. He might have noted the sturdy farm-buildings with good barns, though they are less lofty than elsewhere so as to resist the winds which must often sweep through the village. A work-a-day place off most tourist routes, it looks determined to stay where it is, not to be lured to take life easy in some soft valley. One feels that the Anglo-Saxon Cod would have approved of his foundation's present solid and honest appearance.

A mile downstream, Temple Guiting owes its distinctive name to the Knights Templar who acquired the manor in the twelfth century and to the Anglo-Saxon name for the upper Windrush; it seems they suffered wetter weather circa 780, for the name derives from 'gute', a rushing out, a flood. Temple Guiting has, among other good houses, a remarkably fine Manor House Farm perched high above the river—now widened and watery enough to make a pond—complete with its Tudor-arched windows set in square-headed, drip-stoned surrounds. It was probably built as a summer residence for the bishops of Oxford—which would date it to about 1545, for the see was one of the few established by Henry VIII's short-lived ecclesiastical reforms. The nearby church was largely reconstructed about 1740, not a time for much village-church building. The knowledgeable may amuse themselves picking out the surviving medieval details: the fifteenth-century settings of the Georgian windows, a little 'Decorated' work here and there, the fearsome gargoyles on the largely rebuilt tower. Perhaps more noteworthy are the Royal Arms of George II, uncoloured but splendid, and the font of about 1340. This last is, for its time, stolid and plain but for a row of flowers. A mile south is the hamlet of Kineton, once 'King-ton' and a royal manor, now a group of mainly Stuart farms and cottages, and the Halfway House, a nicely kept village inn invitingly gay with flowers through the summer.

Set above the Windrush, Guiting Power is a pleasant place if a little self-conscious. The older houses along its street and grouped around its tilting green are all very trim and very well restored. The church is Norman plus a chancel of 1903, a little chill and improbable. The suffix 'Power', by the way, derives from the le Poer family who owned the manor in the 1200s. Across the fields is Castlett Farm, once the Domesday manor of Cateslat, the wild cats' valley, a reminder that the villagers of early medieval times had more than an occasional marauding fox to deal with.

Naunton, two winding miles downstream, is usually viewed from the main road along the ridge to its south. From there it appears to lie comfortably along the valley, screened from the winds that chill the wold, a compact little place. To the visitor it spreads itself a mile along its lane, with the church at one end and the Black Horse near the other. 'Niwetone' in Domesday Book, it probably began as an offshoot of the nearby Harford which was first recorded in the eighth century. Its church was, except for the tower, almost entirely rebuilt during the Tudor century. The most remarkable feature, a pre-Conquest cross in the north wall of the nave, may have come from elsewhere. The nave roof has some of its Tudor timber, but more eye-catching is the pulpit of about 1400. A number of medieval stone pulpits are still to be found on Cotswold; Naunton's is one of the finest.

Of Naunton's houses, from the sixteenth-century one near the church to the mill—seventeenth-century but much adapted when it became a house in the 1960s—some may be of more than usual interest. Near the mill is a group of cottages, including Dale Terrace hidden away through an archway, of about 1864, showing that the Victorians could emulate the Cotswold style of the seventeenth century. The pigeon-house halfway along the street, the only survival from a rebuilding about 1560 of the manorhouse (before another rebuilding of about 1890), is a good example, with below the birds' entry in each of its four gables a bold moulding to keep out rats. Cromwell House, now plastered, has a four-centre-arched doorway telling that it was built before the Lord Protector's time. During the rebellious mid-seventeenth century it belonged to the Aylworths, staunch Parliamentarians; in 1644 Richard Aylworth commanded the forces which successfully stopped the Royalists at Stow. Subsequent Aylworths built their country house at Aylworth a mile to the south of Naunton and the site of another Domesday manor.

Below Naunton the Windrush meanders to Bourton. The motorist will have to climb up to find the last mile and a half of Buggildway; the walker can follow the waterside path which at Aston Farm finds the remains of the long abandoned railway linking Bourton and Cheltenham near the site of the far longer abandoned Roman posting station. Or, if another call at Bourton is not wished for, one can turn aside and after taking the Foss Way for half a mile southwards make for Clapton-on-the-Hill.

At first glance the rather work-a-day hill-top village may seem hardly worth a pause—except for the views of the Windrush valley and the pattern of field and copse rising up the far side. But a closer look will show quite a lot in little Clapton. The church stands between two good houses, the manorhouse, tall with projecting gabled entrance and a large dormer matching on either side, and Church Farm, longer and triple-gabled, both from early Stuart times and looking as if they have been earning an honest living ever since. The church has that appeal which comes from smallness and thirteenth-century simplicity; it is barely five paces across, eight paces would take the local brides from the door to the altar. It seems lucky to have survived, for a note in the church tells how in 1636 the vicar 'albeit [he] has in tithes to the yearly value of £30 ... has with oathes protested that there shall be no prayers read there but has offered £5 to pull down the chapel' in order apparently to make Clapton people go into Bourton. The villagers petitioned the Archbishop of Canterbury ... though, according to the historian Atkyns writing in 1712, they had to wait nearly eighty years before 'the church and chapel were new built'. It appears that Atkyns exaggerated, for some of the windows are still of about 1300, as is also the chancel arch on the north side of which a rare inscription has been incised. Its Latin, abbreviated as was usual in the thirteenth century and here and there so worn that the experts are unsure of its exact phrasing, probably reads in translation: 'Whosoever shall say devoutly a Pater and an Ave on his knees and in person: lo! there is a reward then and there of a thousand days'. The opening words are those sometimes questioned; the ending leaves no doubt that the inscription refers to the grant of a thousand days' indulgence ... a generous and, to Protestant eyes, offensive grant which, we must suppose, has been until comparatively recently hidden under plaster in order to survive post-Reformation 'restorers'. The most likely date of the work is 1239 when the newly rebuilt abbey of Evesham (which possessed Bourton-on-the-Water and also the chapelry of Clapton) was dedicated; it was a medieval custom for indulgences to be granted to those who had in some way contributed to church-building.

Having reached Clapton one almost must go on southeasterly along the Windrush valley. The lane skirts Sherborne—a place once of considerable local importance which will be looked at later —to reach Windrush, a high-standing village of cottages about a triangular green shaded by lime-trees. The church is more than locally well-known for its Norman work: the leaning chancel arch with its variations on the chevron pattern, the south doorway with its surround of strange long-beaked birds' heads and long-snouted animals' heads, and the leering animals that support the nave roof .. which make one wonder what such un-Christian beings are doing in a church. Sometimes one can assume that the faces which peer down from corbel or gargoyle are expressions of medieval humour, crude though it may appear to us. But at Windrush—and, as we shall see, elsewhere on Cotswold—the visitor who takes more than a passing glance may find himself feeling that they are much more than attempts at jollity or decoration ... and even more than had been suggested by the Bestiaries, those books describing the incredibly improbable monsters and beings supernatural (or would 'sub-natural' be the word?) which medieval man believed in.

The lane goes on to the Barringtons, arriving by way of the riverside Fox Inn—a call at which may be welcomed by those who have found the very strange carvings at Windrush unsettling. Little Barrington with its houses set above a long green through which a stream trickles, seems a sober, open place and its church, also in part Norman, is simple and undisturbing. Great Barrington village across the Windrush is mostly an adjunct to Palladian and imposing Barrington Park, imitating the Corinthian style though the embellishments to its grounds include one Doric and one Gothic temple. The church, inside the park, has a late Norman chancel arch but is otherwise very fifteenth-century and very much tidied up by a Victorian restorer. Quite a good effigy of Stuart date is tucked away behind the organ. Another more prominent monument to the Bray children being guided heavenwards by an angel, though dated 1720, hints of Victorian fashions to come. The children, and a young cousin, too, all died of 'the Small Pox'.

If any unease still lingers from Windrush's carvings they should be dispelled, at least for the time being, by a call at Taynton—which should be something of a place of pilgrimage for everyone who has delighted in Cotswold stone. The area about Barrington and Taynton and Burford was formerly famous for its quarries, and Taynton was the home of two of the great seventeenth-century families of masons, the Strongs and the Kempsters, who built several of the great houses of Cotswold and—such was their more-than-local renown—were called in by Sir Christopher Wren to undertake much of the stone-work for churches rebuilt after the fire of London, including St Paul's cathedral. Edward Strong, brother of Thomas who with the bishop of London laid the foundation stone for St Paul's in 1675, asked for the following inscription on his tombstone:

> In erecting the edifice of St Paul's several years were spent, from its foundations to his laying the last stone and herein (equally with its ingenious architect Sir Christopher Wren and its truly-pious Diocesan Bishop Compton) he shared the felicity of seeing both the beginning and finishing of that stupendous fabric.

Sir Christopher, we may be sure, would not have queried the 'equally'; he knew very well that the creation of such a building as St Paul's depended on the partnership of architect and mason, both geniuses, both guiding and using the skills of the thirty-five stone-working craftsmen, many of them from the Taynton and Burford neighbourhood. Similarly Vanbrugh, the creator of Blenheim Palace, worked with Valentine Strong, son of Thomas.

Though records do not tell of the humbler homes the craftsmen of Taynton built, the village must be their handiwork. Many of the houses, grouped along little streets seemingly by chance and yet achieving a unity, appear to date from the time the Strongs and the Kempsters and those they trained and employed were working. Taynton church, however, tells that the seventeenth-century mason-families had long lines of fine craftsmen in their ancestry ... and, indeed, we know that Taynton stone had been used in New College, Oxford, in 1396, in St George's chapel, Windsor, in 1474, and that several churches in the villages around, many of which date from Norman times, have Taynton stone.

Taynton church itself is a masterpiece and a memorial to the ancient skills ... and it seems the old craftsmen were an individual lot for, though the church was rebuilt about 1450, the masons have for the most part ignored the contemporary architectural fashion—which was creating the rather stilted 'Perpendicular'—and either reused earlier work or made theirs look as if of about 1340. For this we can be grateful. Except for Victorian remodelling of the chancel, Taynton church looks—and largely is in feeling—of the 'Decorated', the most graceful phase of Medieval Gothic. Many of the windows have flowing tracery, the capitals have flower-based decoration, and the corbels—twenty-six of them and all in good condition—show a delightful array of what we may assume to have been portraits. (In fact, as the knowledgeable will recognise, the fashions of headwear are more nearly contemporary with the date of the church's rebuilding, but the heads have nothing of the strangeness either of the earlier Norman grotesques or of the monstrosities that often stare or grin down upon visitors to fifteenth-century churches.) Perhaps even more appealing is the font, of extraordinarily delicate workmanship.

The 'slight History' of Taynton church and village on sale in the church—a nicely produced, informative work—besides drawing visitors' attention to the many architectural attractions, includes some items from the parish records which enable us to see a little of the activities of the churchwardens (and, no doubt, those hard-working and unpaid officials elsewhere were similarly helping to run their villages):

> 1590, buried a poor man from Watledge whose name we knew not ... 1625, Thomas Fryer being unnaturally murthered, his head cut off and otherwise wounded by his own sonne ... 1630, Edmund Damport to wear a nightcap in Church in Winter, and not his hat ... 1753, gave Richard Howes in his illness, 1s od; gave Anne Harris in her lying in, 3s od ... 1805, Joseph Harris of the Parish of Taynton, being desirous of withdrawing from the Militia, provided William Bolton to be his substitute ... 1808, received at the Church Door, the third day of July, for the British prisoners in different prisons in France, Five Guineas....

From Taynton it is barely two miles to Burford which is reached across its bridge. Immediately the little town begins with a cluster of creamy grey houses about its church at the lower end of its distinguished street. Wide, direct, and grass-verged, the street climbs almost to the cross-roads on the Oxford–Gloucester road. The visitor can spend hours merely collecting hints of the varying ages of the buildings: the Tudor four-centre-arched doorways, the stone-mullioned windows, the later Georgian sash-windows, the early Victorian bays. And then, having decided that the street has grown up from about 1550, he can glance along the side streets and see in the seemingly haphazard grouping of stone gable and chimney and dormer that many a house-front masks earlier work. Burford grew up its hill from the 1450s, from the time when its church, originally Norman nave, chancel and tower, was being enlarged with 'Perp' chapels. Since then the church has acquired a considerable collection of monuments, including one to Elizabeth White who in 1651 'willingly and peaceably exchanged her vile enjoyments here for those rich, precious and unspeakable', and a large, ornate one of 1625 to Sir Lawrence Tanfield, whose long inscription, had it been in English instead of Latin, would have seemed a bitter joke to his poorer contemporaries. He was, later, more accurately described as 'corrupt and avaricious in public life, grasping and overbearing as a landlord'; and his only child, whose little effigy kneels on his tomb, he treated brutally because she was not the hoped-for son.

Burford's story begins with a synod in A.D. 683, and then on through the wars between Wessex and Mercia, the struggles of its Norman lords, its slow growth through the medieval centuries—it appears to have benefited only marginally from the wool trade. Its humbler townspeople are recorded as showing anti-Catholic tendencies decades before the Reformation. Burford saw two skirmishes between Royalists and Parliamentarians and also Cromwell's suppression of the Levellers who, after the king's execution, found their new rulers little more to their liking—and three of them were shot for their 'mutiny' in Burford churchyard. The town gained from the quarries near by in the late 1600s and from paper-making and malting—this last adding to its attractions when, in the 1760s, Burford became a regular stopping-place on the coach route from London to Gloucester, until in the 1860s it began to suffer from the indifference of the railways. . . .

Those wishing to see what Burford has left from its long story should consult Sherwood and Pevsner's *Oxfordshire*; those wanting to know what is behind the present façades should read Mary Sturge Gretton's *Burford Past and Present*. Though now thirty years old, it is unlikely to be bettered. Mrs Gretton tells of all that was and is, and she includes one item that the visitor can no longer see: the monument that we might expect to mark, perhaps grandiloquently, the burial-place of William Lenthall who bought Burford Priory in 1634 to be lord of the manor, became Speaker of the Commons during the House's most momentous years, and ended as Burford's most pathetic figure.

It was Lenthall, who, when Charles I led troops into the House on 4 January 1642 to arrest the rebellious Five Members, earned a place in the history books by replying, when asked by the King if he could see the offending Members: 'May it please your Majesty, I have neither eyes to see nor tongue to speak in this place but as the House is pleased to direct me'. That was, one feels, Lenthall's great moment. When, in July 1647, the London mob invaded the

House, he was compelled to put to the vote whether the defeated King should return. A few days later he escaped to join Parliament's army (though some believed that he feared more than the London crowd the threat of prosecution for embezzling public money). During August 1648 he accepted reluctantly the chairmanship of the conference which debated whether to put Charles on trial (he said afterwards that he only did so because he assumed the majority would vote against such an extreme measure). He had by then come to believe that events had gone too far, and yet he continued as Speaker through 1651 and 1652 because, as he said, of his 'own baseness, cowardice, and unworthy fear to submit my life and estate to the mercy of those men that murdered the king'. On Cromwell's death Lenthall tried to evade the question of the Stuart Restoration, but secretly wrote to the future Charles II offering advice and £3,000, and when a motion affirming the republican opposition was to be put to the House, pleaded illness and absented himself. Though in 1660 excluded from the Act of Indemnity, he was saved by General Monck's appeal—and then shocked both friends and enemies by appearing as a witness against one of the 'regicides'....

Perhaps Clarendon's later judgment on Lenthall as Speaker—he was 'a very weak man and unequal to such a task'—is not unjust. Other contemporaries dwelt more on the lavish way he lived at Burford Priory and how after Charles's execution he graced its walls with pictures from the royal collection; 'he minded most', says one who knew him, 'the heaping up of riches and was ... besotted in raising and settling a family'. He left the Priory to his only son, but for himself he ordered not the customary impressive and virtue-recording memorial but 'that no monument be made for me, but at the utmost a plain stone, with this superscription only: "Vermis Sum"'. Mrs Gretton records that the stone was in Burford church until 1872; it has now disappeared. One day, perhaps some student of history seeking a subject for his thesis will tell us Lenthall's story in detail; it could help us to understand what it was like to be caught up in the events of those disturbed times.

Before leaving Burford there is a point about its street—and, indeed, about many a Cotswold street—that may make us compare our own ways of building with those of the past. Though in fact built through four centuries, Burford's street has achieved a satisfying unity. That unity comes from more than the stone and the similarity of proportion. It comes from the way the differing buildings have been set close together, each contributing to the whole. We may build in stone taken from decaying Cotswold buildings or devise reconstituted stone to imitate the old, we may employ architects to copy the traditional features; but while we persist in demanding our detacheds and our semis, we will never achieve that feeling of unity which is at the core of our admiration ... though whether in truth it arose from intention or from the cost of frontages on to the street, or for protection against intruders or from neighbourliness, not even Burford's long history can tell.

FIVE

The Ways to Winchcombe

As has been mentioned, after attaining Broadway Hill, the prehistoric Way must have turned southwestwards along Cotswold Edge. The going for the best part of ten miles would have been easy and fairly direct. Though here and there combes mould the escarpment, the ridge has not been eroded by rivers large enough to break its line. There is always a narrow strip of the ridge to provide continuity . . . until Winchcombe lying in the curving valley which gave it its name is neared.

The approximate line of this part of the Way survives in the sequence of lane and bridle-path that now follows the Edge. For the first two miles from Broadway Hill it is taken over by Buckle Street, but when that lane bears southwards for Bourton-on-the-Water, the line of the ancient Way continues southwesterly. As a metalled lane it keeps just below the summit of Oat Hill above Snowshill until after a mile the lane turns more south. The Way keeps straight as a track, screened from the west by the ashes and other trees of Stanway Ash Plantation, and giving wide views over the landscape rolling southeast, the swelling and sinking pattern of field and copse that makes up High Cotswold. Approaching Stumps Cross where the road from Stanway attains the upland it becomes briefly metalled, but almost at once it is off again, a bridle-path signposted 'Farmcote, Hailes Abbey, Winchcombe', keeping along the high ground until the next dip where Lynes Barn Farm stands above the source of the south-flowing Guiting Brook and the steep-sided combe in which lies the ruin of Hailes Abbey. From there the Way appears to climb up on to Sudeley Hill where it would have turned southwards and so reached Roel Gate, a lonely meeting-place of ancient routes, from which a choice of path or lane leads down to Winchcombe.

During the centuries while Roman Cirencester and Gloucester struggled to keep some urban identity in a country which had been seized piecemeal to become more nearly one of self-supporting Anglo-Saxon villages, Winchcombe grew to more than local importance. Now small, grey and often overlooked, it once possessed a residence of Mercian kings and an abbey among the greatest in Anglo-Saxon England. During the century before the Normans arrived it was the administrative centre of Winchcombeshire.

Many of those who were drawn thither in the days of Winchcombe's greatness must have travelled along the ancient Ways. But by then most of the villages that lie under the Cotswold scarp had been established and today's visitor can follow their linking paths—the motorist will have to use the parallel A 46 to which they are joined by lanes—in the probability that he is approaching the place by the route the Anglo-Saxons used when visiting Winchcombe's market or paying their respects and their tithes to its abbey. The lowland route leads through some of Cotswold's most interesting villages.

The homes of Buckland, the most northerly of these villages, are dotted about among trees on little lumps and rises below the wooded escarpment. Buckland possesses a manorhouse which has been remodelled since it was built in the 1500s but is still a haphazard cluster of gables, and a rectory which claims to be the oldest in the country still in use. Opened to the public on summer Mondays, the rectory still has its great hall with the fifteenth-century timbers supporting the stone roof, and some contemporary glass in its windows showing the badge of Edward IV.

Buckland's name tells that it was once a place of some distinction, for it owes its first syllable to the word from which 'book' is derived. The manor was not casually founded by a gathering of peasants, but was established by a written charter—probably when the land was given by Kynred, king of the Mercians, to Gloucester abbey. As might be expected, the church is distinguished and large for the village. It was rebuilt during the thirteenth century, was given its tower about 1320, and had some of its windows enlarged and its chancel remodelled about 1480. It is, however, the details that make a glance inside more than usually memorable. Three panels of glass in the east window are survivors from a set depicting the Seven Sacraments, given by William Grafton, rector from 1466 to 1483. They show Baptism with the newborn stiffly upright, Marriage with the bride's father in contemporary custom wearing his hat in church, and unfortunately less distinctly Extreme Unction. Near the door and curtained from the light is an altar frontal probably used later as a pall. On blue velvet is an intricate motif repeated several times: 'conventional flowers' a note in the church calls them: Verey in his *Buildings of Gloucestershire* suggests 'pomegranates showing their seeds' which, being Catherine of Aragon's badge, implies a date after her arrival in 1502. The Crucifixion is shown on the lower border; along the top beside the figures of Saints Peter, Paul and Michael (slaying dragon) is a rebus on the name of William Whychurch, abbot of Hailes from 1464 to 1479. It seems that the frontal was made up of portions of different dates from different places.

Approximately contemporary are some fragments from a reredos, perhaps from Hailes abbey. The painted figures are unusually delicate, simple and really delightful.

Another later rarity is the seventeenth-century wall-seating in the south aisle, complete with wainscotting, tester heads and even some of the hat-pegs. It, too, is simple and unpretentious. Gloucestershire's historian, Sir Robert Atkyns, records that in 1690 all the seating in the church was 'made new by James Thynne as also the handsom gallery'. But already in 1615 the north aisle seats had been provided. It is unusual to find so much seventeenth-century woodwork; Victorian restorers often did away with it. Also in the church is a maple-wood bowl, nicely shaped and decorated, which probably served as the parish bridal bowl at about the time the church was reseated.

If Buckland's church has been fortunate in its restorer of 1885 who allowed so much to remain, it has been less fortunate in some of its twentieth-century visitors. A note in the little collecting box asks that money should not be left as it has been broken open several times.

Little more than a mile across the fields is John Wesley's 'dear, delightful Stanton'. The footpath probably was the way he often rode, not as the much-travelling evangelist but as a young man in his twenties, recently graduated and ordained and, from March 1726, a fellow of Lincoln College, Oxford. Though by nature serious and deeply religious—his father was rector of Epworth, Lincolnshire, and his mother had instilled her very determined religious attitudes into her family—young Wesley was then 'eager and enthusiastic, gay without being frivolous'. He had acquired many friends, among them the Granvilles of Buckland and the Kirkhams of Stanton. The sons of the families were, like young Wesley, newly graduated and hoping to enter the Church; but it is much more of the daughters that Wesley confided in the diary he scrupulously kept and to whom, between his visits, he wrote long and affectionate letters over a period of several years.

Superficially Wesley's association was merely friendly and enjoyable on both sides: days spent in walks, evenings in card-playing or dancing, and conversation ranging over most matters of the day and turning ever and again to religion. But underneath, as V. H. H. Green shows clearly in his *Young Mister Wesley*, the future evangelist was undergoing a formative experience—though himself can never have fully understood it. He came near to falling in love not once but several times, and yet no romance ever developed. He was first attracted to Sarah Kirkham, understanding and witty, and soon his sister Martha was complaining to him: 'When I knew that you were just returned from Worcestershire where I suppose you saw your Varanese [a joke-name for Sarah Kirkham] I then ceased to wonder at your silence, for the sight of such a woman, so known, so loved, might well make you forget me.' But, a few months later, Sarah married the local schoolmaster. Later, her sister Betsy appears to have taken her place in Wesley's eyes and her brother is writing to him: 'You have often been in the thoughts of Miss Betsy, which I have curiously observed, when with her alone, by inward smiles and sighs and abrupt expressions concerning *you*.... I subscribe myself your most affectionate friend (and brother I wish I might write) Robert Kirkham.' But by 1730 she, too, had married. And there was Mary Granville whose company, Wesley confessed in his diary, brought that 'soft emotion with which I glow even at the moment'. And Mary Granville's younger sister Anne who was for a while his 'Selima'....

The paths and lanes about Buckland and Stanton must be those they walked during Wesley's many visits from Oxford. The young ladies must have been flattered by the seriousness with which he answered their questions, treating them not as objects for trivial chat or a flirtation but more (and more gratifyingly) as thoughtful students—and probably more attentive ones than those he taught. Yet, though often attracted to them, Wesley could never bring himself to consider marriage. To be sure, as his sister Emily had warned him early in his acquaintance with Stanton, his 'worldly affairs' were not 'in such a posture that you may marry'; not until he had achieved a living could he afford a wife. But, as Dr Green suggests, it may have been as much Wesley's make-up as his circumstances which held him back and when, much later, he married he did not find happiness. That was long after he had ceased to visit Stanton. From the company of friends there he went with his brother Charles to Georgia where they hoped to turn the 'primitive innocence' of the Red Indians towards Christianity and where Wesley hoped, as he told a friend, he might 'attain such purity of thought as suits a candidate for that state wherein they neither marry nor are given in marriage, but are as the angels of God in heaven'.

Much of Stanton must still look as young Wesley saw it—though it has certainly been tidied up. Thanks mainly to Sir Philip Stott, its architect-owner from 1906 to 1937, it is something of a showplace. To its twisting street of gently dignified Stuart houses with, set back a little among trees, a once-Norman church and gabled, Elizabethan Warren House, Stott added three good barns (brought from elsewhere), two of which have now become homes. With so much affection for his chosen village, Stott also saw to it that the houses were very carefully restored. The result is pictorially delightful if a little inert. Visitors stand admiring or sit sketching, cameras are brought out—but do the residents do much beyond trimming the patches of lawn at the corners and tidying their gardens? It is hard to imagine labourers after their day's work trudging up to the Mount Inn, converted from a cottage at the steep end of the street, though no doubt visitors appreciate the view from its window of the landscape stretching away beyond the grey-stone roofs.

The walker from Stanton will reach Stanway across Stanway Park, finely treed and sweeping up towards the crest; motorists following the lane will approach along an avenue of massive oaks (on which, if they should pause for a little while, they may have the company of perky and trusting nuthatches). The core of Stanway is the great house and the church, with the gatehouse appearing almost to link the two and, to one corner of the churchyard, the tithe barn: to us a memorable group, though the locals in the fourteenth century may not have appreciated the architectural merits of the barn in which much of the produce of their land and their work had to be gathered for the benefit of Tewkesbury abbey. The gatehouse, though perhaps the least significant, seems to overshadow the others. Built about 1630, it is three storeys tall and surmounted by the elaborately-shaped gables with which architects knowledgeable in Renaissance forms were replacing the neater traditional ones (and Stanway's are in turn topped with scallop shells, the badge of the Tracys, owners during the seventeenth and eighteenth centuries, whose arms break the pediment supported by Doric columns).

Though the claim that Inigo Jones was responsible for the gatehouse is not now accepted, it was certainly intended to impress in an age when the landowner was keen to demonstrate in building his superiority over his lowlier neighbours and even, perhaps, over visitors.

Fortunately for us, the Tracy builder of the gatehouse could not run to a new manorhouse as well. His Elizabethan ancestors had done their work well, as the fine but simpler house now almost hidden by the gatehouse shows. With scarcely a hint of ornament to disturb its clean lines, the west front with its tall, stone-mullioned windows and its sharp gables, shows late Tudor building at its best.

Though proximity to gatehouse and tithe barn (now the village hall) attracts visitors to the church, it has little to show. Originally late Norman, it was treated with far too heavy a hand in 1896. The external walls of the chancel have corbels showing grotesques, animal or distortedly human, which must have formed part of the original building, but some appear to have been touched up. And where have the monuments to the former owners of the manorhouse gone?

At first glance Didbrook is a scattered, unremarkable place, but one pair of cottages attracts the architectural historians who include humble dwellings in their interests. Unexpectedly timber-framed, the pair shows at one end the ancient crucks, the pair of substantial timbers forming an inverted V to support the roof. As the method of construction was used from early medieval times into the seventeenth century, its age can only be guessed. The pair of cottages could be contemporary with Didbrook church which is known to have been rebuilt about 1475, after, it is said, desecration of the earlier church by the killing inside of refugees from the Yorkist victory at Tewkesbury. The holes in the door are sometimes assumed to have been made by shot from an early hand-gun ... though it is odd that an occurrence which caused the rebuilding should have been allowed to leave such an unwelcome memento. Yet the holes are there and have the haphazardness of shot. Could out-of-the-way Didbrook have suffered another conflict, perhaps an unrecorded skirmish during the King versus Parliament quarrel?

Hailes is only a mile away, a little group of church, a cottage or two, a farm or two, the traces of a moat that once defended a castle, and a few arches from the cloister to one of the greatest of abbeys. For the enlightenment of today's many visitors, the foundations of the abbey church and of some of the conventual buildings have been uncovered and a small museum displays maps showing what is and what was, some fragments of stone found and notably some of the bosses from the church roof.

Reaction to a ruined monastery is always a personal matter. At Hailes one can assume that Henry III's brother, Richard earl of Cornwall, who founded the abbey in 1246 as a thanksgiving for escaping drowning by shipwreck, was acting from motives only of piety, as piety was accepted in the thirteenth century. One can assume that the services of the Cistercians, originally an austere order striving to return to the simplicity that the earlier Benedictines had abandoned, were beneficial not only to the founder and his descendants but also to those who came to contribute to the abbey's well-being and, indeed, to the world at large. With such assumptions one can feel the pathos of the place; the few forlorn arches and the rough fragments of wall that were once a church larger than some cathedrals may become much more than sightseers' curiosities. They tell of departed beliefs and hopes. Even though one cannot share those beliefs and hopes, there is always something infinitely pitiful about their loss.

Or the visitor can be more factual and more critical. In the founding of a monastery, more (or less) was involved than an act of selfless piety. The foundation was essentially for the assumed benefit of the founder and his family; the monks' services would, in medieval thinking, assure preferential treatment for the family's souls after death. It would scarcely be harsh to assert that it was an attempt to use this world's goods in the next world, a practice in which lesser benefactors could hope to join by their gifts as well as by their devotions. And Hailes had many benefactors, rich and humble. It came to amass 13,000 acres of landed property, it drew countless gift-making pilgrims to see its most precious relic, 'the blode of Crist that is in Hayles'. Without reviving the old argument as to whether the relic was or was not 'but honey clarified and coloured with saffron' as was asserted at the time when Henry VIII ordered its destruction at St Paul's cross, it can hardly be questioned that the purpose of monasticism was not to acquire large lands or to trade on the credulity of those who came for spiritual benefit. Not that such a reflection makes the ruin at Hailes any the less pathetic. The pathos inevitable upon the loss of inspiration remains whether the loss was brought by internal materialism or external politics.

Not all those who wander around the remains of the abbey

looking curious or intent or as if unsure how to react cross the road to Hailes's older and more complete attraction. The little church was built by the villagers a full century before Richard of Cornwall's nearly disastrous voyage, though it was from about 1300 made to serve as a chapel for pilgrims. From that time date its wall-paintings, sufficient of which remain to give some impression of what the place must have looked like to medieval visitors. Besides the almost inevitable Christopher—here so faded as to look almost ghostly—there are St Catherine and St Margaret, and a knight on foot with shield apparently indulging in coursing (and what he is doing there we can only guess). The chancel is patterned with Richard of Cornwall's eagle badge and castles for his nephew's queen, Eleanor of Castile. Above these are fading panels showing, sometimes rather strangely, Biblical episodes. The east window has some fifteenth-century glass from the abbey, pale and gentle; and some contemporary woodwork has survived including the screen—even though during the century after the Reformation the church was reseated, both nave and choir, and was given a neat box-pew for the local 'family'. All told, an interesting summary of much that has happened at Hailes.

Less than two miles across the fields is Winchcombe.

The hills seem almost to encircle it—which does not suggest a geographical setting suited to becoming an important centre. How much Winchcombe in the past owed to royal patronage and how much to the legend which prompted the building of its Benedictine abbey—whose abbot was to attain the rare distinction of a mitre and a seat in the House of Lords—is difficult to determine. The royal residence did not last until the Conquest and, due largely to Lord Seymour of Sudeley, brother-in-law to Henry VIII and a beneficiary from the dissolution of the monasteries, the stone of its once-famous abbey is more likely to be found in nearby Sudeley castle than on the site in Winchcombe. Indeed, nowadays, Winchcombe still seems almost superseded by Sudeley. The bulk of its traffic, at least during the holiday months, arrives merely to pass through en route for the part-ruined, part-refurbished castle with its associations with Henry VIII's last queen, Catherine Parr, its accompanying Wildlife Park, Aviary, Children's Play Park, Gardens, an Entertainment depicting the visits to Sudeley of historical characters, cafés, restaurant ... all apparently made more noteworthy by the castle having served as the setting for a television serial.

For the historically inclined a visit to Sudeley is, of course, also interesting. The castle was built about 1440 by Ralph Boteler who, as Leland recorded during his visit in Henry VIII's time, 'was a famous man of warr in Henry the 5 and Henry the 6 dayes ... whereupon it was supposed, and spoken, that it was partly buildyd by spoyles goten in Fraunce'. Boteler among others who took part in what for us is the Hundred Years' War apparently found ransoms made feudal conflicts profitable. He did not fare so well in the subsequent Wars of the Roses. The Yorkist Edward IV, continues Leland, 'suspectyd him to be in hart Henry the 6 man; wherapon by complaynts he was attachid ... After he made an honest declaration, and sould his castle of Sudeley to Kynge Edward'. After remaining in royal possession for over seventy years, the castle was given in 1547 to Sir Thomas Seymour (who became then Lord Seymour of Sudeley), brother to Queen Jane Seymour and uncle to the young Edward VI. Seymour thoroughly remodelled it, giving it its banqueting hall (which was reduced to a ruin by the Parliamentarians in the Civil War). Seymour, however, enjoyed his possession for barely two years. Having plotted to overthrow his brother as young Edward VI's Protector (and in effect head of government), he found himself in the Tower and subsequently on the scaffold.

At Sudeley, however, it is not so much Seymour that the visitor tends to recall as his wife, Catherine Parr, Henry VIII's ultimate queen who, being shrewd enough to evade the royal displeasure, became also his widow. Sentimental visitors, gazing upon the effigy in the chapel that marks her grave, may like to think that her brief time as mistress of Sudeley castle was idyllic compared with her years as wife to the overbearing and ageing Henry. They can perhaps overlook that the opportunist Seymour had, before winning Catherine's hand, tried to win the Princess Elizabeth and also, if the French ambassador's suspicions were justified, both the Princess Mary and Anne of Cleves. As the ten-year-old Edward VI's stepmother and probably the only woman to whom he felt much attached, Catherine would have had for Seymour politically useful attractions; she, after three childless marriages to husbands old enough to have been her father, was probably ready to assume that she had other charms, too. Within eighteen months, however, and just as her thrusting husband was starting on the course that was to lead him to the block, Catherine died from puerperal fever following the birth of her only child—a daughter Mary about whom, after a few months, history is curiously silent. The effigy carved in 1859 and allegedly 'rendered as correctly as it could be from the portraits which are extant', probably gives an over-gentle impression of a woman who, as readers of Anthony Martienssen's recent biography will know, was by no means always the passive figure that the history books suggest. (Incidentally, Mr Martienssen records the ghoulish treatment the queen's body suffered when in 1782 the coffin was discovered in the ruins of the chapel—at which time the habitable part of the castle was serving as an inn. Visitors to Sudeley who, having come via Cheltenham, may imagine that the eighteenth century was peopled only by cultured ladies and gentlemen, will not find it pleasant reading.)

The castle, as now, is a remodelling of both Boteler's and Seymour's work by Lord Chandos in the 1570s, plus considerable Victorian additions from the time when the Dent family rescued it from complete ruin.

Like so many tourists about this part of Cotswold we have been drawn by Sudeley away from Winchcombe. The little town is certainly worth an hour or so. Its main street is a mixture of stone and black-and-white and plaster, mostly from the sixteenth century onwards though the George Inn, which served as the pilgrims' lodging in the last years of the abbey, has half its original half-timbered yard (in which may be seen a bath-like stone basin said to have been used by the pilgrims).

The George was built before 1525, for on the spandrels to its doorway are the initials of abbot Richard Kidderminster who resigned in that year after becoming involved in a politico-religious dispute which, though often overlooked by historians, was of more than temporary significance. The trouble for abbot Kidderminster arose from the imprisonment of a prominent London merchant, Richard Hunne, on a questionable charge of heresy. Hunne appears to have intended countering the charge with one based on the ancient law of Praemunire which forbade appeals from English courts to Rome; but before he could do so he was found hanged in his prison cell. The bishop of London, aware that Londoners were in an anti-clerical mood, assumed suicide and hastily had Hunne's body tried, condemned and burnt at Smithfield; but the London coroner, investigating less impulsively, uncovered evidence of murder together with a confession from Hunne's gaoler implicating the bishop's chancellor. Feeling among the London populace became violent, and the Commons, then sitting, also showed keen interest in the matter—they had only a few days before failed to get past the Lords a bill by which clerical offenders would be tried not in Church courts but by the ordinary law of the land. The Church had to issue stern warning; it chose as its spokesman Richard Kidderminster, abbot of Winchcombe. Preaching at St Paul's Cross on the text 'touch not Mine anointed', he warned the Commons and the populace at large that questioning the Church's ruling could be taken as heresy—only to be answered by another churchman, a Franciscan known personally to 24-year-old Henry VIII, who argued that 'such things as be thought necessary for the King and commonwealth ought not to be said to be prejudicial to the liberty of the Church'. The unfortunate Hunne became almost forgotten as the dispute about the clergy's immunity from trial by Common Law, left unsettled since Becket's time, was suddenly revived. After more arguments and counter-arguments, young Henry called a conference of Lords, Commons, judges and clergy, to settle the matter. Abbot Kidderminster cannot have been pleased with the outcome; nor could Thomas Wolsey, newly made a cardinal, who had on behalf of the Church to offer its apologies, and so for the time being avoid the dangers of Praemunire. Henry had, meanwhile, taken the opportunity to make his own position very clear: 'We are, by the sufferance of God, King of England, and the Kings of England in time past never had any superior but God; know, therefore, that we will maintain the rights of the Crown in this matter like our progenitors.' We do not know if the abbot of Winchcombe or any other cleric present heard the omen in the royal pronouncement. Hindsight allows us to see how Henry may have been thinking—though Anne Boleyn was at the time only eight years old.

Apart from the pilgrims' hostel which became the George, Winchcombe has nothing to show of its once-great abbey. The legend of St Kenelm's martyrdom which had brought it into being had long been overshadowed by the relic at Hailes ... and it must be admitted that few legends are more suspect. The story tells that Kenelm, a ninth-century boy-king, was murdered by his elder sister, Quendrida, in order that her lover might gain the throne. The crime was disclosed by the unornithological behaviour of a white dove which took a note to the pope of the time, and the uncharacteristic activities of a white cow which led the search for the young king's decapitated body. This was reverently carried to Winchcombe where Quendrida, on seeing it, was smitten blind in an unnecessarily horrible way as divine vengeance. The alleged subsequent miracles at the shrine prompted Kenelm's canonisation and attracted numerous pilgrims. Later investigation has, however, questioned the few facts on which the legend was based. Kenelm son of King Kenulf is now known to have died before his father (who was, incidentally, succeeded by a brother); the villainous Quendrida ended her days as abbess of a Kentish nunnery apparently sufficiently well sighted to have become involved in a prolonged dispute over land. And for what it is worth, two coffins of thirteenth-century date, alleged to contain the remains of King Kenulf and his son 'King' Kenelm, opened after the dissolution of Winchcombe abbey were found to contain the skeletons of a man and a boy, the latter showing no signs of having been beheaded before both crumbled into dust.

If Winchcombe can show little of its abbey, it still has the church which abbot William Winchcombe began in 1456 and finished in 1474, helped by £200 from the townspeople and more from Ralph Boteler of Sudeley. In the style of the 'wool churches'—though Winchcombe abbey's great days as a wool-producer were then past—it is internally less elaborate than many of its time. It has its contemporary screen, fine seating for the clergy, and some of its medieval glass. Among the many monuments is one which may be unwittingly memorable. In Stuart fashion Sir Thomas Williams kneels before an open Bible opposite the space which his widow's effigy should have come to occupy. But she remarried and is buried elsewhere. Sir Thomas's round-eyed stare suggests that he is still waiting.

The major interest of Winchcombe church is, however, outside. Few churches have such a fine and disturbing collection of gargoyles and grotesques. They vary from the obviously comic—a cheery, moustached jester to one side of the door and a hatted, nauseated fellow near the other—to the horrific: a bearded, jeering demon, a fearsome harpy, a monstrous pig-like beast, several repulsive variations on the ape. One cannot wonder that the mitred abbot who ends the collection along the south wall looks surprised at his company. If five centuries of weathering have softened their lines, what must some of them have looked like when first carved? If we accept the comic ones as expressions of the sculptor's humour, what are we to think of the hideous ones? To dismiss them as intended to 'scare away demons' seems hardly adequate when many of them are demoniac themselves. More than a casual glance may leave the uncomfortable feeling that they may not be attempts at beings of the Bestiaries but perhaps expressions of a fear-filled mind. They were fashioned during the century and a half following 1349 when the dreaded plague persisted in returning intermittently. Though we, studying the incomplete records, can assert that each visitation was less destructive than its predecessor, to contemporaries a reappearance of the symptoms must have awakened fears of a return of the hideous season when the Black Death first struck. The disturbing strangeness of many of Winchcombe's grotesques is still to be felt five hundred years after their carving.

By the time Winchcombe's church was rebuilt, the town was losing its local importance. Though in a region where wool was synonymous with wealth, Winchcombe seems to have lived more on its market for horses and cattle—or so we may assume from a street once named 'Horsemarket' and occasional references to purchases of horses and cattle there by the royal exchequer. Later, in Stuart times, some of the locals made a living by growing tobacco which they 'daily bring to London by secret ways, and do usually sell it for Virginia and Bermudas tobacco'. Charles I, prompted by the Virginia Company, tried to put a stop to that, but the growing continued into the Commonwealth. The visitor leaving by the Cheltenham road—and so past the Old Corner Cupboard Inn, a welcoming house which was probably a hundred years old when the tobacco was being grown—may notice that the former occupation has been remembered in the name of a street of new houses. By its tobacco days, however, Winchcombe had long been a half-forgotten town. Leland, writing about 1540, found it 'a place where a fewe poore housys be'; fifty years later Camden called it 'a poor beggarly town'. Not only had its abbey gone; the abbey's great flocks of sheep had gone too ... though the records do not suggest that the people of medieval Winchcombe had gained much direct benefit from them. In the Middle Ages the main source of the abbey's income had been kept literally out of sight of the townspeople on the lands stretching eastwards from the hillcrest above the town—to which we must be returning.

SIX

From Prehistoric Barrow to Nineteenth-century Town

At Roel Gate, the meeting-place of ancient routes on the plateau southeast of Winchcombe, will be found little to detain those who travel in search of views to admire and subjects for photographs. There is not a building in sight, no hint of Roel Farm in its hollow a mile and a half to the east, all that survives of the Domesday manor of Rawelle, the roebucks' well ... though the farmhouse under its great sweep of roof has retained two medieval windows and much of the building is that in which Lord Chandos and his Royalist tenants took refuge in the summer of 1644 while Sudeley Castle was being battered by the Parliamentarians. Of that, the meeting of lanes at Roel Gate tells nothing. The ways meet under the sky, cross, and go on along the ridges. The very emptiness seems to hold a memory of the time when the hills were man's dwelling place, before he had won the good land of the Vale and the valleys from the forest.

The Neolithic Way must have approached the meeting-place from the north or northeast. Two routes, one a lane, one a footpath, follow its approximate line. The lane is now marked as the Salt Way, the footpath is called Campden Lane, both names of medieval origin. As the original Way must have been a wide track—or more probably a series of tracks as its early users avoided natural hazards such as miry patches and thick clumps of scrub—it is not unlikely that those two roughly parallel ways indicate the two outermost paths trodden first by the New Stone-agers, becoming separated and more defined when, in early medieval times, the land was apportioned between the newly established villages. The two offer interesting contrasts. The Salt Way, here following close to the Edge, overlooks Winchcombe and its all but surrounding hills; Campden Lane is more secretive, going by track and footpath across the easterly slope and looking down the combes that contribute to the Windrush valley.

About Roel Gate it seems the prehistoric Way turned west or southwest. After following what is now the Salt Way for a further half-mile, it may have borne southwest to become above the hamlet of Brockhampton the bridle-path making the long descent to the next gathering-place of the ways, the hollow in which Andoversford now stands. Or perhaps originally it took a more westerly line as is suggested by the forts, earthworks and other lumps on the plateau above Cheltenham, and even more certainly by the great long barrow of Belas Knap. The lane from Roel Gate past the partly ploughed-down ramparts of an Iron Age fort looks the likely route. Beyond the col between the little Isbourne and the Coln, however, the course becomes uncertain. The walker can assume the unmetalled lane which will eventually land him on Cleeve Common. The motorist will have to take the lane through Charlton Abbots where is a good manorhouse of about 1600. Either way, Belas Knap should not be missed. Its odd-looking name, by the way, comes from 'bel', a beacon, and 'cnaepp', a hill-top, and tells of the barrow's use for the Anglo-Saxons. Standing high on the fringe of the upland, the barrow is indisputable evidence that wherever the prehistoric Way went, the New Stone-agers lived thereabouts some five thousand and more years ago.

To pacify the purists it must be admitted that Belas Knap, as now, is in part a reconstruction. Those archaeologically infuriating people, the Victorian antiquaries who between 1863 and 1865 dug into the large mound to see what they could find, left the monument looking more of a mess than five thousand years of weathering had made it. Recently, after another much more careful investigation, their damage has largely been repaired and we can again see Belas Knap much as it was built.

To the north two walls, curving inwards from the revetting walls of the barrow, form the sides of what appears to be a stone-blocked entrance; but the four burial chambers are not and never were accessible from there. They are to be found at the sides of the mound: one roughly centrally on either side, one towards the southeast, and a fourth, later one—perhaps much later—at the lower south end. The early investigators' reports suggest that these chambers were constructed as small, separate barrows grouped round a circle of small flat stones, all later being covered by the large mound which was finished with a roof of stone slabs.

Each burial chamber was entered by a dry-stone-walled passage. Each was walled with slabs of stone, infilled with dry-stone-walling.

Two had stone-slab roofs, the other two probably had skilfully constructed corbelled roofs formed of small slabs laid overlapping until they met to complete the chamber. In these tombs the remains of more than thirty people have been found. Behind the 'false portal' the bones of five children and a man's skull have also been found, almost certainly a later interment.

The pattern of Belas Knap, found elsewhere, raises the first of many questions which have not as yet been completely answered. In the majority of Britain's megalithic tombs, all apparently raised between 3500 and 3000 B.C., a single stone-framed entrance begins a passage from which the burial chambers led. This pattern shows variations; there may originally have been from two to five chambers of differing shapes. But the construction of a false entrance, of a courtyard ending in what appears to be a blocked doorway but was clearly built not to lead anywhere, and with the all-important tombs set, as it were, in subsidiary positions in the sides of the mound, leaves us baffled. Clearly the false portal must have been of great significance, but what that significance was we can only guess. Experts in such matters offer choices: it may have served 'ritual purposes', and the traces of burnt animal bones have hinted at 'ceremonial feasts' or sacrifices; or the contrivance may have been intended to keep out of the burial chambers robbers and/or evil spirits; or the false portal was perhaps a shrine for a Mother Goddess whose hermit-like priests or priestesses dwelt alongside the tombs of the royal (or at least chieftainly) dead; or they could have been tribal meeting-places, for with most early and many later peoples religious and social occasions were inseparable.

Adding mystery to puzzlement is the fact that barrows with the feature of the false portal are geographically intermingled with the more usual and, to our thinking, more logical pattern of the passage graves. Were they perhaps a later development? Or can we assume that, despite the usual conservativeness of most early peoples on such a matter, the local tribes-people expressed their own ideas, that as Eric S. Wood in his general and thorough *Field Guide to Archaeology in Britain* says, 'prehistoric burial rites were marked by great fluidity and variety, as though personal ideas of what was fitting were allowed free play'? Such an assertion implies that Neolithic peoples showed far more religious toleration than most of their successors have done.

Another curious and gruesome feature of megalithic tombs—of the passage type as well as those with a false entrance—is that in many the bones discovered within a single chamber often represent far more bodies than could, in a complete state, have been laid there. The northeast chamber of Belas Knap, for example, barely eight feet square, contained one complete skeleton among the 'confused remains of eleven other individuals', and elsewhere even more remains have been found in more limited space. And usually only one skeleton, assumed to have been the last, is more or less intact. The other remains are usually incomplete, and often the actual bones have been deliberately broken. Sometimes, too, there are traces of burning or charring, insufficient to imply cremation but enough to raise another question-mark. Such conditions have prompted interpretations varying from the lurid to the incompletely plausible:

1. That the one complete skeleton was that of a chief whose slaves (including presumably their wives and children for the remains cover both sexes and all ages) were killed and buried at the same time to accompany him into the next world, and that ritual feasting, including cannibalism, accompanied the burial.

2. That the chambers were used for successive burials, the earlier bones being accidentally broken by the 'undertakers'' feet and burnt, also accidentally, by the torches required in the darkness (a theory which ignores that except for the single skeleton, the other remains are often so incomplete that merely discovering the number of individuals represented is difficult).

3. That, during the years in which the tombs were constructed and the mound raised, the dead were deposited elsewhere and only on completion of the barrow did actual interment take place (a theory which, though accounting for the large numbers found in a confined space and perhaps for the loss by accident or carelessness of parts of many of the skeletons, leaves unexplained the frequent breaking and burning of the bones).

Certainty, it seems, is still far away.

If the visitor to Belas Knap has chosen a bright day he may perhaps overlook another important matter. Seen in sunlight with the field beside which it stands spreading out and the woods backing it drawing the eye, the barrow may not appear very impressive; in duller conditions its brooding bulk is more obvious. It represents an immense amount of work. With stone tools, antler picks and shoulder-blade shovels then the only equipment, it would have taken thousands and thousands of man-hours to collect and trim the necessary stone, to build the chambers, walls and false entrance, and then to raise the mound. All was done at a time when the local population can have numbered only a few hundred, and done not only at Belas Knap but in thirty other places on Cotswold. Whether we assume that the work was done in a few seasons or spread over generations, Belas Knap and its like must have been the products of close-knit societies which, however humbly they lived, had developed a means for collective action on a large scale and who were moved to such great undertakings by religious convictions that we can scarcely even imagine.

If the prehistoric Way passed Belas Knap it must soon have curved southwards to follow the Edge above Cheltenham and so reach the hollow in which Andoversford now lies. And, we may suppose, part of this route saw much traffic in Iron-Age times for on the fragment of Cotswold stretching northwards from Cleeve Common are two considerable forts—on Nottingham Hill and Oxenton Hill—a long bank which is positioned as if intended to protect them from the south, and another smaller fort at the southern end of the near-precipice known as Cleeve Cloud.

These are for the walker; there is a network of tracks and paths giving access across wide Cleeve Common. And giving fine views, too, as the westerly rim is reached. Cheltenham sprawls almost from the hills' foot before the great patchwork spreads out to the Forest of Dean and the Malvern Hills. The motoring visitor can enjoy at least the view, for a lane from near Andoversford climbs gently (and narrowly) up to the Edge. It has been metalled for access to the radio station, but the view soon takes one's eyes away from the masts. . . .

Cheltenham down below has hotels enough to make it a good centre for exploring this area of Cotswold; but it is hardly part of it. An insignificant village until the late-Georgian craze for spas and 'taking the waters', it has long been separated from the rural life of the hills. Even its stone, most of it from quarries on Leckhampton Hill a couple of miles to its south, has been hidden behind layers of plaster and paint. It has, however, an interesting story of its own, as readers of Simona Pakenham's *Cheltenham: a Biography* will discover. In addition to a rich collection of visitors—after

George III had enjoyed a stay, almost everyone of any note had, it seems, to go to Cheltenham—Miss Pakenham tells of such diverse residents as astute Captain Henry Skillicorne who married the heiress of the first medicinal spring, founded the first Pump Room, and is remembered in the longest epitaph in Britain; the Reverend Francis Close who turned the 'merriest sick resort on earth' into the sedate educational centre; and Sally Saunders, postwoman, who too frequently for correspondents 'had something else to do than take a single letter to the bottom of the High Street'.

More overlooked, metaphorically and literally, is Bishop's Cleeve below the fort on Nottingham Hill. If the visitor ventures down the steep slope he will find there one of the outstanding churches in the region. It has something from every period from the Norman to the seventeenth century, plus sundry gargoyles of note, wall-paintings and a collection of monuments ranging from a chain-mailed effigy of about 1270 to a very costly alabaster effort of 1636 complete with the allegorical figures of Peace, Faith, Hope and Charity. And there is a rare survival in a musicians' gallery of about 1620. With donations of church-organs from the early 1700s onwards, such interesting but no-longer-necessary adjuncts were usually destroyed—and Bishop's Cleeve's is a fine example.

Even if the visitor to Cleeve Common is not tempted to descend from the Edge, perhaps for a few moments as he looks down on Bishop's Cleeve he might like to remember one Girold who, thanks to the thoroughness of a clerk who recorded the bishop of Worcester's land there, has happened to add a little to our knowledge of the economic history—and the social history, too—of seven hundred years ago. The time was one of expansion, of growing population which needed more food, and so more land had to be won from waste and woodland, had to be 'assarted' in the word of the time. Girold, it seems, was an industrious, go-ahead serf determined to take on the work and the opportunities. The record begins with a statement of his modest family holding: 'Girold holds 12 acres at a rent of 3 shillings.' Perhaps his father or grandfather had found such a small acreage insufficient for the family needs for the survey continues: 'Also an assart of 12 acres, for which the customary rent is 3 shillings; and another assart, of 4 acres, which used to render 12 pence.' Girold has added more, perhaps from neighbours unable to continue working, perhaps from ageing relations: 'And another assart, formerly belonging to Sefare, with a way leading to it, 3½ acres ... and 3 acres, formerly Godfrey's

... and 4 acres, formerly Richard's....' But for Girold these had been only beginnings. To rise above his lowly status, to have a marketable surplus, he was willing to undertake much more: 'And in addition 143½ acres of assart, including woodland which remains to be assarted. Total of Girold's assart: 170 acres, of which a moiety lies in one field, and a moiety in the other. For this he pays a rent of one mark [13 shillings 4 pence] by grant of Bishop Roger.' All told, Girold was determined to work very hard and to pay considerably (unskilled labour cost about 2 pence a day) to increase hugely his holding. And elsewhere throughout much of England other serfs were similarly striving—perhaps not on such a scale as Girold but collectively it was a great effort—to take the first step that was to lead the descendants of some of them to become the yeomen of Tudor times. As can be seen from the Edge above Bishop's Cleeve, the place has grown much since Girold's time. It is to be hoped that some of his hard-won acres are still bearing the good grain for which he worked.

However the ancient Ways—the Neolithic route past Belas Knap, the Iron Age way from the forts northwards of Cleeve Common—crossed the bastion of Cotswold above Cheltenham, both used the hollow in which Andoversford lies. Prehistoric travellers must have taken the col a little to the west of the village between the sources of the little Chelt and the young Coln, avoiding both valleys before bearing southwards on along the Edge. But before going that way, there are at hand the villages of Whittington and Sevenhampton, the one on the fairly level ground close to the site of a Roman settlement, the other a mile or so up the valley of the Coln.

If the name Whittington prompts hopeful recollections of pantomimes, the visitor must restrain himself a little longer. It is probable that the family originated there, but neither Dick nor his cat has any immediate association, though his mother's effigy lies in Coberley church, five miles to the southwest. The village of Whittington would not, however, be unsuitable pictorially as the setting for the beginning of the old story. Its street, level for Cotswold, suggests the adjective pretty; it is a mixture, mostly small scale, of all ages from the sixteenth century to the nineteenth, the stone, as so often happens, giving it unity. Nearer the main road is Whittington Court, gabled and bay-windowed, the manorhouse of about 1550 and still moated. Almost dwarfed by the house and great yew trees is the church, originally Norman, enlarged about

1450, as can be seen from the headdress worn by the lady whose head forms the stop to one arch. Two Whittington lords of the manor of the early 1300s are shown in cross-legged effigies and one of its ladies. They are of the Crupes family whose arms are repeated under the window of about 1510 near the chancel; but within ten years Whittington passed to Sir John Cotton who built the present manorhouse. His brass is in the church, dated 1556, 'in the reygne of Kinge Phillypp and Quene Marye'; few references are to be found to those unhappy years.

Sevenhampton up its placid valley is memorable for its cottages and houses along lanes leading to fords, its unexpected church, and its name. This last is not, as often happens, a corruption of something else. Since before the Domesday Book it has meant 'seven-homestead-village'; but the 'seven' probably meant something other than the number of dwellings. Elsewhere in the Domesday Book are hints that it had been the custom for the tax liability of the Anglo-Saxon nobility to vary according to the number of manors held; on six or fewer manors a thane paid 'three marks of silver' (£1) to the local sheriff, on seven or more manors he paid £8 direct to the royal exchequer. Sevenhampton's name suggests that at some unrecorded pre-Conquest date it had become the seventh estate of a thane who thus achieved (and suffered from) the Anglo-Saxon equivalent of the higher income bracket.

Sevenhampton church, set in a garden of a churchyard, will interest even those not architecturally inclined. It tells its story more than usually clearly. Originally a simple Norman church of nave and chancel, it was at about 1280 lengthened and given new windows, the slim lancets then in vogue (those now in the south transept then formed the east window). Apparently remote Sevenhampton shared in the rising prosperity of the thirteenth century, probably selling the wool of its flocks via Winchcombe abbey, which had acquired the advowson. Less to be expected is that the place should have benefited from the period after about 1450 when wealthy wool-merchants undertook the rebuilding of their home-town churches. Sevenhampton, one would have thought, was too far from the contemporary business life to have attracted the notice, much less the residence, of a thrusting businessman; or perhaps it was that John Cambre, wool-merchant of Worcester, retired there after a successful business career. He it was who gave Sevenhampton church its distinctive appearance. Cambre, however, did not order the rebuilding of the entire church, nor did he disturb its proportions with a chantry chapel for the benefit of himself and his family. Instead he had the central portion added: the tower between the earlier nave and chancel and on either side a transept, so making the building cruciform at a time when, incidentally, that earlier plan was out of favour. He also added the south porch, re-roofed the nave, inserted the 'Perpendicular' east window, but he re-used the earlier windows in his transept. The whole work, though reflecting in part the architectural fashion of the time, has clearly been designed to fit. Not infrequently, fifteenth-century efforts at remodelling have spoilt the earlier proportions or added adornments which, though often interesting in themselves, look a little out of place in a setting of earlier simplicity. That did not happen at Sevenhampton. The central tower is plainly battlemented and not elaborately pinnacled, the porch is not determinedly embellished, and the details throughout the building have added to rather than detracted from the feeling of unity.

The author of all this lies in the church—though, when compared with the monuments of contemporary benefactors elsewhere, the smallness of Cambre's brass makes one wonder whether perhaps his family considered he had done enough for Sevenhampton and so were tempted to skimp on his monument. Or perhaps Cambre himself asked for a modest monument, hoping rightly that the remodelled church should be his memorial.

Along the high ground east of the Sevenhampton valley runs the best-known of the salt ways. It is time to be taking a look at it.

SEVEN

The Ways of Salt and Sheep

Salt was an essential to medieval housekeeping. It was the only preservative of the stores of meat resulting from the autumn slaughtering of the beasts for which there was insufficient winter fodder. From Anglo-Saxon times if not before, through much of summer and early autumn there must have been salt carriers trudging beside their pack-horses all over the country. As we know from medieval records much of the salt was produced from the sea by evaporation in shallow enclosures known as 'salt pans'. The Romans had worked the salt deposits around Droitwich; the Anglo-Saxons, as soon as they had penetrated so far westwards, saw the benefits of such a supply. When Christianity became established and more salt was needed to preserve the fish eaten each Friday and during Lent, it became an act of piety to grant 'salt rights' at Droitwich to a monastic house.

Why only a few of the many paths and tracks which the salt carriers must have used have retained the name of Salt Way seems another example of the haphazard process by which the otherwise unknown Cod named the hills and the lady Burghild has been remembered in Buggildway. As was noticed further north, the route which linked Chipping Campden with the prehistoric Way passing the Rollright Stones, and another which branched off to pass Stow, have both left in the ancient records a scattering of minor place-names mentioning salt. Similar traces occur further south. The Salt Way distinguished by name on the map would seem to be one of several which crossed Cotswold.

The named Salt Way approaches Cotswold from the northwest and climbs the Edge above Hailes before following the upland between the Coln and the Windrush. It is traceable to Lechlade, the highest navigable point on the Thames. Considering the country through which it passes, it is surprisingly direct and level. After crossing the Warwickshire Avon, probably between Pershore and Evesham, its users had to ford only the most insignificant of streams.

For half its first four Cotswold miles—between Hailes abbey and Roel Gate—it appears to take over the prehistoric Way ... which hints that this Salt Way is something of a newcomer to the landscape. Hailes was not founded until nearly 450 years after Winchcombe abbey and during much of that time Winchcombe had enjoyed salt rights at Droitwich. There can be little doubt that Salter's Lane climbing up from Hailes and so bypassing Winchcombe is a later addition. The salt carriers must earlier have gone through Winchcombe and from there climbed more directly to Roel Gate.

From there the Salt Way continues southwards bypassing the villages of Hawling, Salperton and Hazleton, and marking parts of their parish boundaries, an indication of the Way's existence in the eleventh century. It also goes near a 'heathen burial place'—so named by the Anglo-Saxons—two earthworks of unknown age on Pen Hill and the remains of a Neolithic long barrow which, when Victorian investigators reached it, was distinguished by two upright stones at its southeastern end. A mile west of Hazleton its line is taken up by the A 40; but when that road bears off to Northleach—a length constructed during turnpike days—the Salt Way persists along the ridge to cross the Foss Way at almost its highest point between Stow-on-the-Wold and Cirencester. Thereafter it keeps to the high ground between the Coln and the Leach until it reaches the Thames, passing on the way Crickley Barrow above Coln St Dennis.

All this suggests, again, that the medieval salt carriers were not original in their choice of routes ... which is not surprising. Faced with long journeys across a land still thickly green, often marshy and largely devoid of anything we would call a road, they are scarcely likely to have deliberately trodden new routes. They would have used the ways that were there; and the Salt Way's persistent liking for ridges suggests that the salt carriers followed a route trodden first by prehistoric peoples.

Though most of the Salt Way is not unsuitable for cars, the traveller should not hurry along it. As so often with ridge-following routes, there are frequent glimpses over the quieter reaches of Cotswold. And there are villages nearby.

Hawling, the northernmost, is true Cotswold, high, exposed to all the winds going, but thanks to many trees about it not bleak in appearance. The little street of varied stone houses slopes gently down from the manorhouse and church, the traditional neighbours. The manorhouse was Elizabethan, the church medieval; both were partly remodelled about 1760 but not disturbingly so. In the church, except for those who demand an invariably medieval appearance, the two blend surprisingly well, for the round-headed Georgian windows are, apart from their key-stones, of almost Norman plainness; and the manorhouse has kept some of its Tudor gables. All told, a satisfying village though one less featured than many a show-place on Cotswold.

Salperton, a couple of miles south and similarly skirted by the Salt Way, owes the first two syllables of its name to 'salt-paeth', the salt path. Its inclusion in the Domesday Book leaves no doubt that the salt traffic had been well established before the Conquest. To today's visitors it looks a quiet, gentle place of neat houses along a valley; a seventeenth-century lord of the manor found its earlier homes too humble to be included in the view from his great house and so had the village rebuilt a half-mile away from Salperton Park and its church. Many of the houses remain from that rebuilding, though the visitor seeking refreshment will find that the Old Bell, despite the carved tablet of its sign, has long been a private house. Salperton's great house is now more a Victorian attempt at the Jacobean than the original, and a hotel—which is perhaps not unjust. The church, too, was heavily treated about the time of the rebuilding (when it must have acquired the painting on the west wall of a skeletal Father Time). The fifteenth-century tower has, however, survived. High on its south side, demonstrating that women are not to be easily overlooked even by high-handed lords of the manor, is the head of Eve, still with that Apple in her mouth.

Past a long barrow and a little southeast stands Hazleton up and down across a dip. The village street is along one ridge, the church and the two large houses—one has Tudor gables and mullioned windows—on another. The church, a mixture of Norman and fifteenth-century, is almost empty of monuments; it seems that the family who came to own the village after it had at the Reformation passed out of the possession of Winchcombe abbey, never lived there. The relations of later villagers in the 1700s were, however, able to afford the restrained Baroque tombstones that are to be found in many a Cotswold churchyard; Hazleton's are typical of this distinctive work which owed its inspiration to the Painswick family of the Bryans. Hazleton's name, by the way, is often spelled

'Haselton'; it should be 'Hazelton' from the hazels that grew about it before the Conquest.

Where the A 40 now takes over the Salt Way a lane leads down to Compton Abdale, a place of good farms with a mixture of cottages and newer houses set in a deep combe. At the lane-side is a stone crocodile from whose mouth the local water-supply has gushed for the last two centuries. Those who find earlier carvings more intriguing should climb the path to Compton Abdale church set high and almost hidden by yews. What appear from a distance to be pinnacles to its fifteenth-century tower will be seen to be animals squatting on their haunches, each holding in its fore-paws a kind of post and each with mouth agape. Are they attempts at the comic or were their wide-open mouths intended to imply praise? Below are some grimacing gargoyles, animal and sub-human, while on the buttresses rest what appear to have been sphinxes—though why they should be there we can only guess. Over the west window is a good horn-blower. Quite an interesting little collection.

Though, as will be considered later, travellers along another Cotswold route, the White Way, may have passed through Compton Abdale, those frequenting the Salt Way probably knew nothing of the place. They would have kept to the ridge-top, approximately along the line of the A 40, past where stands the Puesdown Inn—built for the stage-coaches and the entrances to its stable yards are still there—until the branch where once stood a hangman's stone. There the Salt Way kept southeast and so bypassed Yanworth, a hill-top cluster of houses at all angles to the lane, and Stowell, little more than great house and church hidden among trees. Whether the traveller will think a diversion through these villages worth making will depend on his liking for the ancient and rare, for each has an item giving a glimpse into the ways of the past.

Yanworth's item is in the church set apart from the village among fine, prosperous-looking farms. The church has traces of Norman work; but older still is the font, tub-like, with by way of decoration a moulding suggesting rope—and that is what catches the eye of the experts in such matters. The font is certainly pre-Conquest, perhaps quite a lot so; for the rope effect hints that it was modelled on the large wooden (and rope-encircled) fonts used during the period of the Anglo-Saxon conversion when it was customary for adults to sit or stand in the font while the baptismal water was poured over them.

Stowell's curiosity, even rarer, consists of two figures in the painting on the wall of its mainly Norman church. The painting itself is, unlike much medieval work, aesthetically attractive as well as curious. Two full centuries older than most surviving wall-paintings it was painted more sensitively than the later work and is without the disturbing luridness that seems to be associated with work of the century following the onset of the Black Death. As was customary it showed the Last Judgment; the upper part which would have depicted Christ in Majesty was lost when the roof was lowered, probably in the 1600s. What is left is Our Lady, seated and attended by the Apostles, and below, among what was originally a crowd of souls awaiting entry to Heaven or damnation, are two figures unexpected in such a context and probably the only surviving representation of a custom that was old when the work was done. They appear to be fighting, but each is armed only with a square shield and what looks like a pickaxe; neither has the customary protection of armour or helmet. They suggest not a chance encounter but an illustration of the ancient practice revived by the Normans and retained through medieval times, known as Trial by Combat. A man accused of a crime against another, if unable to establish his innocence by 'oath-helpers', could appoint a champion to settle the dispute in a contest with a champion appointed by his accusers. The proceedings were carried out in the presence of ecclesiastics—justice was then a concern of the Church—and the fourteenth-century legal treatise known to historians as 'Britton' sets down the conditions which governed the decisive fight: the combatants should be 'armed without iron and without any armour, their heads uncovered, the hands and feet bare, with two staves tipped with horn of equal length, and each of them with a four-cornered target [shield], without other arms by which either might annoy the other'. The two fighting figures in Stowell's wall-painting fit Britton's description.

On the ridge northeast of Stowell the Salt Way as a lane has crossed the Foss Way to follow the high ground between the Coln and the little River Leach. After passing Crickley Barrow, Neolithic or Bronze Age, and Saltway Farm, it becomes on Saltway Hill a track until approaching Coln St Aldwyn where it was crossed by the Roman Akeman Street, now only a dotted line on the map. Eighteenth-century park-making thereabouts has obscured the Way's curve round a sudden bend of the Coln; but a half-mile further south, at another prehistoric mound, it reappears as a lane heading for Lechlade.

Roughly parallel a mile or so to the southwest is the Coln, here less of an upland stream, more leisurely in its going down a valley dotted with copses above which the cornfields spread. By the river are the villages linked by a lane that takes first one side of the valley, then the other.

Coln St Dennis, owing its distinctive name to having been given in 1069 to the church of St Denis in Paris, is small, compact and grouped around its Norman church half-hidden by beeches and yews. Coln Rogers has more to show the visitor. Its church hidden away down a side-lane has a nave which was already standing when St Dennis's was built. Those knowledgeable in such matters can enjoy themselves picking out the long-and-short work at the corners, the surviving Saxon window cut from a single slab of stone, and the pilaster strips characteristic of pre-Conquest work. Coln Rogers also has a priest's house probably dating from the fourteenth century, and an Old Rectory with Tudor windows (though the 'Perpendicular' south front is Victorian handiwork). Less than a mile downstream is Winson with a church essentially Norman, into which windows representative of the four succeeding centuries have been inserted. The survival of so much early work hereabouts, however, should be attributed not to a medieval love of the past but more probably to the local poverty. The Salt Way is leaving the sheep country; these Coln-side villages must, during the Middle Ages, have concentrated more on producing their own needs than on winning a little of the enrichment that wool brought. Having acquired about the time of the Conquest a church adequate for the small populations, each village probably had little surplus wealth or time to rebuild or reconstruct. Necessary re-roofing, an occasional window to let in more light (and more draught if there was not at hand a benefactor to provide expensive glass) and perhaps if, as at Coln Rogers, a local abbey had acquired the advowson, some skilled help with the chancel—the nave was the parishioners' responsibility—and that was about all that could be done through the seven centuries until Victorian restorers took over, fortunately hereabouts not too enthusiastically. (Winson also has a good example of a manorhouse of about 1740, solid and formal, and telling of the lord of the manor's determination to keep up with contemporary ideas of architecture in early Georgian times.)

Ablington is perhaps the most visually satisfying of the Cotswold hamlets. It is a place of good farm-buildings and a strikingly fine house of about 1640, complete with ball-finials to its gables, dripstones to its stone-mullioned windows and even its lions on its gateposts. The manorhouse, dated 1590 and looking nearer the medieval even though plastered, is more discreetly hidden by a high wall. It was the home of Arthur Gibbs, author in 1898 of *A Cotswold Village*. One of the first of the intimate studies of Cotswold life, Gibbs' book has become a classic—though so many changes have come to Cotswold and to England since Gibbs wrote that a modern reader may find that it awakens more than nostalgia. Through the inter-war years Gibbs' book was more a source of information for local historians and a record of passing rural quaintnesses; recently it has become wider regarded and is being reissued. We of the 1970s, less assured about the way society is going than our fathers and grandfathers were, may come to look on *A Cotswold Village* less sentimentally.

Since William Morris asserted that Bibury was the most beautiful village in England it has become the subject of so many photographs that even a newcomer must feel he has been there before. It has just about everything, all in the local stone and with the river Coln, widening now, to reflect its charms: a curving street of varied houses, more about the green under woods climbing up the sheltering hills, a church planned before the Conquest on an impressive scale and, since its medieval and later restorers have been restrained in their efforts, now an ecclesiologists' delight; and long, many-gabled Arlington Row, the most photographed of the surviving weavers' cottages and once dependent on nearby Arlington Mill (now restored and a folk museum). It has Bibury Court, gabled and Tudor, and Arlington Manor only a century younger. It has its village lock-up of about 1720, and even the junior of its bridges is two centuries old. Bibury is, in short, all that is claimed for it. And yet . . .

It must be admitted that the village is very well cared for and very well mannered. The notices drawing attention to attractions for tourists are discreet, and it cannot in fairness be blamed for its many, many car-loads of visitors who wander around camera in hand and get in the way just as you have got your own shot in the viewfinder. The more experienced visitor would avoid summer weekends and public holidays. Seen when spring sunshine is opening the first leaf-buds of its many trees or when October sunlight is catching the last yellows and coppers and reds, Bibury is more restful. At such times one can wander around and see all that is to be seen, and perhaps realise that though so much has survived, there is one building that has disappeared. Up to Stuart times Bibury had its church house—a village meeting-place, not the present Church House built in 1802—for in 1636 the churchwardens turned out from its 'small and unfitting room' a man who 'formerly with great inconvenience had hard shift to dwell in, and so thereby with his wife and children he is enforced to lie in the streets'. The local J.P. commanded the churchwardens to give the family decent lodging and, when they ignored his warrant, he ordered the constable to fine them £1 which was to be devoted to poor relief. With the annoying habit of old records, we know only that the churchwardens paid the fine, not what happened to the homeless family. Not that such a glimpse into Bibury's past need disturb the occupants of the houses about its green or along its street; few of them, one suspects, are descended from those heartless churchwardens. If any of those Stuart Biburians' descendants still remain in the neighbourhood it is unlikely that they will feel concerned about their ancestors' behaviour; most probably they are, these days, hardly part of the village, for they would live on the housing estate of circa 1953 discreetly sited away along the Burford road.

Across the stretch of Cotswold traversed by the Salt Way ran another route of local importance not named on any map. Going more northwest-southeast, it linked Winchcombe with Sherborne near the Windrush. A clue to its usage is to be found in the name Sherborne, the 'clear stream' named before the Domesday Book and early recognised as an ideal place for sheep-washing.

The precise line of this route cannot now be determined. It must have passed through Charlton Abbots above Winchcombe, and through Hawling, Salperton and Hazleton, and probably had offshoots north to Snowshill and south to Yanworth. The motorist can guess that it followed the present lanes and so find himself a quiet, very rural route across High Cotswold. The walker can assume that it took the footpath that climbs from above Sudeley to Roel Gate and thereafter used the track that is now Campden Lane until a mile south of Hazleton it may have curved into another, more easterly bridle-path along the ridge north of Hampnett from where, after briefly becoming the A 40 it drops down as a footpath to Sherborne. Either way, the traveller will end up along the valley of the Sherborne brook with the pattern of field and wood rising up over the gently swelling hills and, because the main road on the ridge takes the traffic, giving a feeling of being half forgotten.

This nameless Way had its origin both on the ground and in its purpose in Winchcombe. Though there is very little to see of Winchcombe's once-great abbey, by a chance of history quite a lot is to be found in its surviving records. As R. H. Hilton tells in his paper in *Gloucestershire Studies,* a large collection of documents varying from papal decisions and royal grants to bailiffs' accounts and notes of wages paid to abbey servants has survived, covering several decades between 1350 and 1520. From them can be gathered an impression of the organisation and business activities of a medieval monastic house ... and the phrase 'business activities' is not inappropriate. On the wolds above the town and stretching the dozen miles to Sherborne grazed the abbey's wealth, and the processes to turn wool into cash were conducted in as business-like a fashion as any contemporary laymen could have undertaken.

Domesday Book records Winchcombe abbey as possessing only a few estates, half of them out in the Vale. Only Snowshill and Charlton Abbots were on sheep country, while Sherborne lay beyond the Foss Way. But during the next two centuries Winchcombe's abbots invested shrewdly. They bought the manors of Hawling, Hazleton, Yanworth and Roel—the last from the abbey of St Evroul for the large sum of £550 plus £20 annual rent. A glance at the map shows their purposes. The abbey had, by the 1320s, turned their former randomly-sited wold manors into an almost continuous twelve-mile-long sheep-run across which ran adequate communications by contemporary standards: the prehistoric Way leading southwest towards the growing port of Bristol, the Salt Way to the Thames valley, and the Foss Way linking the Southwest with the East Midlands and beyond.

Having acquired the manors, the abbey seems at times to have taken land outside its own demesne into its hands ... or so we may assume from what happened to John le Knyt, in the 1350s one of the surviving free landholders of Hawling. In the thirty years up to 1380 eighteen documents record Knyt's parting with portions of his land to the abbey, sometimes for the 'good of his soul', more often for an agreed price 'owing to his great necessity'. Finally, about 1382, he exchanged his last acres for a pension of his board, lodging and clothing.

Before then a visiting Florentine businessman named Pegolotti had been impressed with Winchcombe's wool production. He placed the abbey twelfth in a list of over two hundred English monastic houses producing wool, and estimated, probably cautiously, that its flock totalled 8,000 sheep providing an annual revenue of over £350 (which was more than many a noble of the time could have achieved and was only part of the abbey's income).

The extensive sheep-run was only the basis of the abbey's wool production. The business end was not at Winchcombe but at Sherborne, and the records tell how that manor was organised. On the North Field swelling over the rise across the Sherborne brook and the South Field reaching at least to the present A 40, were grown the necessary food crops—though, to judge from summaries of acreages, more important than wheat for the villagers' sustenance was 'drage', a mixture of oats and other grain, used in making the abbey beer. Northeastwards along the valley of the Windrush spread large meadows capable of producing hay for winter fodder for the abbey ewes and also at times a surplus to sell. Above them spread the village common.

It seems that comparatively early the villagers were relieved of the 'day works' by which, in medieval custom, so many paid for their strips of land in the common fields. Two decades before the Black Death—which historians used to tell us had begun the process of commutation of services—the abbey's Sherborne tenants were paying cash rents, and had only to provide up to four 'boon reaps', four days on the lord abbot's land gathering his harvest. Otherwise the villagers—the records imply a population of about 300 which was more than Winchcombe itself—were free to work their own holdings, except for a few weeks in early summer. During that time took place one activity in which all had to join; and the abbot himself, accompanied by a retinue which included his steward and his master shepherd, travelled the nameless Way from Winchcombe to stay at Sherborne while it was done. It was, of course, the washing and the shearing of the abbey's huge flock.

The shallow 'clear stream' which had given Sherborne its name was ideal for the washing. Each villager, as part of the bargain by which he held his land and his home, had to provide washing and shearing service—up to 15½ days of each from those who held a full virgate of land. Not until the wool was dried and baled did the abbot and his staff leave, having meanwhile lived on the stores of bread and beer, meat and cheese (ewes' milk was specially favoured for cheese-making) that had been stored against their coming ... and, though the records do not include so uncommercial a matter, no doubt the villagers joined in the shearing feast mentioned elsewhere and featured in Shakespeare's *The Winter's Tale*. And among the hundreds of bales of wool that were soon after the feasting on their way to the Flanders markets were the fleeces of other than abbey sheep. It seems that the abbot acted as middleman for the more prosperous of his tenants.

That was in the heyday of Winchcombe's wool-producing. From about 1350 onwards monastic (and noble) production gradually declined, while tenant farmers enlarged their flocks (often renting land formerly held by their lords as demesne) and increasingly supplied the needs of the growing wool-cloth industry. By 1485, the year which saw the first Tudor on the throne, Winchcombe's output had shrunk to 2,900 fleeces a year, little more than a third of the production estimated by Pegolotti in about 1320.

As it approaches Sherborne, the nameless route bypasses two villages which never came into Winchcombe abbey's possession: Hampnett and Farmington. Now quiet and out-of-the-way, Hampnett was once a lively little place, for until the coach-road was diverted through Northleach its lane was the main road from London and Oxford to Cheltenham. A large green with cottages and houses about it spreads across a slight hollow and rises to where the church stands almost among the barns and outbuildings of a good farm. The church is more than locally known for its Norman work; it has retained through eight centuries the original groining to its chancel, its chancel arch and some of the narrow, round-headed windows to its nave. Though the visitor may have his own opinions about a Victorian rector's painting of the chancel, there are many details worth more than a glance, notably the unusual fluted shaping of the capitals in the chancel and the pairs of slim doves that adorn the capitals of the arch. One pair, with the birds drinking from a chalice, is believed to represent Holy Communion; the other pair, breast to breast on the corner, is even more unusual. Such details suggest that about 1180 there must have been a finely skilled and sensitive craftsman at Hampnett.

Farmington, reached along a lane that passes plough-subdued Norbury Camp, also has a part-Norman church—which has the oddest of east windows. In his *Buildings of Gloucestershire*, Verey says it is 'very Late Perp with curious tracery'. It may be hazardous to query such an authority, but it is hard to imagine a medieval mason ever perpetrating—or allowing an apprentice to produce—such an excruciating effort of strips and eye-like holes.

Sherborne, standing a little above where its brook has been widened enough to reflect the trees along its far bank, has changed much since the abbots of Winchcombe's time. It is now a 'model village', the creation largely of its owner about 1820. The prim cottages, built in rows, are each complete with stone porch, drip-stone topped windows and neat dormer above. Few are individual though one house has a Norman doorway complete with tympanum, presumably from an earlier building than the present church. This was rebuilt at about the same time as much of the village. Its main interest is for those seeking social significance in monuments. On the earliest, dated 1661, John Dutton 'who was master of a large fortune and owner of a mind equal to it', is portrayed in his shroud, following the fashion of John Donne's monument in St Paul's. There are also a large classical figure, a young mother and child on their way to Heaven, and what Verey calls a 'life-sized angel' trampling Death—surely 'human-sized' would have been a more appropriate adjective. These last two, dated 1807 and 1791 respectively, are of that uneasy period when the classical was going out and a return to medieval submissive recumbency was impossible and something near to story-telling was coming in with varying effect. All are of workmanship befitting ancestors of the Lords Sherborne—though it seems that, while employing the best sculptor of the time, Sir John Dutton's children were a bit slipshod over his maternal grandfather's christian name, and making an amendment in carved stone is a tell-tale matter.

Between the last few miles of the nameless Way from Winchcombe to Sherborne and the Salt Way as it goes southeastwards from its crossing of the Foss Way stands Northleach. It was founded as a new town in 1227 by the abbot of Gloucester, owner of the manor of Eastington, the parent settlement. For the first three centuries of its life Northleach thrived on wool; but when mechanisation began to take over, the little River Leach had not power enough to compete with the Stroud valley. Through the Tudor century the place must have had a thin time and we know that in the 1600s its lord of the manor, William Dutton, left his great house—which was pulled down in 1937—and £200 to help the unemployed, hoping that the revenue would provide for 'some honest tradesman in freestains or stuffs or in any other such trade as may keep the people from idleness'; his brother Thomas in 1616 founded the almshouses which still stand in the High Street. Thirty years later Northleach suffered from the rival armies in the Civil War. Charles I was there in 1643; in 1645 after the battle of Naseby, Sir Thomas Fairfax quartered his troops in the town and they, though restrained from damaging the church, did not endear themselves to the people. Armies, even semi-civilian ones, have to be fed and supplied, and Northleach was then barely able to maintain its own people. The place had something of a boost when its main street became part of the turnpike route across Cotswold. Northleach is, therefore, mainly of the 1600s and 1700s, trim, grey and, thanks to its market-place, possessing a feeling of spaciousness. Little survives from its great days as a wool town, but among that little is one of the best of late-medieval works: Northleach church, the most gracious of the Cotswold 'wool churches'.

Whatever the original church, by about 1420 Northleach's leading families had become wealthy enough to begin rebuilding first the tower and, during the next hundred years, the whole church. Fittingly most of them are still remembered in the portrait-brasses in the church: Thomas and Agnes Fortey (1447) and her first husband, William Scors, tailor (1420), John Fortey (1458) who rebuilt the nave and added the clerestory to make the church 'more lightsome', another husband and wife of 1485 whose inscription is missing, John and Joane Taylour (1490), Robert and Anne Serche (1501), Thomas 'mirchant of ye Staple of Calis' and Johan Bushe (1526) ... though, unjustly, of the brass to William and Margaret Bicknell who added the Lady Chapel in 1489 and possibly gave the church its enchanting south porch only the children survive. The matrimonial pairs suggest that in each case husband and wife acted as one, and we have no reason to think otherwise though it happens that one Northleach woolman, Will Mydwynter—whose brass is believed to be that which has lost its inscription and now has only the identification of a wool-mark based on the letters W and M—has inadvertently contributed to our knowledge not only of wool-business in the late fifteenth century, but also of marriage business.

It was from Mydwynter that the Cely family, 'marchants of the stapall at Caleis', bought 'good cottyswolde woll'. The Cely letters, like their more famous contemporaries, the Paston letters, often mingle business and family matters, and so allow us to see something of personal lives as well as business transactions ... as when, on 13 May 1482, young Richard Cely wrote to his brother George:

> I have been in Cotswold this three weeks and packed with William Mydwynter twenty-two sarplers ... and in our communication he asked me if I were in any way of marriage. I told him nay and he informed me that there was a young gentlewoman whose father his name is Lemryke and her mother is dead and she shall dispend by her mother £40 a year, and her father is the greatest ruler as richest man in that country.... And ere matins were done William Mydwynter had moved this matter to the greatest man about the gentleman Lemryke, and he said and informed the aforesaid of all the matter and the young gentlewoman both.... I came to Northleach again to make an end of packing and on Sunday next after the same man that William Mydwynter brake first to, came and told me that ... if I would tarry May Day I should have a sight of the young gentlewoman and I said I would tarry with a good will ... and to matins the same day come the young gentlewoman and her mother-in-law [stepmother] and when they came into church and when matins was done they went to a kinswoman of the young gentlewoman and I sent to them a bottle of white Romnay and they took it thankfully for they had come a mile on foot that morning and when mass was done I come and welcomed them and kissed them and they thanked me for the wine ... and the person pleased me well as by the first communication she is young, little, and very well-favoured and witty and the country speaks much good by her. Sir, all this matter abideth the coming of her father to London that we may understand what sum he will depart with and how he likes me.... I pray send me a letter how ye think by this matter.

It seems, however, that for all the young lady's being 'whery whellfavyrd and whytty', Northleach did not provide young Richard Cely with a bride. A little over a month later he was writing to his brother that 'Sir Harry Bryan ... labours me sore to go and see Rawson's daughter', and Lemryke's is forgotten. Nor does Will Mydwynter appear from the correspondence to have benefited much from his association with the Celys. Later in 1482 he is writing to Richard Cely that wool prices have risen and that his suppliers 'nedys haffe halle ther money', and asking that he 'may haffe the £200 that ye sayd y solde nott haffe tyll Nowhembyr'. The Celys were not helpful; and later Richard is writing to brother George that 'Mydwyntter ys com; God ryd us of hym'.

From the moment the visitor approaches Northleach's exquisite south porch, the church gives more than any other wool church a feeling of lightness and grace. Inside one is less aware of the technical mastery which made possible its lofty arcade, and there seems less of the chill rigidity of much of the 'Perpendicular'. Perhaps it is that Northleach's scale is a little smaller than that of many another 'wool church' and so one can take in, from the first, its wholeness.

As noteworthy as the church but in a very different way is the long, rather severe building ending with a smallish, box-like room at each end, which stands at the crossroads of the High Street and the Foss Way. It was built in about 1790 as Northleach prison—the cells which once stood behind have been demolished and the stone reused in the Mill Inn and the Mill House at Withington. Until a few years ago it served as the local police station; now much of it stands empty and risks demolition ... which would be a pity for those who, in their pieces in the press and on the television, like to tell us that prisons of the past century and a half were built as places in which criminals could be locked away and forgotten.

As Northleach prison should remind us, the builders of nineteenth-century prisons had very different intentions. Their buildings expressed the ideas which were early demonstrated at Northleach by Sir George Onesiphorus Paul. Son of a family of 'gentlemen clothiers' rich and influential enough for him—after a youth spent enjoyably and expensively—to be appointed high sheriff for the county, Paul undertook his duties more seriously than most high sheriffs of his time. He even looked into—literally as well as metaphorically—the prison accommodation for which he had become indirectly responsible ... and was horrified by what he saw, much as John Howard, high sheriff of Bedfordshire, was similarly disturbed and so was beginning the investigations which were to lead to his great work on prison reform. The two met and their views coincided. As he records, Howard found the cramped, ancient gaols of Gloucestershire as revolting as those of Bedfordshire. At Berkeley the building was, he says, 'quite out of repair; only one room for men and women; no chimney; yard not secure; no water; no straw'. At St Briavels, where also the medieval castle served as the prison, he found 'no yard; no water; no allowance; no firing; one of the two sickly objects I found there had been confined a twelve-month, and never once let out of that dismal room'. And many of the prisoners, as Paul was later to tell his listeners on his many lecture tours, had done no more than 'stolen turnips from a field, or apples from the trees in an orchard'; some he found in Gloucester castle were innocent of any crime.

Like Howard, Paul determined to do something about the conditions he had found. Being by nature a vigorous character, he launched into a prolonged series of meetings, speeches, addresses, letters, pamphlets, appeals. For over thirty years he demanded that new prisons should be built in which 'bread, water, and air, as the means to beneficial existence, should be denied to no prisoner', that washing facilities should be provided for all, that each prison should have an infirmary where sick prisoners could be treated. He also demanded an end to the custom of herding all prisoners —male and female, young and old, those awaiting trial and those found guilty, and in some areas lunatics, too—into a single and totally inadequate room. Apart from the health risks, Paul was concerned that newcomers might be 'contaminated' by those already there. He strove against the mere imprisonment, the useless shutting away. Imprisonment, he said, 'should be a state of continual occupation and of complete seclusion, by the one to create a habit of industry, by the other to force reflection on the mind'. When he built his prisons with a cell for each prisoner, Paul was not trying to impose solitary confinement as a punishment; rather, he visualised each prisoner spending the greater part of his time working alone in order to have ample opportunity to acquire a useful skill and to reflect on the misery to which he and his family had been brought and so, aided by the prison chaplain, to become able and determined to reform himself.

Paul's ideas were followed by those who, during the fifty years after his death, built prisons in many towns of Victorian Britain. The bareness of the buildings, essential to cleanliness, and their apparent restrictiveness, may repel us. We may consider Paul's assumptions naïve and his methods crude. But we should not overlook that he and Howard as well as those who put their ideas into practice were trying to ensure that at least some prisoners came out more able to find a satisfying place in society and so less likely to return to prison ... as we in our changes to their system are also trying to do.

EIGHT

Iron-agers' Way

From the dip in the Edge above Cheltenham where in Roman times stood a small market-town runs the A 436 linking Gloucester and Stow-on-the-Wold. It is often regarded as part of the Cotswold Ridgeway though in truth it owes much of its modern course to the local enclosure commissioners. There can, however, be no doubt that across this area ran a route that was in existence in the Iron Age if not before. As a glance at the map shows, from Andoversford southwestward the route is continued by some miles of the prehistoric Way and then by ancient tracks through the hilly country around Painswick. Across the lowest Severn ford it reaches the Forest of Dean with its iron and, beyond, Welsh gold and copper. East of Stow the route picks up the prehistoric Way again a mile before the Rollright Stones. The Andoversford–Stow length of the A 436 appears to represent an Iron Age short cut to the original, more meandering Way.

Only by detailed study of the maps and records surviving from pre-enclosure times would it be possible to assert with fair accuracy the medieval route and from that to assume the Iron Age one. Certainly about Andoversford there have been considerable changes. A century and a half before the recent by-pass, the road up from Cheltenham, which until then used steep Dowdeswell Hill, was diverted in a long curve northwards for the easing of the stagecoach going. A map dated 1748 of the parish of Hawling, two miles northeast of Andoversford, shows that the main road then went directly east; the enclosure map of 1821 gives its present course cutting northeastwards across what had been Hawling common. The up-and-down last four miles to Stow, crossing three valleys, suggest that earlier the route may have curved northwards to keep more consistently to the higher ground—and so would have passed some unclassified tumuli and two Neolithic barrows. Or it could have gone more directly east—about the route of the B 4068—past Notgrove's long barrow to reach the Windrush valley at the Iron Age fort which was the first Bourton-on-the-Water.

However the earlier routes went, in the century before the enclosure commissioners tidied them up piecemeal they saw other travellers besides those going peaceably about their business. In the seven-year contest between King and Parliament, there was much coming and going across this part of Cotswold.

The adherence of Gloucester and the Stroud neighbourhood to the Parliamentary side, in part the outcome of the incessant interference of the governments of the first two Stuarts with the wool trade, was a major cause of the armies' visits. After Charles had established his headquarters at Oxford from which he planned to attack London, he always had hostile Gloucester in his rear. By the summer of 1643, he had decided to take the place and end its nuisance; on August 10th he arrived to organise the siege in person.

Parliamentary strategy demanded that the town should be held, and there followed three hectic weeks during which the people of Gloucester made what defences they could and the Parliamentary leaders in London urged the young men of the capital—not such willing fighters except when their homes were threatened—to march to break the siege. At last, on August 26th, the Parliamentary commander, the earl of Essex, had sufficient strength to risk the march—and risk it was, for defeat en route would have left London all but defenceless.

At Stow-on-the-Wold a strong contingent of Royalist cavalry waited for the Parliamentary army—unwisely and unsuccessfully, as they could not make one of their devastating charges among the hilly fields and streets of the town. Even so, the Royalists assumed that Essex would not continue across Cotswold 'near thirty miles in length', as the earl of Clarendon wrote later, 'where half the King's body of horse would distress, if not destroy, his [Essex's] whole army, and through a country eaten bare, where he could find neither provision for man nor horse.' Essex, however, persisted, his men resisting Cavalier harassment until at last, on September 5th, the weary, hungry and battered Londoners saw from above Cheltenham the towers of Gloucester. More significantly, they saw smoke rising from the Royalist camp. Charles had ordered the destruction of what equipment could not be carried away, and had abandoned the siege. The relief of Gloucester, with its strategic and psychological benefits, had been achieved ... though the people of Stow must have wondered how decisive Essex's march had been when, within a fortnight, the Royalist army passed through, hurrying to intercept the Parliamentarian Londoners on their way home. But when the two armies met in the fields outside Newbury, the Royalists could only delay, not defeat them.

Stow was to see more action on 21 March 1646, a last despairing effort from the remnants of the defeated Royalists. The King's man, old Sir Jacob Astley, trying to make his way back to Oxford, encountered a stronger force of Parliamentarians just north of the town. The battle was one-sided and brief. As old Astley watched his men, now prisoners, being marched off to spend the next few days locked in Stow church, he told the Parliamentarian commanders: 'You have done your work and may go play, unless,' he added prophetically, 'you will fall out amongst yourselves.'

Such is Cotswold's share of the Civil Wars according to the textbooks, but there was much more marching and counter-marching along the more usable roads. Stow on the Foss Way saw much of it, and passing armies ever need supplies and are not always scrupulous about paying for them, as John Chamberlayne, Esquire, of Stow, Maugersbury and Oddington, was by chance to let us know. Having supported the king, he was liable on the Parliamentary triumph to a heavy fine. To diminish his liability he drew up 'a note of quarteringe contribution & provisions sent to the Armyes for the land I hold'. It gives an impression of what the Civil War had meant to non-combatants:

> Imprimis: quartered upon the Commings up of Marquesse Hartford with the welshmen 120 foote souldiers & 20ty officers and the Horses 5 dayes att £5 a daye Comes to ... £25 0. 0.
>
> Item: Pd. to Colonell Gerards Regimt. and my Ld. Percyes regimt. 14teene month Contribucion att £3 3s 4d the month ... £44 6. 8.
>
> When my Ld of Essex His Army Marched to the reliefe of Glouc. they spent mee In Howsehold Provision of Bread Bere cheese meate & provender ... £6 0.0.
>
> Quartered upon the Breakinge up of Glouc: seidge 20ty men and Horses of the kings army 3 dayes which comes to £4 0. 0. ...
>
> I Had Corne upon the Growndе Spoyled by the two armyes Prince Rupert facinge me Ld. of Essex at Stow worth £40 att the least ... When Sir Wm Waller laye att Stow the cariadge Horses

> were turned In my Corne & did mee att the least £30 worth of Hurte....

And so through fifty-seven items until at the end Chamberlayne tots up his losses:

> Summ totalis is £446 10s od beside I Have quartered many more wch I Have forgotten I Have lost 17teene Plowe Horse taken out of my teemes upon that land and many tymes payed greate summes of mony to stave of quarteringe & for post Horses and to avoyde carriadge and other chardges Incident to warre wch I Reckon not I lost above a Hundred sheepe by souldiers all wch I leave to your consideracions and referre my selfe wholy to yor mercyes.

The commissioners appointed by Parliament accepted much of Chamberlayne's claim for he was in May 1649 let off with a demand for only about one-sixth of the value of his lands ... until an informer drew attention to property he owned elsewhere and had not mentioned. Though Chamberlayne pleaded that this property was heavily mortgaged, he found himself finally mulcted of £1,246—about two-thirds of the value of his estates. His efforts, to be found in full in the Gloucester Record Office, seem to have benefited him little.

The Iron-agers' Way, like the other early Ways, passes through few villages. Near Andoversford and a mile south of the Way are Shipton Oliffe and Shipton Solers sharing a twisting valley. Before the Conquest they probably comprised one sheep-run owned by the abbess of nearby Withington; by the Domesday Book the valley had been divided into two manors, one belonging to the Olive family, the other to the Solers. Both are pleasant little places, though slate roofs here and there intrude. Oliffe church lifts its unusual, heavily-capped thirteenth-century bellcote against a backdrop of chestnut trees. Inside it has an item which may be noted for future reference. Beside a window to its early chancel is a carved head with the tongue sticking out, but an assumption of bucolic humour is probably incorrect. The face looks to the altar; the protruding tongue may imply readiness to receive the Holy Wafer.

The local hereabouts is the Frogmill Inn cut off from the village by the A 436 and now itself bypassed. Such almost brutal siting is due both to unsympathetic planners of turnpike roads and their successors of the motor age. Built for the stage-coach traffic, the inn served as the first stop on the Gloucester–London run of the famous 'Glocester Flying Machine'—105 miles in two days could in the 1700s be likened to flying. Appropriately the inn now looks to motorists and has, of course, sprouted Olde Worlde extensions and modern notions of catering ... though a visitor may wonder what, if the Toadmill Inn were to remain unaltered into the twenty-first century, our descendants would make of people who coyly labelled two necessary doors 'Boys' and 'Girls'.

After keeping high and bypassing Naunton along its valley, the Iron-agers' Way, now the A 436, descends to Lower Swell about the little River Dickler. Several well-preserved houses cluster around its still-homely inn, the Golden Ball; up a side lane is its church which must infuriate the ecclesiologist. Alongside a small, very Norman village church was added, in 1860/70, a new old-imitating nave and chancel. With much good medieval work about to inspire or guide him, the Victorian architect could surely have done a more convincing job; but one should at least be grateful that he did not destroy the chancel arch to the original church, perhaps the most remarkable on Cotswold. Though small, it has three orders conventionally carved and, beyond the outer one, a series of emblems and figures: a pair of symbols suggesting hot cross buns, three linked rings, a stylised hare, a more recognisable stag, three fishes, a large-headed human, a wolf or a dog on its back, a horned beast, twining cord, a bird.... Below, on the north capital, are a dancing figure, a woman with a stick (distaff?) and what appears to be a hoop, and a prone figure. A note in the church suggests that the 'buns' are the fateful Apples, that the central figure represents Man, and the animals show his ascendancy over them. The three figures below are said to show Man grasping the serpent and so triumphing over evil, the woman 'holding the serpent to her breast, fostering evil', and the inner one Man lying on the serpent 'fallen, yet superior to evil'. Even accepting early medieval interpretations of the Fall and that the Normans were not naturally inclined towards notions of equality between the sexes, that explanation seems to omit much. The linked rings were used as a symbol of the Trinity, the bird could have been intended as a dove, fish were emblems of Baptism, but as for the rest.... Most of us, knowing our Bible far from thoroughly and the many legends and pseudo-gospels current in the twelfth century not at all, have to be content with feeling in the work a strangeness that separates us by more than time from the Norman sculptor.

There are other things to see in Lower Swell, including the Lady Well a little way along the drive to Bowl Farm, minutely canopied but still bubbling. Small though it is, the Whittlestone which once marked the long barrow a half-mile to the west was said to come down to it to drink when it heard the clock strike twelve. About a century ago, however, the stone was removed and placed in the vicarage garden ... which must have disturbed the local legend-addicts for it had long been known that, having been supernaturally set up, the Whittlestone could not be moved by 'all the King's horses and all the King's men'. Across the river is another sight not less noteworthy in its way: Spa Cottages, a prim row with its windows distinguished by curiously-shaped surrounds and an attempt at geometric patterning along the cornice. The row was Lower Swell's effort to gain from the discovery of a chalybeate spring (now under the floor) at a time when the alleged health-giving custom of 'taking the waters' was fashionable. But no second Cheltenham grew at Lower Swell, and the little terrace remains only a pleasant reminder of a lost hope.

Like Lower Swell, Upper Swell a mile to the north is a streamside village. Its church, also originally Norman, tells that it was a separate parish from early days. Beyond the churchyard its manor-house, handsome Jacobean with a good columned porch, is now boarded up and empty. Upper Swell's mill is still there in its early nineteenth-century version, complete with mill-wheel and, alongside, its row of once-dependent cottages.

Stow-on-the-Wold was originally the Iron Age fort which the Romans crossed with their Foss Way and the Anglo-Saxons labelled 'Mailgaresbyri'—Maugersbury to us. Though having been a recognised meeting-place a full half-century before the Conquest, it did not become a market centre spontaneously. It was deliberately founded as a town in 1107 by its lord of the manor, the abbot of Evesham. That it was expected to thrive is demonstrated by its wide Market Square—so wide and open that on chilly days those who loiter will test the accuracy of the local saying: 'Stow-on-the-Wold where the wind blows cold.' Its medieval rise appears to have been not so much as a wool town but as the market for sheep. When cloth-making brought a reorganisation of the Cotswold industry and the decline of many early towns, Stow was able to maintain its position as a market—its Horse Fair is still famous—and developed boot- and shoe-making; while, as its many inns still show, it later benefited from the coach traffic. Now, like Campden and Burford mainly dependent on tourism, it wears an eighteenth-century look, though those who venture along some of the side streets will find hints of Stow's earlier days. Here and there are timber-framed houses and 'Tudor' work, and the rather dejected long building standing near the entrance to the churchyard was in 1594 the grammar school. Once Stow could boast a local museum recording its past from the Stone Age into Stuart times; its collection of Civil War relics was said to 'give a vivid picture of this unhappy period when the shopkeepers and other inhabitants of Stow must have often deplored the fact that their town was on a high road and thereby open to the marauding visits of soldiers of both parties'. Today's visitor will not find such an experience. The Civil War exhibits were some years ago transferred to Worcester museum, the prehistoric collection to Bristol ... which may be advantageous to the general student but is a little hard on those who visit Stow and look for tangible reminders of its long past.

Stow church in which for a while in April 1646 Royalist prisoners were kept is, though large, not a 'wool church'. It has retained more of its original work—it must have been started about 1120 soon after the founding of the town. Additions during the thirteenth century and 'Perp' enlargement of many of its windows tell of Stow's times of prosperity. Its monuments, however, are not to wealthy wool-men but to local landowners like the Chamberlaynes.

The alternative and probably ancient way to Stow, the B 4068, passes two villages which may appeal to those interested in archaeology, tapestry-work, or the curious.

The first of them, Notgrove, has its major sight a mile and a half to the west beside the road: the long barrow which has stood on the crest for most of 6,000 years and is now more a monument to the thoughtlessness of Victorian antiquaries than to Neolithic peoples. About a century ago it was so brutally treated that the uprights of what was its passage and burial chamber now stand roofless. It was then assumed to have contained two interments. Far more careful examination in 1935 revealed not only the remains of ten more skeletons but also, apparently completely sealed, a separate circular domed chamber containing a stone cist in which was the crouched skeleton of an elderly man. It seems that it was for this burial that the mound was originally raised and that later-comers, though still New Stone-agers, added their own, more characteristic tombs reached by an entrance passage. But the atmosphere that might stir today's visitors has departed. The monument, sited in a slight dip in the ridge so that the fieldscape spreads out on either side, gives one only the view and a feeling of pathos.

The honey-coloured houses of Notgrove village stand in random fashion about the upper end of its combe. Farms and cottages intermingle; the church and the manorhouse form a group apart behind a farm at the end of a short by-lane. The manorhouse, though rebuilt after severe fire damage, looks dignified Stuart. The church, small and originally Norman, has a tower and a spire of about 1340. Outside the east wall is a curious little Crucifixion—the face wears an expression of amused surprise—said to be of Saxon workmanship. Inside are five good effigies to the former Whittington lords and ladies of the manor, ranging from about 1585 to 1630, and two of earlier fourteenth-century priests which age has unfortunately worn. And there is the tapestry which serves as the reredos. The work of the local Anderson family—men and women, parents and children worked on it from 1936 to 1954—it shows the village set among colourful trees, with a surround of religious emblems and some flowers and animals said to have been prompted by family nicknames. It is a delightful piece of work; about the twenty-second century or so, it may well be more than a local sight.

A mile and a half to the east, Aston Blank stands high. The suffix 'Blank' was Old English for 'bare' though the village has now gathered about it several clusters of trees; the alternative name of 'Cold Aston' must still be appropriate in winter for the village must catch every wind that blows. Its houses line the street or group around the triangular green on which a large sycamore gives an impression of shelter; and near by, for those who visit on a chilly day or who on a warm one need refreshment, is the 300-year-old Plough. The church has something to show from Norman times onwards, but is curiously empty of monuments. Only one, coloured, classical and cheruby, greets the visitor as he enters under the patterned tympanum of the south door. Did Aston Blank never attract a local 'family' of note or wealth?

This Way meets the Foss Way near Bourton-on-the-Water and so must have used that road to reach Stow. Eastward from Stow the Iron-agers' Way went to link up with the earlier route past the

Rollright Stones. It is now for most of the eight miles overlaid by the A 436. As ever the villages lie off it along loop lanes.

Oddington, just west of the River Evenlode and the railway, has a pleasant winding street and several good houses on little side-roads that make one wonder why it seldom gets much notice in the guide-books. It also has a remarkable old church a quarter-mile along a lane to the south. Alone and almost surrounded by trees, it began as a small, narrow building, thick of wall, small of window and of an age that the experts disagree about. Verey, in his *Buildings of Gloucestershire,* gives twelfth-century, a note in the church claims a pre-Conquest origin. Certainly the arch leading through a very thick wall from the original nave to the original chancel is so severely plain that one suspects a Norman mason would have provided something more visually impressive. On to this original church was built, about 1240, a larger church, the wall between the two being pierced by an arcade and a tower added; and then, perhaps a century later, some of the windows were enlarged and given their gentle tracery, and in the fifteenth century the building was re-roofed. It has, in short, just about everything medieval, architecturally speaking, all in village scale.

It has even more. The stone seats in the porch show scoring, said to have been made by medieval arrow-sharpening. Inside, a rich Jacobean pulpit complete with sounding-board reminds that the 1600s were days of great sermons. (While the church was neglected during Victorian times, a vixen is said to have reared her cubs in the pulpit, an occasion remembered in a tapestry kneeler in the chancel.) But what draws the experts to Oddington church is the Doom painted on the north wall. Once very large, it has lost much of its colouring during the five hundred and more years since it was painted (and for two centuries it was hidden under lime-wash). Conventionally, Christ is shown at the top attended by Apostles and angels; below are the dead, some being ushered into Heaven, some being forced into Hell's Mouth. There are individual touches: a demon applies a bellows to the fire, an angel gives a helping hand to a soul hopefully trying to climb Heaven's wall, some of the doomed as well as the saved are crowned. More unexpected is the impression of Heaven, not because the artist has suggested a rather earthly collection of buildings but because in this persistently stone country he has shown them as built of brick. It may be that he was merely copying a Continental original: it could be that, brick-making having at the time only recently reappeared in England, he was constructing his Heaven with the very latest materials.

Across the Evenlode from Oddington are Adlestrop and Daylesford. Adlestrop once had a railway station where, as readers of poetry anthologies which include works of the first decade of this century will recall, Edward Thomas tells:

> . . . one afternoon
> Of heat the express-train drew up there
> Unwontedly. It was late June.
> The steam hiss'd. Someone clear'd his throat.
> No one left and no one came
> On the bare platform. What I saw
> Was Adlestrop—only the name

Adlestrop has other claims to be remembered—and so should have Edward Thomas who was killed in Flanders in 1917. The work of his contemporary, Wilfred Owen, has recently been revalued, and deservedly so. One day perhaps others of those essentially life-loving and cruelly killed poets may come to be seen as more than recorders of what to many of us is the half-unreal world of pre-1914.

Adlestrop has lost its station—the name-board now serves the bus-shelter—but has acquired few more houses since Thomas's pause there. It remains a scattered place, its cottage pairs and threes dotted along twisting lanes, its former great house Adlestrop Park—part-Tudor, part-Georgian—now a children's home, and its church too thoroughly restored to be interesting. The former large rectory is now the House. There stayed frequently Jane Austen, niece to Theophilus Leigh, Adlestrop's rector for over forty years. Those who like to indulge in the game of guessing the scenes of fictional happenings will find no clue that Adlestrop House featured in any of Jane's novels. The rest of us may recall that Miss Austen was usually too discreet to make her backgrounds readily recognisable and so can believe that she might quite probably have transported her characters' houses to other counties . . . and so, Jane addicts can imagine that the finely sited Adlestrop House was visited by Mrs Norris, always so intent on arranging good works for others to do, or could have served as the home of the handsome and vain Sir Walter Elliot whose only reading was the entry in the Baronetage beginning: 'Walter Elliot, born March 1, 1760...'

Daylesford, on the far side of the Iron-agers' Way, now the A 436, has very different associations. It is little more than a church, a few groups of 'estate cottages'—very good ones carefully designed to show a variety of traditional features—and the House which was the home of Warren Hastings, 'one of the immortals of the British Empire'—to quote a guide-book obviously written a full half-century ago. Is he ever mentioned in school history lessons nowadays?

Screened by fine trees and set at the end of a long drive so that the casual visitor will see nothing of it, Daylesford House is not quite what might be expected by those who can recall only Hastings' achievements. Much of his career was, by eighteenth-century standards, a triumph, and the overcoming of an unpromising start. His mother died early, his father disappeared leaving him in the care of an illiterate village-woman from whom he was rescued by his grandfather. He knew little affection. As 'a solitary isolated wanderer'—his own description—the boy Hastings indulged in dreams, the most persistent being of regaining possession of the ancestral home at Daylesford. According to Sir Keith Feiling's *Warren Hastings,* his ancestors had in fact been unremarkable people, and the stories the boy came to believe in—that they had arrived with the Conqueror, that they had come near to achieving the throne, that they had become impoverished by supporting the king in the Civil War—owed as much to his grandfather's imagination as to family tradition. However he came by his dreams, Daylesford and the desire to possess it one day had taken hold of young Hastings long before, almost by chance, he became a 'writer' in the East India Company and so at the age of eighteen landed at the half-port, half-fort of the future Calcutta.

His dream remained in his mind during the next thirty-five years as he worked for the Company, rising by effort, tact and determination to nominal ruler of Bengal. Like other Company's servants, he supplemented his income by trading ventures of his own—but unlike most, he never did so to the Company's detriment. He came to play a part in the tangled politics of the numerous, recently formed and persistently quarrelsome states which then comprised India, scheming to maintain his employers' interests and —rare for his time—trying to benefit the people by establishing orderly rule wherever possible and bringing some discipline to the ineffectual and graft-ridden local governments. Inevitably his activities brought him enemies, among both his fellow Company servants—many of whom had accepted poorly-paid positions on the assumption that by illicit trading and corruption they would speedily make fortunes—and Indian rulers who were incessantly scheming against one another. More serious opponents were, however, among those who, when he had become governor of Bengal, were sent out to form his council of advisers; they had been appointed by rival factions within the Company and by rival factions within the Home government in order to oppose him. Often Hastings' schemes were thwarted; sometimes when opportunity offered he took decisions which were regarded as high-handed (and in times of danger, when it took several months to get instructions from London, they had to be). When at last he retired, his enemies, mainly for political reasons, had him impeached. Pitt and Burke lent their support to what would have been a fiasco of a trial had it not been spread over seven wearisome years. The evidence against him, fashioned largely out of innuendo, had scarcely any basis in fact....

Through all those long years he had remembered Daylesford and his young dream. Even before he had been back in England a fortnight, he was trying to buy the estate; his building of the House coincided with his protracted trial, and with his impoverishment. Long before the trial had ended with his unquestioned acquittal, Daylesford House had become his home. The generosity of friends and, later, of the East India Company enabled him to complete it, and to live out his remaining twenty years as squire of the village. And yet throughout most of the long wait to realise his dream he had known that the family he was so determined to reinstate would die with him. The two children of his first marriage had died young, and his second marriage had been childless.

The siting of the House, withdrawn from the passer-by, seems to fit; and its appearance has nothing of the ostentation then expected from one who, even after his unjust treatment, still shared the eighteenth-century pride at having achieved so great a position. The building is almost severely plain. Its architect was Samuel Pepys Cockerell who a few years later was to design the improbably Eastern Sezincote which was to inspire Brighton Pavilion; but at Daylesford he restrained himself to a single decorative feature, the domed and Doric-columned entrance. Knowing Cockerell's Indian leanings, we must assume that Hastings discouraged such reminders at Daylesford.

The medieval church which Hastings restored was in 1860 replaced by a rather ponderous imitation of French Gothic, but immediately outside the east window his monument still surmounts his grave. After his acquittal, it was suggested that Hastings might be granted a title in recognition of his services to India; but the government, still including some who had joined in the impeachment proceedings, were unwilling to make the recommendation. Friends wished to protest on Hastings' behalf but he, learning of the government's reluctance, said that rather than plead for recognition he would 'go down to the grave with the plain name of Warren Hastings'. At a time when fashion and custom expected elaborate monuments and lavish epitaphs, the simple Grecian urn has only the inscription: 'WARREN HASTINGS, 1818'.

NINE

The White Way

Andoversford, where the Iron-agers' Way branches off the prehistoric Way and where now the A 40 crosses the A 436, might be expected to be a place of some note. In fact its street, now bypassed, has little to show but the Royal Oak. The guide books seldom deign to mention it . . . though to Cotswold farmers its frequent Sales and Shows of livestock give it an importance the tourist knows nothing about. And before the Saxon Onnan or Anna left his name to the ford across the diminutive Coln, the Romans had found its situation to their liking and had built nearby 'a constellation of villas', says H. P. R. Finberg in *Gloucestershire Studies,* because the place 'was well placed to attract local trade.... In 1863 remains extending over nearly thirty acres were found to include a street eight to ten feet wide, a temple, and a number of private houses, with a mass of coins dating from the beginning to the end of the Roman period'. Perhaps one day archaeologists will get to work and insignificant Andoversford will blossom with signposts: to the Roman Town.

As has already been mentioned, the prehistoric Way, taking the ground which avoids both the dip to the Coln and the source of the little Chelt sliding down to Cheltenham, went a little to the west of the village; a lane linking Whittington with the hamlet of Kilkenny a mile west of Andoversford would seem the likely course. Nearby are two forts, one contour-following and suggesting Iron Age construction, the other more rectangular and perhaps Roman. Close to Kilkenny is another earthwork as yet uninvestigated, possibly of the Belgic half-century before the Romans arrived.

The ancient Way would have taken the crest running southwest from the Andoversford hollow through Birdlip where the Roman Ermin Way makes its zigzag descent to the Vale. For the motorist the A 436 must approximate to it at least as far as Seven Springs where the Way may have curved northwards over Leckhampton

raditional gables, windows and drip-stones, Painswick

COTSWOLD STONE

oveday's Mill and mill-house, Painswick

Neolithic burial chamber, Notgrove

COTSWOLD STONE

Eighteenth-century tombs, Painswick

-rotesque, Winchcombe church

Grotesque, Barnsley church

COTSWOLD STONE

orbel in porch, Horton church

Corbel in nave, Whittington church

Capital, circa 1200,
Mickleton church

COTSWOLD STONE

Font, circa 1150,
Rendcomb church

Manorhouse, circa 1600, Aston-sub-Edge

COTSWOLD STONE

Manorhouse, 1702–5, Nether Lypiatt

Thirteenth-century Poor Soul's Light, eighteenth-century Gazebo, Bisley

Lock-up, 1824, Bisley

Medieval Dovecote, Daglingworth

SURVIVALS

'Teazle Tower', Woodchester

Village inn: 'The Greyhound', Barnsley

COTSWOLD INNS

Town inn: 'The Old Corner Cupboard', Winchcombe

Hill to return to the line of the road where the Air Balloon hotel now stands, thereafter keeping along the crest. For the walker it is possible to follow a sequence of footpaths from Andoversford to beyond the long barrow a mile west of Kilkenny and then, after a spell on the road, to take the lane which, becoming a footpath, curves round the great bastion of Leckhampton Hill.

From there, where a cliff-like drop steepened by quarrying protects the north and west sides of an Iron Age fort, the whole basin of the lower Severn opens out; Cheltenham is below, and across twenty green miles rise the Malverns. The view and the curious and much-photographed rock-column of the Devil's Chimney—the result more of quarrying than of natural wear and tear—attract many visitors. Formerly the fort's defences were of more interest for, after the Iron-agers, the Romans and the Saxons found the place useful—or so we may suppose from coins including a hoard dating from A.D. 835 to the end of King Alfred's reign. This last has suggested to imaginative visitors a fight against the Danes, though Alfred's Wessex was far to the south. Perhaps a clue to the hoard's being there may be found in a round barrow just outside the modern entrance to the fort. It has not yielded up its secrets in two investigations and, though round barrows are often Bronze Age, both Romans and Anglo-Saxons occasionally raised them.

In the two-and-a-half miles to Birdlip are two more forts and if the motorist has not been tempted to walk to the one on Leckhampton Hill, he will find that on Crickley Hill is near the road. It is archaeologically the more interesting, and as a viewpoint not inferior to Leckhampton's. The main fort was begun about 550 B.C. and, after its timber fencing had been destroyed by fire, was reconstructed in about 100 B.C. and again its entrances were burnt down, presumably by the last and most aggressive wave of Iron-agers, the Belgae. Making it even more interesting, a lesser bank and ditch within the present fort is now known to have been Neolithic work, a 'causewayed camp' to the archaeologist which probably means a large cattle-pound. The site seems a little odd for the New Stone-agers. The sharp fall on three sides would have been very helpful for defence and yet, unlike many of their causewayed camps elsewhere, it must have been on the extreme edge of the tribal grazing ground.

A third fort is half a mile before Birdlip, capping a tree-covered spur called the Peak. From nearby Barrow Wake came several rich accompaniments to an Iron Age burial including the Birdlip Mirror

—in bronze, finely engraved and enamelled—now in Gloucester City Museum. If such a series of forts is not enough for the archaeologically tending visitor, there is in a copse immediately south of the Air Balloon, another largish lump . . . and, when he has struggled through the nettles and undergrowth to find it, the visitor can decide whether it looks prehistoric or was the motte of a medieval castle.

At Birdlip, almost on the edge of its famous hill, the prehistoric Way is crossed by the Roman Ermin Way. If the Royal George Hotel, once a very necessary resting-place for the coach-horses, suggests the need for a pause, the visitor might find matter to exercise his (or perhaps more probably her) imagination in the name Birdlip. It offers intriguing possibilities to those who like their place-names to hint of stories; for before 1675 it had been 'Brydelepe' or, in modern spelling 'Bride-leap'. Beyond that the experts cannot go, and so the rest of us can guess. Had it been in the woods clinging to the hill that had troubled the Roman engineers that some girl had made the leap which ever since has distinguished the place? Where, whence, and why had she leapt? From the top downwards in desperate escape from the bridegroom her father had selected? Or had she leapt from the parental coach, slowed by the road's steepness, on to the back of her lover's fleeter steed? The visitor resting in the Royal George or merely admiring the view can make up a story to suit his or her mood without risk of contradiction from some knowledgeable and unromantic busybody.

Across the country southeast of the Andoversford–Birdlip length of the prehistoric Way, two ways lead to Cirencester. The more southerly is Ermin Way, direct and indisputably Roman, though here and there it may have utilised parts of earlier routes. The other, known for the last three centuries as the White Way, is less assured both in its age and in its northern terminus. The source of the name is also uncertain; the derivation often suggested—that, having served as a salt way, the 'White' arose from the salt the carriers spilled—assumes a carelessness so protracted and thorough that long before their journey had ended the salt-carriers would have been out of a job.

Before considering a possible northerly end for the White Way, it might be advisable to glance at the map which shows, less uncertainly, its start at Cirencester. After a slightly curving couple of miles, it heads straight along the ridge east of the Churn valley.

This straightness has prompted claims for Roman workmanship, and there can be little doubt of its use in the Roman centuries; but its persistent ridge-following hints at an earlier origin. This becomes more probable on the high ground west of Chedworth. From there the White Way is often said to have gone twisting down through the woods to give access to the famous Chedworth villa and a lesser known one near Withington, and in Roman times there must have been such a lane hereabouts. But before those villas were built, the White Way could have continued its ridge-top going by curving northwestwards along the high ground between Churn and Coln and so reached the prehistoric Way junction near Andoversford. A level sequence of path and track along this line is claimed as prehistoric by Milward and Robinson in their study of *The West Midlands.* A little below it, hidden in Withington Woods, is a long barrow much damaged but still indisputably Neolithic. It looks as if the lane that now continues the White Way past Chedworth villa and Compton Abdale to meet the Salt Way near Hazleton is a part-Roman, part-medieval addition.

The northern few miles suggested as the original White Way are for the walker, and they will take him through some of the quietest stretches of High Cotswold. A mile and a half southwest of Andoversford, just beyond the Kilkenny Inn, a lane bears southwards to pass the round, tree-circled barrow known as St Paul's Epistle. At a right-hand bend of the lane, a path now traceable more by field-walls than by footprints continues along the ridge. Above Withington the route becomes more defined ... and the walker, while enjoying the quiet green going, may like to reflect on that oddly named tumulus he left behind near the main road. A. H. Smith in his *Place Names of Gloucestershire* has an interesting idea. Recalling that elsewhere Gospel Oaks mark the boundaries of ancient parishes, and that they derived their name from the custom of reading a few verses from one of the Gospels while beating the bounds was in progress, he suggests that 'St Paul's Epistle' might have similarly gained its distinctive name. The round barrow still marks the boundary between the parishes of Dowdeswell and Withington, an indication that it was there at least nine hundred years ago.

To follow an approximately parallel route, the motorist has to take the lane signposted Withington a half-mile west of Andoversford. For the first two miles it is very straight and has been assumed Roman, though it is known to have been made—or was it only made up?—about 1820 when Withington parish was enclosed. Withington village is in two parts on either side of the Coln. To the west, brief streets, their houses half-hidden by trees, meet at the church and manorhouse; across the river are more houses, some old, some yet to lose their newness. By the river are the Mill Inn and the Mill House, recently converted from their ancient usages (the Mill House is of fourteenth-century origin but much of it is a re-use, circa 1960, of stone from Northleach prison) to serve visitors needing food and refreshment.

The village was 'Withiandun' in the eighth century when it possessed a nunnery founded by St Aldhelm of Malmesbury. The original name, meaning 'Widia's hill', is a reminder that the early Saxons valued the grazing ground above the valley rather than the lower land and that, Widia being in Germanic legend a son of Weland the Smith, the heroic and heathen stories had yet to be ousted by more nearly Christian ones. According to the researches of H. P. R. Finberg, the boundaries of the early Saxon settlement (and mainly of the present parish) coincided with those of the Roman estate centred on the villa that stood on a spur a half-mile south of the church ... which gives an ancestry few villages can claim.

It seems that a Withington abbess in the tenth century had as good a business head as many of her monkish contemporaries for she acquired the nearby Shiptons, Oliffe and Solers, whose first names tell that they had become known for wool production. By the time of the Domesday Book, however, the manor of Withington had passed to the bishops of Worcester for whom was built the original manorhouse (which was largely rebuilt during late Tudor times and now has a Jacobean appearance). It is probably to the bishops of Worcester that Withington owes the church which Cobbett thought 'like a small Cathedral'. There is Norman work—the south doorway is particularly good with its carved chevrons alternating with unusual flower motifs—but the general effect is of about 1420 with a good tower from which fierce gargoyles glare down and inside a spaciousness unusual in a parish church. Though no record suggests that it was ever other than a village church, a curious niche in the south wall of the chancel may make the knowledgeable wonder. The niche was made for a cistern for water to wash the Communion vessels, a rare feature and only known elsewhere in a monastic context.

Such a church has gathered several monuments among which is

one that may interest those with a taste for fashions of thought as well as of costume: that to the Howe family of 1651 now near the southwest corner of the nave. It seems that Father and Mother, shown as busts above, were very well aware of the transience of the flesh for, besides each resting a hand on a skull, they saw that space was provided after the name of each offspring in readiness to record the date of his demise (and a son was on 15 June 1670 'slayne at Limbrick in the kingdom of Ireland'). But to give a skull apiece to the youngest of the boy and girl 'weepers' below seems, to our twentieth-century thinking, carrying parental convictions a little far.

The tourist attraction of this part of the Coln valley is the Roman villa at Chedworth. The wise visitor will go early or late in the season when the remote, tree-screened setting is lovely and the narrow lane is less thronged with traffic.

What the visitor will see at Chedworth villa depends largely on what he brings to it. Everything so far discovered is laid out for inspection: the major rooms—the ones with the mosaics—have been protected by neat buildings, the foundation walls of the lesser apartments are carefully capped with minute stone roofs to prevent further decay, and everything is clearly labelled. In the centre stands the rather suburbanly 'Tudor' house of 1870, now the box-office plus museum. To the expert a visit must be absorbing—as it also seems to be to the school children writing up notes for their projects and social studies. Though the major mosaic, depicting allegorically the seasons and portions of satyrs and nymphs, is the show-piece, perhaps more moving is the mystical symbol based on the first two Greek letters of the word Christ and known as the Chi-Rho. Elsewhere in Britain this rare survival is to be found on monuments in areas where the Celtic Church kept Christianity alive beyond the reach of the heathen Anglo-Saxons. The symbol in a late Roman context, scratched on slabs of stone which once formed part of a shrine to the local water-goddess (and are now in the museum), hints of possibilities about which the imagination can get to work.

At Chedworth the Romans' liking for varied forms of bathing seems taken to excess. There were two considerable ranges of intercommunicating rooms given over to warm baths, hot baths, cooling-off baths and cold baths, plus the necessary furnaces and fuel stores. Once one range was assumed to have been built for washing, fulling and dyeing wool but that now-disproved theory, if mentioned at Chedworth, is liable to prompt slightly disdainful looks and over-patient explanations. And yet, in a Cotswold context, a sizeable dwelling-plus-production-centre without some association with wool and weaving—known on a commercial scale to the Belgae before the Romans arrived and to the Anglo-Saxons after they left—seems almost incomprehensible. Or will, one day, the unearthing of the still-buried east wing of Chedworth villa reveal the almost inevitable dyeing vats and weaving sheds?

The fame of the villa tends to make visitors overlook Chedworth village, an uphill mile to the south by footpath, three miles along winding lanes for the motorist. It is a long place, spread about the slopes of a combe that reaches to the Foss Way. Many of its houses and cottages, grouped wherever a brief level made building practicable, are small-scale eighteenth-century, more or less, and some are older. The bridges and embankment of the erstwhile railway unfortunately intrude in places; without them corners of Chedworth might have been featured in the Olde Worlde calendars. And the church shows, perhaps more clearly than any other on Cotswold, the change the late-medieval wool-based prosperity brought. As you approach the church, the fine large windows with their flattened arches and vertical tracery, the battlements around the tower and along the nave-parapet, the fearsomely gaping gargoyles, are reminders of the 'Perpendicular' triumphs of Chipping Campden and Northleach; but step inside and you go back another three hundred years. The massive pillars of the nave, the great round-headed arch to the tower, the bold, unsubtle mouldings, suggest power and strength and the determination of the Normans to be dominant—and, according to some, a conviction that their ecclesiastical handiwork would stand until the Last Day.

Though Chedworth's striking church shows the change that four centuries had brought to Cotswold, we cannot in fact be sure who ordered the remodelling of the Norman church about 1460, or that it was directly due to wool. Until his death at Barnet in 1471, Kingmaker Warwick had been lord of the manor—it had been in his family for four hundred years. The manor seems then to have passed to his son-in-law, George, brother of Edward IV, that duke of Clarence whose ultimate liking for Malmsey wine has assured him a place among those snippets of history we all remember. Both, as owners of large estates, must have been interested in wool production, and either of their widows, both related to Edward IV, might have undertaken the work at Chedworth. Or the benefactor may have been the Richard Scly or Sly who is commemorated by a Latin inscription on a buttress of the newer work. He was almost certainly the Kingmaker's bailiff and, as a note in the church suggests, could easily have acted the middleman for his employer's more prosperous tenants and so become a wool-merchant himself. In 1485 the manor reverted to the crown. Henry VII's queen, Elizabeth of York, is known to have visited Chedworth in 1491. One of the corbels supporting the church roof is said to show her portrait.

In three places about the church are dates—1461, 1485, 1491—in Arabic numerals. In Church and government circles Roman numerals were to remain in constant use, even for the Exchequer, into the 1700s. It seems that already in 1461 the businessmen of Cotswold had found Arabic figures far more convenient in their international trading.

Somewhere about Chedworth, probably near the church, one of the green bulges in the landscape was known up to the eighteenth century as Scummington or Skimmington Hill. The name seems to be forgotten now ... which is as it should be. A skimmington was a procession organised to draw attention to an unfaithful spouse and was, no doubt, accompanied by ridicule and ribaldry enjoyed by all—except the accused. Readers of Hardy's *The Mayor of Casterbridge* will remember how cruel such bucolic justice could be. That the hill was so named suggests that former Chedworthian husbands and wives treated their marriage vows casually; or were they merely more careless than elsewhere? The fact that the name has been forgotten may suggest comparable alternative explanations, about which a mere visitor dare not speculate.

Just off the White Way to the west, in the narrow, steep-sided green valley of the Churn, are Rendcomb and North Cerney, two very different villages. Rendcomb is the smaller: three good farm-groups on the valley floor, and the great house and the church up a little combe. The village has known two very different lords of the manor. Sir Edmund Tame, son of the builder of Fairford's masterpiece, about 1510 gave Rendcomb its present church. Perched high and backed by woods, it is on a more modest scale than Fairford church and though Sir Edmund, following his father, gave it a set of stained-glass windows, Rendcomb's are unfortunately now incomplete. Some good panels survive in the north windows ... though it seems that Sir Edmund was concerned mainly with Biblical stories rather than attempting, as his father had done at

Fairford, a summary in pictures of the whole Faith. Many other details from Sir Edmund's work have also survived: the door and its ironwork are his, and also the nave roof supported by angelic musicians, and the screen (now painted dark brown—in Sir Edmund's time it would have been enlivened with coloured figures).

The church stands between the house and the stable-block (both now serving as a school) of a later lord of Rendcomb, Sir Francis Goldsmid. Built in the 1860s both are cumbersome and pretentious, the tower of each appearing to be designed for the impression it would create, and they were probably also judged to be necessary, for, from their summits it can be seen that Sir Francis imposed himself on the landscape, too; the clumps of trees that grace the park are shaped to make Hebrew characters spelling out his name.

Below Rendcomb the Churn winds down to North Cerney and Baunton. It is a valley to take leisurely, both for itself and for what is to be seen in its villages.

North Cerney's cottages, an eighteenth-century farm complete with contemporary outbuildings, an older mill-house, and the long, inviting Bathurst Arms, are grouped under the hills on the east; across the river and main road are the church, the William-and-Mary rectory hidden among trees, and 'the Church House which has stood finely on its hill since about 1470. The church is something of a show-place, thanks to very careful preservation by a local benefactor. It is substantially of about 1470, the earlier church having been severely damaged by fire. From that time date the fine pulpit and the glass in the east window showing the Yorkist Edward IV's Sun-in-Splendour badge. In 1880 the church was restored, gently, after which it has been given several items of decoration including a chancel screen and a side screen by F. C. Eden—a follower of the Cotswold tradition revivers mentioned at Chipping Campden—some coloured plaques and some wooden figures possibly late medieval. The result is impeccable but a little sentimental. One hesitates to carp about good intentions and fine workmanship, but the items give the effect of having been set up for our approval, and this diminishes the feeling that many generations (some of whom doubtless were not well-intentioned and some of whose skills were limited) have met there for worship and for the memorable moments of their lives.

Overhead in the nave are three portrait corbels supporting the fifteenth-century roof. One of these is William Whitchurch, the rector of about 1465 who, we know, rebuilt after the fire. The other two are said to be Henry VI and, nearest the chancel arch, Edward Stafford, duke of Buckingham, wearing his coronet ... and the association of those two is interesting and odd.

As at Chedworth we are back in that confused and confusing period we know as the Wars of the Roses. It was no doubt an uneasy time to live through, and carvers of church ornaments—among others—must frequently have had to watch their political steps. From 1465 to 1470, when North Cerney church was being rebuilt, Henry VI, the most kindly, devout and politically incapable of kings, had been removed from the throne by Edward of York, and to have included his portrait would have been a risky matter. To be sure, after Henry's sudden and politically convenient end—by murder, his Lancastrian supporters asserted, 'of pure displeasure and melancholy', claimed his Yorkist opponents—he was to become revered and almost canonised; but around 1465 his death was still five years ahead. There was, however, the period between October 1470 and April 1471 when the earl of Warwick indulged in his last effort at kingmaking by ousting Edward IV and reinstating the pathetic and enfeebled Henry VI. It could have been during those few months that the corbel in North Cerney church was carved.

The third contemporary head, that of the duke of Buckingham, makes it unlikely that the king's portrait was a later expression of sympathy. Such feelings had to await the triumph of Henry Tudor, by which time Buckingham had been executed for treason after becoming involved, at least in popular rumour, in what has been called the 'most famous unsolved mystery in British history'.

As will be remembered by those familiar with Shakespeare's *Richard III* or with Sir Thomas More's story on which it was based, it was Buckingham who in 1483 encouraged Richard to achieve the throne. After the young sons of Edward IV—thirteen-year-old Edward V and his brother, the duke of York—had been set aside in the belief that their father's marriage to Elizabeth Woodville had been bigamous, Buckingham led a concourse of nobles, members of the Commons and clergy to persuade Richard to accept the crown as the legal heir. But within a week or two, Buckingham, having declined to join Richard on the customary post-coronation progress through the realm, was plotting to lead a rebellion against him. Such a change of attitude has puzzled historians ever since; and, as a contemporary chronicler records, it occurred just as 'a rumour was spread that the sons of King Edward [IV] had died a violent death but it was uncertain how'. The coincidence has led some recent investigators into the tricky subject to suggest that Buckingham might have been aiming for the crown (he was, after Richard's sickly son, well in line), and that the rumour 'was spread' in order to win support from Elizabeth Woodville's many and politically powerful brothers, cousins and relations who at the time were planning to reinstate the dethroned Edward V. Rumour seems to have spread the truth. The two Princes in the Tower disappeared ... until what were assumed to be their fragmentary skeletons were discovered nearly two hundred years later.

Whatever its objective, Buckingham's rebellion failed and he was duly executed ... and thereafter his part in the events of 1483 have been little regarded. With the death of Richard at Bosworth two years later and the triumph of Henry VII, the assumed murder could be foisted on to Richard but otherwise, except for an occasional murmur, inquiry into the circumstances of the Princes' deaths could be left in abeyance. Not until after Sir Thomas More's death in 1553 and the discovery among his papers of an unfinished 'History of Richard III' was there available any account of what had happened to the boys and how their bodies were buried, as More says, 'at the stayre foote metely deepe in the grounde under a great heape of stones'. Though More's story, based on an earlier version in bad Latin, contains several misstatements of fact and many improbabilities, it seemed confirmed when, in 1674, during alterations to the White Tower, two part-skeletons of youngsters approximately of the ages of the Princes were discovered 'at the stair foot' though not apparently 'under a great heap of stones'. Thereafter, due largely to Shakespeare's popularising of More's story, few people have noticed that there had been, about the time of the Princes' disappearance, a belief that Buckingham might have been involved. Writing some years before More, Jean Molinet, a Burgundian chronicler, reported that shortly after Richard's coronation 'there came to the Tower of London the duke of Buckingham who was mistakenly believed to have murdered the children'. One wonders where Molinet heard of Buckingham's visit and why he assumed the belief 'mistaken'. One wonders, too, where he heard another rumour that the boys were not smothered in their beds and then buried, as More tells, but walled up alive in a small apartment in the Tower ... because, about seventy years before the discovery 'at the stair foot', an anonymous account of work being done in the Tower tells that in a walled-up recess near the rooms the Princes were believed to have occupied were found 'a little table and upon it the bones of two children ... [which by] all present were credibly believed to be the carcasses of Edward V and his brother'. Perhaps we should be a little curious about where Buckingham was at the time of the crime. Should we one day require his portrait for a rogues' gallery, there is a corbel in North Cerney church.

It is time we left North Cerney, but not without a backward glance at the strange beast incised below the south transept window. It is a manticore which, according to the ancient Bestiaries, had 'the head of a grey-eyed man with three rows of teeth, the body of a lion and the tail of a scorpion'. Not a being one would welcome in a lonely lane on a dark night ... though as its diet was naked men, if one always went well clad one had little to fear. Unlike most other fabulous beasts which the medieval mind accepted with bewildering credulity, the manticore seems to have had no religious significance attributed to it. The visitor must wonder what it is doing on a church; and Verey in his *Buildings of Gloucestershire* suggests that the work is post-Reformation which makes it even more out of place.

A little over a mile downstream, at the hamlet of Perrott's Brook, the Churn is crossed by the Welsh Way which must be looked at later. Meanwhile, halfway to Cirencester, Baunton's varied street lies beyond its mill-house under the gentler hills. The small, towerless church is another that has surprises. A good Christopher, possibly six hundred years old, meets the visitor as he opens the door. More complete than most medieval wall-paintings, the large red-cloaked figure carries the Child as in the legend across a fish-filled stream flowing through a very rural landscape. Opposite, curtained from the possibility of damage, is a rare and puzzling altar frontal mainly in appliqué work. The central figures above are clear enough as a Crucifixion with St Mary and St John, and the double-headed silver eagles must have been a badge of local significance ... but the rebus in the centre, showing a bird carrying in its claws a donkey from which is suspended a barrel? These medieval riddles are matters of dispute among the experts. Clearly the barrel is a tun, giving the last syllable of the hidden name as 'ton', but the usual assumption that the bird and donkey above represent 'borne' for 'Baun' and so complete the village name becomes questionable as Baunton was Baudington in medieval times. A learned note in the church suggests that the bird is a hawk and the rebus may be on the name of John Hauckborne, abbot of Cirencester around 1510 when Baunton church belonged to the abbey. But then why the donkey and why the 'ton'?

From Baunton one can climb up to the last mile and a half of the White Way and so enter Cirencester along the ridge and past a new suburb of Whiteway and past Saxon Gate (which is old but not so ancient as its name implies); or one can continue along the valley-following and more twisting A 435 to pick up the last mile of the Ermin Way.

Often called 'the capital of the Cotswolds', Cirencester began its life more than 1,900 years ago, and much of its history has been recorded in stone and man's handiwork. The visitor will find enough in the Corinium Museum to stir his imagination about the town and the people who lived in it during its centuries first as a market-town, then as the administrative centre for the province of Britannia Prima. Though by the time the First English captured it, the town had probably become depleted in population and was to become increasingly ruinous, it appears to have retained enough urban identity to revive as trading increased during the centuries of the Anglo-Saxon kingdoms. The growth of the wool trade gave it a more than local importance. By 1100 it had acquired a castle which was destroyed in Stephen's reign and never rebuilt. By 1117 it possessed an abbey of such importance that its abbot, like Winchcombe's, was 'mitred'. Through the medieval centuries, however, it seems never to have grown to fill the Roman area, perhaps because its abbots opposed the granting of borough status; Cirencester remained in a legally and commercially ambiguous position until having supported Henry IV against the rebellious earls of Kent and Salisbury—they were captured in the town and beheaded by the townspeople—the necessary charter was granted (and the royal pleasure was expressed in a gift which enabled the building of the present church-tower). It lost its abbey at the Reformation but it did not lose its trade and its local importance, though inevitably it felt the ups and downs of the wool trade. By the Stuart century it was, like the wool towns of the Frome valley, more Parliamentarian than Royalist in sympathy, and paid for its politics with a fight in its streets. The town must have suffered with the decline of the wool trade, though its position at the junction of four great highways must have maintained it as a market. Most of its older houses are now of the seventeenth and eighteenth centuries, many of them little altered externally since they were built. Of the earlier town there survive the so-called Saxon Gate (Norman work of about 1180), St John's Hospital dating from the 1230s, the Weavers' Hall of about 1430, the Old Grammar School and Monmouth House, both largely Tudor, plus for those who keep an eye on the side streets the backs of several lesser houses ... and, of course, the largest of the Cotswold 'wool churches'.

Such a summary is probably more tantalising than helpful. It should, however, warn the visitor that if he thinks that a few moments' glance into the church and a minute or two in the Corinium Museum will suffice to 'do' Cirencester, he should not even bother to stop. One could spend several days—or, more enjoyably and less intensively, make Cirencester the centre for a Cotswold week or two and so come to know it in several hours spread over a longer time—and still find more to interest in the lively and characterful town. Whether or not the visitor prepares himself with Verey's *Buildings of Gloucestershire* recording nearly thirty pages of the noteworthy, or uses the Town Council's *Cirencester: The Roman Corinium*—oddly, no detailed history has been published for many years—he should allow himself ample time just to wander and let the impressions come.

And, as a bonus, there is Cirencester Park. The House was built in 1714–18; the gardens were laid out with the assistance of Alexander Pope: 'I am with Lord Bathurst ... draw plans for houses and gardens, open avenues, cut glades, plant firs ... all very fine and beautiful in our own imagination.' They are still there, 'fine and beautiful' in maturity.

TEN

The Welsh Way and the Ermin Way

The Roman Ermin Way was built for the fast movement of troops between the first military base at Cirencester and the next near Gloucester before, in A.D. 75, the governor-general Sextus Julius Frontinus succeeded in subduing the warlike Silures across the Severn sufficiently to establish a base at Caerleon-on-Usk. Probably not until then, a generation after the initial invasion, did Ermin Way see many traders and civilians; for, though Cirencester had begun its growth as a centre for marketing local produce soon after the Second Legion had moved westwards, Gloucester remained essentially military.

On the ground and on the map the Ermin Way shows its purpose. With only two concessions to the lie of the land—a slight change in alignment to dodge the combe in which Brimpsfield stands and the unavoidable zigzag to negotiate the escarpment below Birdlip—it carves its way across Cotswold as uncompromisingly as a motorway. Like most military roads it has no interest in the inhabitants of the neighbourhood through which it passes. There is scarcely a building alongside it in the nine miles from Stratton outside Cirencester to Birdlip. Like his Roman predecessors, the motorist can make his way along it heedless of the country on either side.

The other Ways through this part of Cotswold are less direct and more human. While an early Way certainly in use in the Iron Age continued to follow the Edge southwestwards from Birdlip through a tangle of woods and hills to reach the fords across the Frome, the prehistoric Way appears to have curved more southerly. The headstreams of the Frome carve combes into the upland a few miles south of Birdlip, and the Way had to avoid them. Probably a little north of Birdlip it began to change direction; probably, too, a mile or so southeast of Birdlip the Ermin Way took over the ancient route. But on the high ground between Elkstone and Syde—one near the east-flowing Churn, the other close to the west-making Frome—an unmetalled lane leads off southwards from a length of Ermin Way which, M.O.T. having replaced S.P.Q.R., now serves as a lay-by. After passing Winstone near the source of the Churn, this lane follows the curving ridge above the Frome until beyond Sapperton it gains another ridge leading southwest again to the rim of the escarpment. This must approximate to the line of the prehistoric Way.

Across the same stretch of Cotswold leads another Way of uncertain age. Not until it is leaving the hills in the neighbourhood of Cirencester does it achieve a name on the map: the Welsh Way.

The name seems to have been first recorded as recently as 1792 when the Enclosure Commissioners prepared their map of Bagendon parish; but it implies a much earlier origin. From early medieval times drovers from Wales and the Border Country had been bringing cattle reared on their upland pastures to be fattened on the richer lands of central and southern England. W. G. Hoskins in his *Making of the English Landscape,* traces two such drove-roads, one leading to Northampton and another to Banbury. There must have been many more. Some have no doubt become unrecognisable under macadam, others have survived in nearer their cattle-way condition as 'green lanes'.

A characteristic of drove roads is their tendency to avoid towns en route. To drive a herd of several score beasts through the narrow streets of a medieval town would have been a bothersome business for the drovers and liable to cause more than complaints from the townspeople. Indeed, the known routes suggest that villages were avoided, too; the ambling cattle would have been a threat to growing crops. Certainly the prehistoric Ways, often following unpeopled ridges, were used as drove-roads. Berkshire's Ridgeway saw such slow-passing traffic, and an inn on the ancient Icknield Way has for its bar a lean-to on the floor of which, it claims, drovers of a hundred and more years ago slept en route from the cattle-producing West Country to the markets of East Anglia. It is very likely that many Cotswold Ways served the needs of the drovers during the centuries before the railways came to make for speedier going, though only the Welsh Way has preserved in its name the memory of its former users.

The Welsh Way's easterly and named dozen miles making an arc around Cirencester and ending at Fairford are easy to follow—and, suggesting that the drovers may have used a route already in existence, three miles north of Cirencester it goes very close to Bagendon, the site of a pre-Roman settlement. Its approach to Cotswold from the west is more uncertain. The drovers and their charges would not have crossed the Severn at populous Gloucester or Tewkesbury. Perhaps a half-forgotten ford between the two served . . . and climbing the scarp in a line for the known Welsh Way is a track called the Green Way. Having attained the crest and a metalled surface it takes a slightly meandering course across the country, where the headstreams of the Churn rise, before making southwards to join Ermin Way at the hamlet of Beechpike. Three miles towards Cirencester it branches off again and attains its first named stretch.

This northwesterly part of the Way is, admittedly, conjectural. One day, perhaps some expert in such matters will prove another route, but meanwhile the traveller can take the excuse to visit three villages that those who stick to the main road hereabouts know nothing of.

Coberley lies below the Way to the east, its few houses clustering in a valley and a quarter-mile away its church hidden behind the former Home Farm—and all mainly of the Victorian period. The visitor with an interest in curiosities or pantomimes, however, will find a call at the church interesting. During the reconstruction its architect perhaps overdid the realism of the fourteenth-century-type floral motifs, but he retained the attractive windows to the south chapel and three tombs of more than local interest.

The manor was once owned by the Berkeleys of Berkeley who seem as a family to have shared their final resting places among their various estates. Here are monuments to two of them: Sir Giles Berkeley who died in 1295, and Sir Thomas who fought at Crécy and died six years later—though in accordance with medieval custom his effigy shows him in the armour fashionable in his youth. Beside Sir Thomas's effigy lies that of his wife in wimple, hood and gown . . . and one wonders what she is doing here, for she married a second time Sir William Whittington of Pauntley, twenty miles away, and bore him three sons, the youngest of whom became three times Lord Mayor of London. The purist can assert without much risk of contradiction that the legend of the poor Dick Whittington making good is only comparative; the third son of a landed knight may not have had much in the way of expectations, but he was hardly of such a penurious background as the pantomime story suggests—and, regrettably, it is possible that the cat was the name of a ship he came to own. The legend offers no explanation as to why his mother should apparently have been laid beside her first husband. Dare one postulate that in those days a link with noble status took precedence even after death? Or did Sir Thomas, who in all probability built the chapel in which he now lies, demand that his widow should ultimately lie beside him even though she was, when he was arranging the matter, still young enough to have been likely to remarry? Or did he, husband-like, take it for granted that her effigy should be beside his and did she, wifely, not argue ... but made sure that, after his going, she acquired another husband and possibly a last resting place elsewhere?

In a different way as interesting is the monument to the earlier Berkeley, Sir Giles; it has to be looked for low down in the chancel. It shows only the bust and the hands holding a heart ... and so implies that Sir Giles's body lies elsewhere. The significance of 'heart shrines' has apparently escaped expert investigation; at least, a watchful eye on such matters over several years has caught nothing to query the theory that they originated during the Crusades when to return the whole remains of those who died far from home would have been a difficult and costly undertaking. So, it is said, only the embalmed heart was sent to be deposited in a recess in the church wall ... and the practice so begun became customary through the Middle Ages. Heart burials are not so uncommon as the unobservant might assume; most counties have an example or two, though Coberley's is the only one on Cotswold. The custom appears to have survived the Reformation.

Wherever he was buried, Sir Giles appears to have been a man of considerable determination ... for it is said that Coberley's third note-worthy monument, a slight swelling of the ground outside the chancel and near the heart shrine, covers the grave of Sir Giles' horse Lombard. One day perhaps some legend-destroying busybody will check up; meanwhile we can note that even to have asked circa 1290 for a horse to be buried in consecrated ground would have appeared eccentric if not sacrilegious, and to have contrived the necessary permission could, even for a Berkeley, have been no easy matter.

Travellers with a liking for trees and water will go on to Cowley, a mile south of Coberley. Though since the Gloucestershire Education Committee have taken over the house—early Victorian but near the Georgian—wire fences and 'Private' notices have become rather plentiful, the lane that skirts the park gives enchanting views, for the river has been dammed to make a tree-reflecting lake. The village, too, is mainly but not excessively Victorian—as is also the top of its once-ancient village cross. The church was thirteenth-century; its restorer of 1872 made it appear even more so. The characteristic lancet windows are improbably plentiful . . . though that would not have worried one of the Victorian congregation. An uncle to Alice [of Wonderland] was rector, and she often visited Cowley.

Elkstone, nearer the Ermin Way, appears a bleak, upland village of two or three oldish houses and some indifferent early twentieth-century ones . . . until along a by-lane one finds the church. Its tower rising above an old Priests' House and a farm is impressive; but that is only the beginning. Even to the visitor for whom an old church is only an old church, a look around and inside Elkstone church is an experience.

Much of it is as built about a century after the battle of Hastings: it is late Norman and it demonstrates in its doorways, its chevron-patterned chancel arch, and the rare groined roof to the sanctuary, the sombre dignity that the style and the period could achieve. It appears originally to have had a central tower; but that must have become unsafe and was, except for the lowest storey, replaced by the sturdy, embattled tower added to the west end about 1370. All this is unusually good and a delight to the ecclesiologist; but it is when the ordinary visitor looks more closely at the place that he becomes aware that there is more to it than its age and its architecture. Faces and figures peer down from the tower and the wall-cornice, while inside . . .

It is perhaps the contrasts in feeling that they convey which make the strongest impression. The later ones, the gargoyles high on the tower depicting medieval musicians (a shawm-player and a citole-player each with a grotesque animal on shoulder) and, lower down, the animals that stand or recline on the buttresses—they seem little more than medieval attempts at jollity. The collection of older and odder animals along the external nave-walls are said to represent the signs of the zodiac—though one looks like an elephant which has lost part of its trunk, another is a snake, one resembles a griffon, and another is more clearly a horned demon. Their strangenesses we can, perhaps, shrug away . . . until we go to look inside the church. Over the door is the Norman tympanum. It depicts, conventionally, Christ in Majesty with attendant lamb, angel and dove . . . but around it strange faces peer: long-beaked, semi-human birds, a grinning toad-like being, a staring two-fanged creature, a human standing on his head and others with alarmed eyes. And inside are comparable contrasts. The chancel arch, to the Norman builders a feature to be made specially impressive as the entry from the workaday world of the nave to the scene of the sublime mystery of the Mass, has its richly carved surround ended with—of all things—a pair of grinning dragons. The unsettling contrasts pervade even the chancel. Delicate and varied flower carvings frame the window above the altar while overhead the roof-supporting arches meet in four grinning, chinless heads tied together by a strap holding their tangled hair. Such juxtapositions, emphasising for us the haunting strangeness of much of the work, might suggest to our twentieth-century minds more of psychological significance than of religious symbolism.

It is almost a relief to climb the spiral stair behind the pulpit and reach not a rood loft nor an upper chapel, but a dovecote over the chancel. But we cannot think that the doves' religious association led to their being housed there; except for the lancet window that served as the birds' entry, it is all rurally mundane. The doves were for pigeon pie.

South of Elkstone the Welsh Way probably used the Ermin Way or, according to some authorities, followed for a few miles the prehistoric Way a little further west. Either route will give opportunities to glance at the villages along the valley between the two. Winstone, the highest, can be bleak ... though, even so, a few new houses have been built about the old. The church can show pre-Conquest work; the knowledgeable can point to the monolithic door-jambs of the north door, a nearby window formed in Saxon fashion of a single stone slab, the chancel arch crude and early. The Norman south door had the bases of its jambs cut away about 1340 it is believed, when the largest of the church's bells, two inches wider than the doorway, was brought in.

Further down the valley and less exposed to the winds are the Duntisbournes (often pronounced 'Dunsbourne') and Daglingworth. Domesday Book records two Duntisbournes, one of which was subsequently given to the abbey of Gloucester and so became Duntisbourne Abbots, while the other became Duntisbourne Rouse from its association with the thirteenth-century Le Rous family. Meanwhile, the abbey of Lire in Normandy had acquired the intervening portion of the valley where grew up the hamlet of Duntisbourne Leer.

All of them cluster on the western slope of the valley, little groups of wall, stone roof, chimney and gable linking lane and stream. Abbots is the largest, set about a sloping green. The church, once Norman, is now mostly Victorian pseudo-Norman; did its architect really think his work would in time come to look genuine? Leer is a quiet hamlet of good houses, mostly old with two new ones trying to fit in. One of the older houses has what appears to be a medieval church window; it is likely that the monks of Lire had a chapel in the place. Rouse, rather more scattered, has a church which has won the approval of Sir John Betjeman among many others. The stonework of its nave, with traces of herring-bone and crudely-fashioned quoins, suggests a pre-Conquest origin. Inside, it is narrow, simple and early. It must have once served a semi-monastic purpose for in the chancel is a set of misereres with underseat carvings, each of a lion looking cheerful and wide-awake—which is as it should be for according to the Bestiaries, lions slept with their eyes open, ever vigilant like good Christians. Below the chancel is a rarity in a tunnel-vaulted crypt necessitated by the steep slope of the churchyard. There is also a churchyard cross. Duntisbourne Rouse's little church looks as if prosperous wool-man, reforming Puritan and Victorian restorer have all overlooked it, for which today's visitor, feeling its antiquity and its peace, may be grateful.

A little to the west of the Duntisbourne valley, up on the ridge and so near the prehistoric Way, were three long barrows. One, known as the Hoar Stone, was crudely opened in 1806. It appears to have been similar in pattern to Belas Knap with side chambers and a false portal of which the stone standing at the eastern end giving the barrow its name is probably a survival. The second, in a copse a half-mile to the southwest, appears to have attracted no diggers. The third, a little to the north, is now remembered in the name of Jackbarrow Farm. It was destroyed in 1875 when some of the human remains discovered were sent to the Nailsworth Mechanics Institute, presumably as curiosities. Others of the New Stone-agers found a more appropriate and restful end in Duntisbourne Abbots churchyard.

On the map the Welsh Way is marked branching off Ermin Way on the ridge to the east above Duntisbourne Rouse; but, while still in the valley, curiosity-hunters might like to note two items at Daglingworth, a mile to the south. At Lower End is a sturdy circular dovecote allegedly thirteenth-century; dovecotes dating from the 1600s onwards are a feature of many a Cotswold farmyard, but so early an example is rare and Daglingworth's is complete with revolving ladder—a potence to those in the know—to get at the nest-boxes and, outside, a jutting course of stone to keep rats from the pigeon-holes. Three centuries older are three pieces of carving in Daglingworth church, discovered during a mid-Victorian attempt to make the building improbably Norman. They are pre-Conquest and, though set in panels on the wall as if show-pieces, contrive to look early and sincere. The Crucifixion shows Christ appropriately bigger than the soldiers on either side, one holding the spear and scourge, the other the reed and sponge; St Peter's all-important key had to be disproportionately large; the third shows Christ enthroned. They are more curious than beautiful, more naïvely honest than consciously artistic, and so in some indefinable way they convey more of their sculptor's simple conviction than do many of the monuments that have embellished churches during the nine hundred and more years since they were carved.

The lane opposite Daglingworth church climbs up to cross Ermin Way before joining the Welsh Way as it drops down to the valley in which Bagendon lies. Bagendon was once notable only for its sturdy part-Norman church; visitors showing curiosity about the lengths of bank and ditch about the village were told that they were 'supposed to have been thrown up in 536 by the Britons as a defence against Cedric, King of the West Saxons'. Since Mrs Elsie Clifford's excavations in 1954–6, those earthworks can no longer be supposed such temporary efforts. They were for a half-century the defences of the tribal capital of the Dobunni, the late Iron Age people who were occupying Cotswold when the Roman legions arrived.

Mrs Clifford's discoveries and their interpretation can be found in her *Bagendon: A Belgic Oppidum,* a detailed work intended for the expert but much of it fascinating to the rest of us. It shows clearly that the 'natives' the Roman invaders found in Britain no longer lived in primitively equipped hill forts, but in recognisable if crude towns, known to archaeologists as 'oppida'. The buildings were built on stone foundations with wattle-and-daub walls supported by sturdy posts and roofed with thatch—probably as weather-proof as the dwellings of villagers throughout the Middle Ages.

In the land surrounding their settlements they practised agriculture more successfully than any of their predecessors had done. Excavation has yielded evidence of grain stores suggesting good harvests, and ox-goads telling that the people of Bagendon used a more efficient plough than the early Iron-agers had known. 'The enormous number of animals represented by bones indicates that farming was on a large scale,' writes Mrs Clifford. 'Many of these animals had reached maturity, and winter feeding must have been possible.... Bones of oxen are so numerous that, over and above the hides required for clothing and home use, there must have been many available for export.' There is also evidence of spinning and weaving on a scale which suggests that the people made for more than their own needs. In short, Bagendon was a town in the modern sense, a centre of production for market, not merely a self-supporting settlement.

Excavation has also yielded much metal work: brooches, pins, mirrors, and jewellery, mainly of bronze, all of a high standard. Iron from the Forest of Dean (and coal, too) was used, copper from the upper Severn, lead (from which they could extract the silver) from the Mendips, and gold from Wales. Gold, silver and bronze coins, of which examples have been found over most of southern Britain, suggest wide trading. 'Bagendon metal-workers were people of wealth', writes Mrs Clifford. 'Their standard of living can be gauged from the quantity of wares that were imported': table pottery from Italy, red-glazed ware from southern Gaul, fine glass from Egypt and Syria, Continental platters, wine in amphorae, beer in butt-beakers. There can be little doubt that the Dobunni of Bagendon were among the people who contributed to the British exports listed by Strabo writing about 10 B.C.: corn, cattle, gold, silver, iron, skins, slaves and hunting dogs. The notion that the Romans brought what we assume to be civilised business practices to tribes of savage barbarians is disputed by the finds at Bagendon.

As far as the Dobunni were concerned, the Roman takeover was peaceful. They appear to have been allied to the Catuvellauni of the Southeast; when the Catuvellauni were defeated, the Dobunnic leader, Bodvoc, threatened by rivals, appears to have accepted the Romans as overlords. Even so, the Romans must have been unwilling to leave the tribal capital at Bagendon enjoying semi-independence near unconquered country. We must assume that they persuaded Bodvoc and his people to leave their oppidum to become the first citizens of the town that was to become Cirencester. Mrs Clifford's excavations found no indications of fighting on the site which remained unoccupied until, at some unrecorded date before the Domesday Book, the Anglo-Saxon Baecgingas, the folk led by Baecga, began their village on the 'denu' or valley leading to the river Churn.

Almost secretly the Welsh Way passes Bagendon to the south as it drops to cross the river at Perrott's Brook, following on the way the line of part of the Dobunnic fortification. After climbing over the ridge along which runs the White Way and crossing the Foss Way, it takes a quiet, little frequented course out of sight of houses and, as it nears Barnsley, is so hidden among the trees that the blackbirds fly off squawking indignantly at human approach.

Barnsley is surely one of the most attractive of single-street villages, and more demure than its much visited neighbour Bibury. There are so many trees about the place. Wherever one looks they form a backdrop to the cottage-rows which are modest, neatly proportioned and uncluttered with tourist-luring signs. The inn, the Greyhound, is fittingly unpretentious, and its internal modernisation has been kept within bounds. The church, though having a restored look inside, still has externally Norman grotesques to its chancel. Here and there eyes peer strangely or mouths grin disconcertingly, even though seven centuries of weathering must have softened their expressions.

As the A 433 heads for Bibury, the Welsh Way bears southeast to go through an undramatic landscape of cornfields swelling over the last gentle rises of Cotswold. It crosses the Roman Akeman Street at the hamlet of Ready Token named from a departed inn whose landlord insisted on cash. Four more gentle miles and it is approaching Fairford and its end.

Fairford nowadays is visited for the medieval stained glass of its church, the most complete collection in the country . . . which has tended to make visitors overlook the little creamy-grey town's several good seventeenth- and eighteenth-century houses, the earlier Bull Inn and the George Inn—the latter timber-framed and perhaps nearly as old as the church—and a Mill House of about 1670, very carefully restored. Keble House along London Road is as John Keble knew it as a child, long before becoming the author of *The Christian Year*—a best seller which ran into ninety-five editions between 1827 and his death in 1866—and the divine who was said to be 'the most eminently good man in the Church'.

So much has been written about Fairford church that it is impossible to give an adequate impression in a single paragraph. It is the complete 'wool church', entirely rebuilt between 1490 and 1520 by the Tames, father and son, whose tombs with their portrait brasses remain in their church. The building shows the splendour that the Perpendicular could achieve; the light-restraining glass prevents a feeling of chilliness that large windows and lofty arcades sometimes give. It has everything that wealth and piety could give it ... and the observant will notice, among the badges of the then-important families—the Kingmaker's bear and ragged staff, the Yorkist falcon and fetlock—the Tames' arms and their merchant's mark, and shears to represent those lesser wool-men who also contributed. (Those visitors with a taste for medieval carving will find a bucolic collection in the misereres, including such favourite items as the fox and geese, a woman dealing with her drunken husband, and harvest-gathering.) But, above all, John Tame planned not merely a building in which services were to be held but a church in which the Catholic faith could be conveyed other than by the spoken word to a largely illiterate congregation. The famous windows for which Tame gathered the finest artists and craftsmen—probably under the Fleming, Barnard Flower, who had designed and glazed the windows of Henry VII's Lady Chapel at Westminster—were not intended as decorations showing random episodes from the Bible and the then-accepted legends but, rather, as a coherent expression of the bases of religious belief, arranged so as to make each window contribute to the whole. In the Lady Chapel, for example, the windows show in sequence the story first of Mary, then of Christ's birth and childhood. The great east window tells all the episodes of the Crucifixion, while the other east windows—in the Corpus Christi chapel—tell of the Resurrection, partly from Biblical accounts, partly from traditions current in the fifteenth century. In the nave the impression is strengthened by what may be called linked references. In the south windows are the Twelve Apostles, each holding a scroll on which is written a clause of the Apostles' Creed; each is faced by a prophet in the north windows holding an appropriate quotation from the Old Testament. Above, the clerestory south windows show the saints and martyrs in the company of angels; facing them across the nave are the Church's persecutors attacked by demons. The themes end in the west windows' portrayal of the Last Judgment with to one side the Judgment of Solomon, to the other David judging the Amalekite who brought the news of Saul's death. No brief description, however, can do more than hint at a few guide-lines to what John and

Edmund Tame and those who worked for them set out to do. For what they achieved it is essential to go to Fairford, to look and perhaps to understand.

ELEVEN

The Ways to the Golden Valley

That medieval salt-carriers used earlier Ways receives more confirmation a few miles southwest of Birdlip. While the prehistoric Way bears southwards from its Edge-top going to avoid the beginnings of the Frome valley, a lesser route continues the former line to end on Saltridge Hill overlooking the curving hollows that become the Painswick valley. On the way it passes a Neolithic barrow in Cranham Wood, one with a false portal less pronounced than Belas Knap's and, oddly, only a single burial chamber. (This route also passes near to Cooper's Hill, scene of the cheese-rolling where the local youngsters—and these days visitors too—race for what was formerly a Double Gloucester.)

The country southwards from Saltridge Hill is curiously lumpy. In some remote geological time when much of the Midlands was under the sea, the cliff-like Cotswold escarpment was hereabouts subjected to prolonged and tempestuous attack during which portions appear to have been broken from the Edge. The ridges and valleys now run not roughly at right-angles to the Edge but more nearly parallel to it. They have also become richly beech-clad, making this as colourful a part of Cotswold as is to be found; making, too, its hamlets still secret-seeming, so tucked away are they along twisting abrupt lanes.

Which of the many tracks and paths and lanes served the salt carriers southwards from Saltridge Hill is impossible to ascertain. They could have dropped down to Painswick and followed the valley to Stroud. They may more probably have regained the upland after crossing Sheepscombe's steep-sided valley, and then taken the ridge along which the B 4070 runs. Whether or not they paused at Bulls Cross, today's traveller might well do so for its double-sided view. To the west Painswick's spire rises out of a landscape of tumbling and swelling fields and woods, to the east one looks down into the Slad valley where Laurie Lee passed his childhood before taking 'Cider with Rosie'. From Bulls Cross a sequence of path and lane leads along the ridge to above Stroud where those knowledgeable in such matters suggest this route crossed the Frome, though Stroud's existence is not recorded until about 1200 and the name, meaning 'marshy land overgrown with brushwood', does not imply an ideal place for a ford.

Such uncertainty may be disturbing to those who like to imagine themselves following historical footsteps, for through this country passed, on 2 and 3 May 1471, Edward IV with his army seeking battle with the forces gathered by the Lancastrian Queen Margaret of Anjou, wife of Henry VI. Edward had, on a foggy day a fortnight earlier, defeated the Lancastrians at Barnet where that troublesome maker and unmaker of kings, the earl of Warwick, was killed while trying to escape from the battlefield. On that same day Queen Margaret, accompanied by her only son, Prince Edward, had landed at Weymouth from France. The news of Warwick's defeat and death made her think to return to France, but she was persuaded that the West Country and the Welsh would rally to her support. After moving to Exeter she made her way northwards, aiming for South Wales where Jasper Tudor, earl of Pembroke, was gathering men. But, first, she had to cross the Severn.

Edward was hastening from London where he had been crowned a second time. Reaching Malmesbury on April 29th, he heard that the Lancastrians had passed through Bristol and were making for Gloucester. Edward immediately ordered that the city was to be held at all costs and advanced westwards. On the evening of May 1st he camped in the Iron Age fort above Little Sodbury while Margaret lodged at Berkeley castle. For the next two hot, tiring days the armies hustled along roughly parallel courses. The Lancastrians urged their men along the lowland to Gloucester to find that Edward's orders had been obeyed. They were compelled to press on to the next bridge at Tewkesbury. The Yorkists at first followed the ancient Way but kept northwards to cross the Frome which they so muddied that they could not water their horses. They found the Way again at Birdlip and went on to descend Leckhampton Hill, reaching Cheltenham, then a village, on the afternoon of May 3rd. There Edward learnt that his enemy had reached Tewkesbury, and he urged his men on to Tredington, three miles from the Lancastrian camp.

On the next day, Saturday, May 4th, was fought one of those clumsy and confusing battles frequent in medieval history. The

Lancastrians had found, a mile south of the town, good defensive ground 'full difficult to be assayled ... in their front they had so many hedges, trees and bushes, that it was right hard to approche them'. Yet, when the Yorkists appeared, the Lancastrians came out to the attack—incomprehensibly to us who do not share the medieval assumption that battles are decided by God's judgment. The conflict was short but bloody. The Lancastrians were routed, their claimant, Prince Edward, ending his life and his mother's hopes on the battlefield (though Tudor historians, to denigrate the Yorkists, told of his capture and murder by Edward IV and/or his brother, the future Richard III).

The vaguenesses about the Yorkist route may disconcert those who demand accuracy; they should perhaps recall that history, being concerned with human activity, is always less tidy and more disputable than historians have opportunity to allow. The rest of us can travel through this green and hilly fragment of Cotswold assuming that our route approximates to that taken by Edward's Yorkists and so, if we like, may indulge our imaginations without much straining of historical accuracy. And as we go, we should notice that later and more peaceable people hereabout have added to the landscape since Yorkist-versus-Lancastrian times. Perhaps more closely than elsewhere stand the fine houses of the well-to-do owners of the mills along the Frome and its tributaries. For Stroud's waterway did not earn its name of the Golden Valley as sentimental visitors may suppose from its beechwoods' autumnal tints. First mentioned in 1777, it was 'doubtless so called from the wealth that comes from its industries'.

Near Saltridge Hill is Cranham, the village in a hollow at one end of its ridge-top common, the church standing boldly at the other. The woods about the place, sweeping over the ridge and down the escarpment, bring picnickers from bluebell-time to copper leaf-fall. The village, the Anglo-Saxon's 'heron-frequented homestead', seems oddly named; one wonders where among the thickly wooded combes and hillsides the birds found the marshland that is their usual habitat. The beechwoods we now enjoy were planted by eighteenth-century landowners who, unlike us, could plan and plant for their great-grandchildren, but from early medieval times this part of Cotswold was well covered. The great stretch of Buckholt Wood sheltering Cranham from the north owes its first syllable to the Old English for 'beech', and was well known to charcoal burners in the twelfth century.

Cranham is more than a collection of picnic spots. There is, up on the A 46, the Royal William built in 1830 when the new turnpike road from Cheltenham to Stroud was opened. Somewhere in the village once lived a well-to-do colony of weavers ... or so we may assume from the two pairs of shears carved high up on the church tower. Such symbols often denote that the work was, at least in part, paid for by the local members of trade shown. If the Tudor roses that end the drip-mould to the window lower down are contemporaneous, it would seem that around 1500 little Cranham must have been a thriving place.

Prinknash House and/or Abbey in a combe just west of the A 46 is often visited by tourists. Known locally but not always affectionately as 'Prinnish', it was originally the grange-plus-hunting-lodge of the abbots of Gloucester, enlarged about 1514 and added to in the nineteenth century. The older rooms of the finely gabled grey house welcomed Henry VII's queen, Elizabeth of York, in 1502. Her son, Henry VIII, brought his first two queens there. Catherine of Aragon's visit in 1510 probably prompted the rather clumsy carving of the youthful Henry under a window in the great hall. Anne Boleyn came in 1535 when the royal couple's host was abbot Parker of Gloucester who, four years later, had to hand over the house, as a monastic possession, to the king. During the Civil War, Prince Rupert quartered troops there, and one of them scratched a portrait of a fellow officer on the mullion of a bedroom window. A century later Prinknash won the approval of the political-commentator son of the great Walpole; Horace Walpole enjoyed its setting 'on a glorious but impracticable hill in the midst of a little forest of beech', but not the 'barbarous relief of Harry, young'. Since 1928 the house has seen monks again, and is rarely shown to visitors.

The nearby and much more recent abbey is, these days, the attraction for some. Large, ungainly, and of very orange-coloured stone, the building may baffle those whose notions of a monastery are based on the medieval pattern with the living accommodation grouped around the all-important church. They will see nothing to suggest their expectations ... until a notice directs them to the 'crypt chapel'. A call there may make the visitor wonder why a religious organisation should place its core in so lowly a position and why, as the setting for the expression of timeless truths, it should be decorated in an attempt at the contemporary which has a way of looking passé within ten years. There is also the 'Pottery Shop' in which are offered not only Prinknash pottery but also animal pictures, plastic aprons, 'commemoration tankards', 'jewellery', et cetera, which seem to have no connection with either Prinknash or monasticism. Adjoining are the café and, below it, the pottery, very modernly equipped and professional. And if the wife is running short of eggs, milk or vegetables, there is the 'Farm Shop', and to entertain the children, the 'Bird Park'. Only in the surrounding fields may one catch a glimpse of a blue-robed figure. Otherwise there is nothing to suggest that if a visitor should come for spiritual or material succour his need will be satisfied. His gaze will catch only signs guiding him to the varied attractions ... and, perhaps, two other notices. He may see on a field-gate a board: 'BRS [brothers?] not wanted at incence today'; at the sightseers' entrance there is 'Barclaycards welcomed here'.

Southwards the road leads over and around an ever-changing pattern of wood and hill and field that is an endless delight at all seasons, to find its way to the Painswick valley.

Perhaps more than anywhere else in the Cotswolds, Painswick has in the past suffered from its photographers. Anyone unfamiliar with the place might think it has nothing to show but the ninety-nine yew-trees in its churchyard and that its only noteworthy happening takes place on the third Sunday in September, when the school children revive the ancient and once widespread Clipping Service—which is often associated by the uninitiated with the over-featured trees. In fact, Painswick is a lively little place with much to show (it has its annual festival in August), and a lot goes on besides the Clipping which in Anglo-Saxon times meant 'embracing', and was symbolised by the locals holding hands to make a circle around the church to signify their embracing of the faith preached inside. For those curious to learn how such an ancient custom may have originated, Roy Christian in his *Old English Customs* suggests that Clipping had a pre-Christian beginning in

> the old pagan festival of Lupercalia, the feast of the Lycian Pan.... Among its rites were a sacred dance round an altar and the sacrifice of goats and young dogs.... It is a tradition of Clipping day [at Painswick] that the villagers eat 'puppy-dog pie'. This is now a round cake with almond paste on the top and a small china dog inside, but it may be a reminder of the

days when real puppies were sacrificed, just as the Clipping may represent the ancient dance round the altar.

Since Mr Christian wrote, the 'dogs' have disappeared from Painswick's Clipping, which is a pity; old customs should be maintained reasonably *in toto*.

With or without Clipping Day and yew-trees, Painswick churchyard above the valley whose stream provided the power for many mills, is a good place from which to start a look at the place. Architecturally, the church itself is not very appealing. Though rebuilt late in the fourteenth century, there have been extensive alterations necessitated partly by damage done during a Civil War fight in and around it, partly by having had its spire twice struck by lightning. Most of its fittings are recent. The earliest monument—which was damaged either by the lightning or the fighting—has a complex and peculiar story. On a late medieval tomb-chest of Purbeck marble kneel the seventeenth-century figures of Dr John Seaman and his wife, but they were not the first occupants. Before them, in 1540, had been buried there Sir William Kingston, one of the 'foure sad and ancient knightes' who guided Henry VIII in his young days. Later Kingston undertook other, less comfortable duties. He arrested the dying Wolsey at Leicester, and later, as Constable of the Tower, had to take charge of the condemned Sir Thomas More: 'good master Kingston, trouble not your self, but be of good cheer; for I will pray for you ... that we may meet in heaven together where we shall be merry for ever and ever.' Kingston had, meanwhile, entertained Henry and Anne Boleyn at his country house of Painswick Lodge, then the manorhouse, though little of the building which they saw remains. Anne Boleyn was to meet Sir William at least twice again; he officiated at her coronation, he acted as her warder when she, too, went to the Tower. After such a career it is perhaps not altogether unjust that Sir William was not allowed to rest in peace; and he had already purloined another's burial place. The tomb-chest is of a fashion of eighty years before his time and is believed to have been made for Lord Lisle, one of the more unpleasant participants in the tangle of family feuds that were the background to the Wars of the Roses. He will be met again at North Nibley near Wotton-under-Edge.

Outside the church are to be found the resting places of Painswick's former more worthy people, its clothiers. Their monuments now form one of the town's sights. Earlier, the well-to-do had been buried within their local church, but by the 1700s restrictions of space and a wider spread of wealth demanded that even the locally important should lie among their humbler neighbours in the churchyard. And in Painswick, thanks to the Bryans, a local family of skilled and inspired craftsmen, they were remembered in tombstones in the restrained Baroque of the time, showing much variety of design but always dignified. Elsewhere on Cotswold the work of the Bryans and their imitators can be found; Painswick churchyard has a fuller collection showing that Joseph Bryan and his sons, John and Joseph, whose lives spanned from 1682 to 1787, were artists of a high order in their chosen craft. Their work deserves to stand with the finest that skill and Cotswold stone have produced.

Like Campden or Cirencester, Painswick is a place where one might be excused for wandering around with the local guide or Verey's *The Buildings of Gloucestershire* in hand. There is so much to see. The general impression is of the seventeenth and eighteenth centuries, varying from small, trimly proportioned street-side houses to the solid, square and self-aware 'Georgian'. A more careful look will find earlier work: Court House near the church, built about 1600 for one of the first of the gentlemen clothiers, has traditional gables; there is a fine contemporaneous group in Friday Street, and in Bisley Street are to be found some a full century older still, one of which still has the entrance used by packhorses. There is New Hall which was the Cloth Hall in 1429, and not infrequently the eighteenth-century fronts mask earlier houses, even in one instance the medieval cruck construction. And, giving the lie to today's assumptions about Victorians skimping on popular education, there is Painswick National School of 1846 imitating the Gothic. Yet, though visitors wander about camera in hand or pause to delight in some façade or peer at the wares in an antique-dealer's window, Painswick gives the impression that it lives as much for itself as for transient tourists.

Along the stream below Painswick stand several of its mills, now converted to home or workshop, but still showing their Stuart or Georgian origins: Lovedays, gabled and stone mullioned; Brookhouse Mill whose house has acquired more recent Doric columns; small, appropriately-named Damsell's Mill; Cap Mill known to have been there since 1622, and from not long afterwards King's Mill and the Sheephouse up on the hillside above. When Stroud grew and took their cloth-making, Painswick's mills had to go in for more conventional grinding and even for pin-making, but all the same they have retained their traditional and purposeful dignity, making the visitor ask himself again and again why so many other work places of the Industrial Revolution and after had to be such crude, ill-proportioned and dreary excrescences stuck on to landscapes to which they had no relevance. How many of them will, when the twenty-first century draws to its close, be regarded as industrial architecture or have been adapted as homes?

The same questions are less likely to be asked at Stroud. Though it possessed a fulling mill before 1500 when, according to some hopes, Dick Whittington may have lived there, little remains of Tudor or Stuart Stroud. As has been mentioned, the Frome valley became Golden as from the late 1600s increasing centralisation drew the former cottage industries away from the villages. Its heyday was the late eighteenth century, the time of the gentleman clothiers some of whom, like the Clutterbucks and the Playnes, were descended from Huguenot craftsmen driven from France by religious persecution. Stroud's mills and older houses and cottage rows are, therefore, mainly of the Georgian century, built when Stroud and the nearby villages and small towns were thriving on 'Stroud Scarlet' and 'Uley Blue' for the uniforms of His Majesty's forces engaged in the Seven Years' War with France and the later Revolutionary and Napoleonic Wars. By the time of Waterloo there were over one hundred mills along the Frome and its tributaries, and a further sixty in the Cam and the Little Avon valleys. By then earlier transport difficulties were being in part overcome. Formerly packhorses had been the only means of carrying in such hilly country; from the 1780s they were being replaced in the Stroud valley by barges on the canals linking the Frome with the Severn and the Thames.

As we can see by hindsight, Stroud and its neighbours had overreached themselves. The expansion could not be maintained against increasing competition from overseas and from the Yorkshire woollen industry powered by more efficient steam. The 1820s began abrupt closures, rising unemployment, and mill buildings being sold for other purposes or left standing empty. When in 1847 the railway brought the possibility of coal and steam-power, Stroud's valley was no longer Golden, and thousands of weavers and spinners and dyers had migrated—little Uley and Bisley each parted with at least a hundred of their workers, many to America and Australia. Not until new industries could take the place of the old—many were, like Maudsley's of Dursley and Daniel's of Stroud, originally iron foundries equipping the mills but were able to turn over to more general engineering—did Stroud and its neighbours regain modest prosperity.

This later revival has not improved Stroud's appearance. For the needed new building the new railways brought not local stone but cheap, harshly-red brick and dull slate. Around the eighteenth-century core and about the cottage rows that cling to the valley sides are too many terraces and villas of the kind that sprang up everywhere in the economically-minded and tasteless decades before 1910; set against the earlier stone they seem even more out of place than elsewhere (though here and there the hard-looking brickwork now is being covered by paint). Some of the more recent shop-rows and the like in concrete and reconstituted stone look less unfitting. After all, Stroud has always been a workaday place and much as we may admire the proportions of the surviving mills, they were in their time very functional.

The story of Stroud and its neighbours can be found in fascinating detail in Dr E. A. L. Moir's paper, 'The Gentlemen Clothiers', in *Gloucestershire Studies*. Much of the story Dr Moir tells from the correspondence of the clothiers themselves: how they ran their mills, not always efficiently; how they coped or failed to cope with fashion's demands or the need to find ready cash; how they thrived or how they succumbed—except for the five mills still maintaining the local reputation for fine cloth by producing Her Majesty's guards' uniforms and such perfection-needing material as for billiard table covers and tennis balls. Dr Moir, being concerned with the whole industry, tells also of working conditions and of workers' attitudes when new inventions threatened employment ... as when the employees of Paul Wathen, mill-owner friend of the Prince Regent, wrote to him: 'Wee Hear in Formed that you got Shearin meesheans and if you Dont Pull them Down in a Forght Nights Time Wee will pull them Down for you Wee will you Damd infernold Dog.' Later, when the workers tried to take legal action against their low wages, their employers 'removed the Tryals to Westminster Hall, and the Expense of carrying on such Prosecutions have been too heavy for the Workmen to carry on'. It is a tale of booms and closures, of bitternesses and disappointments, and Dr Moir tells it all ... except perhaps for one aspect. When we look at a gentleman clothier's home—at Lypiatt Park, for example, the great house which Paul Wathen enlarged and made Gothic in

1809—we must wonder if some of the employers were not so keen to become gentlemen that they drained the stream of their wealth. Had but a fraction of their immense profits been put back into the business ... but that is too much to expect at a time when ambition demanded that the very few who could climb from business into the gentry should do so.

A few miles northeast of Stroud, the fragment of Cotswold all but separated by the deep Frome valley is crossed by a route which has attracted the name of Calf Way. The name appears to be recent; it was earlier 'calf-haga', the calf enclosure, and applied to the site of what is now Calfway Farm, a mile northeast of Bisley. But the Calf Way's level going through a country dissected by abrupt-sided combes hints of an early origin, and it passes three long barrows and several as yet unclassified tumuli.

Bisley is the chief settlement hereabouts, but before reaching it from the north the Calf Way divides. The more westerly lane goes through the three hamlets of Lypiatt. Upper Lypiatt is mainly gentleman clothier Wathen's house, hidden behind a copse at the end of its drive and looking down into a secret, all but inaccessible combe. Middle Lypiatt also has a great house, finely gabled and still mainly Tudor (from near which the Way gives to the west an unexpected glimpse of the Severn estuary like a serpentine lake under the grey-greens of Dean). Nether Lypiatt has a manorhouse of about 1710, smallish for its time, square, classically symmetrical and delightful. There are times when the symmetry demanded by eighteenth-century architects seems a bit overdone; but in Nether Lypiatt it looks right. The contemporary wrought-iron work enclosing the lawned garden is there, too. The unEnglish-looking name Lypiatt, by the way, was originally 'hliep-geat', a gate which could be leapt by deer but not by domesticated animals, and recalls the time, both pre- and post-Conquest, when an attribute of lordship (and a necessity for winter stores) was the right to hunt venison.

Bisley, a little to the east, is a place to stop and look at. Though the country immediately around it is comparatively level, the original Bisleyans, some time before 1066, chose to make their settlement up and down and in and out of a steep little hollow. No doubt they were attracted by the natural water supply; the Seven Springs of Bisley are more than locally famous, though the visitor might wish that some benefactor in 1863 had not dolled them up in his notions of the Gothic style. However, as Bisley is one of those places where the ancient custom of well-dressing is kept up, in early summer the local children's handiwork softens the Victorian embellishments. And there is much else to see including the George Inn and the Bear which was for two centuries before 1766 the Court House (its chubby pillars are Jacobean but the back part is a century older). There is the double lock-up—it was not every troublemaker of the 1820s who had temporary incarceration in a shapely little 'cage' with a ball finial topping its ogee gable. And in the churchyard is a rare 'poor souls' light', a gem of thirteenth-century work through the trefoiled openings of which candles shone to the benefit of those too poor to buy their own. In the adjoining garden of the great house is a gazebo, one of its windows overlooking the graveyard which one might expect to have had a sobering effect on the ladies and gentlemen chatting within during eighteenth-century summer afternoons. Inside the church there is a knightly effigy of about 1240 in a fair state of preservation, particularly the lively-looking dog on which his feet rest; and there are carvings of fifteenth-century musicians which, before the drastic restoration of 1862, were on the nave roof. And for those who wander round Bisley's tight streets there are many good, grey-stone houses, and such oddments as a mounting block and a tethering ring looking as if they have been long *in situ* and not recently added as antiquating embellishments....

The wandering visitor, if interested in historical mysteries or curious about the willingness with which some of us accept anything but the truth, might like to reflect on the story of the Bisley Boy. It is said to bring Americans and the credulous to out-of-the-way Bisley. Suitably, the tale begins with the discovery of a body—in a stone coffin of extraordinary length and medieval pattern which had for decades, perhaps for centuries, lain in the garden of Over Court, the local great house. This coffin was later buried in a corner of the churchyard until, rather more than a century ago when the nearby school was being built, the coffin was rediscovered and opened. In spite of measuring over seven feet long, it was found to contain the remains of a young girl ... according to the story, the skeleton of Queen Elizabeth I when about ten years old. For, we are told, she had been living at Over Court around 1543 and had died there. Her guardians, too frightened to tell Henry VIII when he called shortly afterwards, substituted a boy 'of the same age and appearance' who passed himself off as the royal daughter not only for the necessary day or two, but for sixty years.

This explains, so the story's accepters assert, why the Virgin Queen never married. It would explain that, of course; but even assuming that the 'boy' could have been briefly deceptive, the story does not explain how, throughout her long reign, none of Elizabeth's ladies ever noticed anything amiss, even though Her Majesty's taste in dress was at times somewhat revealing. Perhaps the oddest aspect of the story is its persistence even though, over thirty years ago, Mary A. Rudd in her *Historical Records of Bisley-with-Lypiatt,* tells how the 'fiction was invented by Canon Keble [brother of the Victorian divine and then vicar of Bisley] and others purely for their own amusement.... There was, and is, in Bisley,' adds Mrs Rudd, 'a family which bears a remarkable resemblance to Queen Elizabeth ... probably this fact suggested the romance to the vicar's mind'. This family is, for the story-tellers, descended from an unrecorded illegitimate child of Henry VIII.... All of which brings business to Bisley's inns; and, though one would hesitate to threaten their well-deserved custom, Bisley truly deserves to be visited for itself, not for some improbable story.

Southwards from Bisley the lane divides, one branch reaching the Frome at Brimscombe which, around 1800, tried to become an inland port on the new Severn–Thames canal, the other branch descending through Chalford. And what a descent it is. In reality Chalford grew upwards from the mills along the river, many of which are still there, including impressive Belvedere Mill House of 1789 built in time to profit from uniforms for the Napoleonic Wars, and earlier Bliss Mills. A nice group of smaller mills is now being converted into homes at the west end of the little town. There being no space on the valley floor, the cottages for the workers had to be built clinging to the hillside, along the zigzagging paths and packhorse trails by which, before the days of canal and railway, the wool was brought to the mills and the finished cloth taken away. Many a cottage has two storeys on its lower side and one or none on the upper; in some the roof drains the rainwater into the lane gutter a mere foot or two below the eaves. Most of the so-called streets are far too narrow and steep for today's traffic; that has to take one of the few roads that twist across slopes so steep that anything gentler than 1 in 4 seems scarcely worth a notice.

Architecturally the most interesting building in Chalford stands, of course, between canal and river, close to a later round-house built as a canalman's home. Once Chalford Place, then the Company's Arms Inn when the East India Company was Chalford's largest customer, it is known to have belonged to Corpus Christi College, Oxford, in the fifteenth century when it was probably the manor-house or grange. The front, looking on to the river, was in part remodelled during the Tudor century when it acquired a fine three-storeyed window. In the days of William and Mary it was given a new entrance and a withdrawing room—possibly by then the Tudor hall was serving as a wool store, for what appears to have been a high entry for the bales was made close under the roof. There would then have been a mill near by, the house serving as the owner's home and office, while the attics under the great beams of the roof were apprentices' and servants' sleeping quarters. Later, as an inn, it was the meeting-place for the local clothiers. For those who can unravel its adaptations, the house tells in summary much of Chalford's history; and, if the visitor chooses his time to suit the owner, he may be given an opportunity to see for himself.

All told, Chalford is a place for those who look not for cloying 'gems of Olde England' but for indications of how the little town has lived. And who would not find appealing a place which has named one of its streets 'Old Neighbourhood'?

A more easterly ridge route through this fragment of Cotswold runs north–south from Birdlip to Sapperton. On the way to it a detour through Brimpsfield and Syde is worth considering. The lanes hereabouts are so twisting and sharp that more relaxed going might be suggested by the valley-following footpaths; these are, however, marked more clearly on the map than on the ground and at times they call for stout footwear and determination. However one goes, the route starts near one castle mound and ends near another ... from which we may assume that this now tranquil and remote valley once saw more aggressive passers-by than the local peasantry.

Brimpsfield's proximity to the Ermin Way must have prompted the construction of a castle to keep watch on the users of that important route. The Conqueror gave the manor to one of his closest adherents, Walter Giffard; it was probably on his orders that the locals raised the mound close to the church. The earthworks show this to have been a considerable structure ... though the visitor may not think it worthwhile to defy the 'Private' notices and the thickets of nettle and bramble to search for the few remains of what were once a square, four-towered keep and a portcullis-defended gateway. Perhaps such a fate was not unjust; the Giffards were a notoriously turbulent lot and the last of them having rebelled against Edward II, the castle was slighted, to use the current euphemism for partial demolition. (The map marks another mound a quarter-mile to the east, nearer Ermin Way on which an earlier and probably wooden Giffard castle is said to have been built. Now a grassy bulge on the hillside, it does not readily suggest a military origin.)

More lasting has proved the Giffards' church at Brimpsfield. The Norman south doorway, a Norman window now blocked, and the Norman chancel arch must be from their original building; the chancel of about 1250 tells of a remodelling during their later days. Probably the Giffards also contributed unknowingly to the church's rather skimped tower. Added about 1470 and too narrow for the nave, much of its stone is believed to have come from the then ruinous castle.

South of Brimpsfield a lane twists up to Syde—and at an awkward bend is a cottage with windows of about 1340 which may have been the chantry chapel founded by William, steward to a Lord Berkeley, 'atte Syde to fynde a pryste to selebrate and pray for the said ffounders ... the pryste shall live chastly and nott come to Marketts Alehouses or Tavernes neither shall he frequent Playes or unlawful Games'. Syde's name suggests that the Anglo-Saxons ran out of adjectives; it means simply and very appropriately 'hillside'. High on the slope stands a memorable group: the little church, mainly Norman, the finely gabled late-Tudor manorhouse, and between the two the tithe barn. This example is not so large as some Cotswold tithe barns, though at the west end are two traceried windows suggesting that part of it may have served as the priest's house. If the locals in late medieval times had thought to dodge paying their dues to the Church, the incumbent, whatever his private feelings on such matters, was apparently too on-the-spot not to know.

Just south is Caudle Green, a nice grouping of houses and cottages, pleasantly varied and one with its external oven, about a green. Beside the cowshed on the upper side a stile starts a footpath which leads along the upper Frome; or a little to the south is a track, motorable if the ford is not likely to be uncomfortably deep. Either route goes through dark, mainly coniferous woods so thick north of Miserden that it is hard to find the mound of the castle raised probably shortly after the Conquest. Excavation has revealed reconstruction in stone during the thirteenth century, though the castle appears to have been abandoned by 1280. Even without its present thick, dark-green screen, its situation seems remote; it was presumably built to guard both the Ermin Way and the nameless track that had, since the Iron Age, linked the prehistoric Way east of the Frome with the Severn crossing below Gloucester, but it can hardly have done so very dominantly. The Musard family who held the manor at the time Domesday Book was compiled and, we must assume, caused the mound to be raised, have left few traces in history—which is perhaps not unexpected if their name is any guide; 'musard' is Old French for stupid. But at least they had the distinction of naming the place itself; before their arrival the village was 'Grenehamsted', a much more suitable name as any summer visitor will testify.

Miserden Park, between castle mound and village, looks over the thickly wooded valley. Elizabethan gabled (with a new wing added in 1920), it was built for the Sandys family of whom Sir William and Lady Margaret have the fine tomb in the church. The recumbent figures, impeccable in their workmanship, must be a delight to anyone interested in historical costume of Charles I's time; and above, as relics of medieval custom, are the funeral helm, gauntlets and sword. Near by is another tomb almost as fine, that to William Kingston who died two decades earlier—though why his feet rest not on the usual dog or lion but on a goat eating a cabbage seems to have baffled even the experts. Between the two in time (but in the chancel) kneel Anthony and Alice Partridge discarding medieval recumbency, and there is an early Victorian weeping angel . . . an interesting collection though their setting, once Saxon, is now mainly of 1866.

Much of the village is of even more recent date. Miserden is near the home and headquarters of the Cotswold tradition reviving architects and craftsmen of the first decades of this century, and one of their leading figures, Sidney Barnsley, designed many of the pairs of cottages about the small green and along the brief streets above the secret, tree-hidden Frome. Individually, the house-pairs are pleasant, their details impeccable; yet their grouping gives the place a slightly 'garden city' look. It has been designed; it has not grown.

Above Miserden runs the ancient route linking the prehistoric Way beyond Sapperton with the Severn crossing. A couple of miles northwest of Miserden it has passed through the hamlet of Whiteway which, though not likely to be on the itinerary of seekers after the photogenic, might interest those who like to take in all the ways of life that have contributed to the variety of England. Whiteway is not so much a village as a scattering of individual places of living. Founded in 1898 by Nellie Shaw—the curious will be interested in her book, *Whiteway*—it became the home of a group of men and women determined to live by Tolstoyan teaching as they interpreted it: to live in kindly and co-operative freedom from government, law, money, and all the other adjuncts to civilisation that the rest of us, sometimes regretfully, assume to be necessities. Sharing out their land—about a quarter-acre to each—they set about building their homes, initially little more than huts, and producing their own needs, and in between whiles they were free to think or work or play as they chose—and they enjoyed dancing, acting and music. It would be encouraging to record that they have lived so ever since, but in the 1930s the younger generation, unsettling as ever, insisted on modifications. A rudimentary form of democracy was set up by way of a 'colony meeting'; and the outside world had to be accepted in part as a supplier of necessities the local land could not provide. The colonists took to selling some of their home-baked bread and home-made furniture, their hand-made sandals and clothes. Something of their way of life persists though one wonders for how much longer. Some of the earlier dwellings are looking sadly down-at-heel even when the may is in blossom, and the more substantial ones have more than a hint of suburban respectability . . . which those of us who feel at times critical of twentieth-century urban society may find a little discouraging.

Two miles south of Miserden and, like that village, set above the tree-hidden Frome is Edgeworth. A few houses and a couple of farms with good barns stand where the lane dives down through woods to cross the little river just south of the long, two-storeyed mill, a reminder that even so remote a village was once involved in the business of the Golden Valley. The manorhouse and the church are half a mile to the south at the end of a drive and screened by sycamores and cypresses. The stately house, said to stand on the site of a Roman villa, was built in Queen Anne's time. The small, dark church may have been of pre-Conquest origin but is now part-Norman, part-medieval and much mid-Victorian. Some sour and grinning grotesques have survived from the Normans, and on the fifteenth-century tower is a mixed collection of gargoyles, one sticking out his tongue, a pair holding what looks like a bottomless urn acting as a water-spout—a more graceful way than usual of fulfilling the gargoyle's function—and what looks like an attempt at that cannibalistic monstrosity, the anthropophagous, though the weather's wear seems to have robbed him of the lower half of his victim. Inside, in the glass of the chancel window, the portrait of a bishop of about 1370 is lucky to have survived the restoration of 1866.

This branch of the Calf Way goes on southwards until the Frome, curving westwards about Sapperton, bars its way. There it is less than a mile from the prehistoric Way following the ridge on the far side of the river.

Sapperton is a good place to loiter in. It has something to suit all tastes—or nearly all. Its varied houses and cottages are set on a shelf overlooking the tree-filled Golden Valley. The local great houses are at a little distance and discreetly sheltered from public gaze. Daneway House dates incredibly from before 1339, for in that year permission was given for a chapel to be added to the great hall and the adjoining solar; a taller addition of about 1620 now completes the house which was for many years at the beginning of this century the workshop of Gimson and the Barnsley brothers, the leading architects and designers among the group who revived the Cotswold building crafts. Their home was Pinbury Park, a mile and a quarter north of Sapperton, which is part-medieval, too, having been a manorhouse of the nuns of Syon. Pinbury was remodelled late in the 1600s when the home of Sir Robert Atkyns, Gloucestershire's first notable historian. His *Ancient and Present State of Gloucestershire* with its seventy engravings of the major houses of his time, is still consulted—and is very rare, most of its two editions having been destroyed by fire before they could be sold. Sir Robert was a perceptive and thorough historian but, as might be expected from the time of his writing, tended to concentrate on noble families and ancient seats—which prompted an envious rival to label his book a 'pompous and injudicial piece'. That critic would be shaken to learn that it has recently been reprinted.

Gimson and the Barnsleys are buried in Sapperton churchyard under finely engraved memorials; Sir Robert's effigy reclines inside the church with his book in hand. He has a more than usual right to be there for he probably took a major hand in restoring the church, and the Jacobean benches and gallery came from another of his houses, Sapperton Manor, destroyed in 1730. The carved woodwork gives the building a distinguished look, and the visitor can pass a pleasurable few minutes trying to identify the allegorical figures on the bench-ends. Though originally Norman, the church is now much as Sir Robert knew it: Queen Anne, which is something of a rarity in church architecture, and almost completely so.

An earlier and more imposing monument than Sir Robert's is that to Sir Henry and Lady Anne Poole. Of about 1620, it is a large Renaissance family effort, heavily and classically canopied, with Father and Mother attended by a son kneeling at each end (though the daughters-in-law, given subsidiary positions, look somewhat indifferent to the whole business).

Another of Sapperton's attractions is to be found near the Daneway Inn standing lonely—except at holiday times—beside the now disused canal. A footpath leads across the fields to the once-impressive entrance to the canal tunnel, a forlorn, almost eerie place if the visitor has chosen to time his visit suitably. And somewhere in Sapperton village is a cottage which, if it should ever be identified, may one day attract Americans, for in it was born about 1730 Charles Mason whose name was rather more than a century ago on all American lips. He was an astronomer and a surveyor, occupations which in the eighteenth century were not the placid ones we may assume. Commissioned by the Royal Society in the summer of 1761 to make observations of the planet Venus from Sumatra, Mason and his associate Jeremiah Dixon were attacked en route by French pirates. Their more remembered joint exploit, a survey begun in 1763 to fix the disputed boundary between Pennsylvania and Maryland, was almost ended by hostile Red Indians. However, sufficient of their marking stones—shipped out from England and probably from Cotswold—were set up to become in the 1850s and 1860s the politically stirring Mason–Dixon line separating the 'slave' states of the South from the 'free' ones of the North.

One last item: the name Sapperton, first recorded before the Conquest, is of course Anglo-Saxon. It offers interesting speculations about our English ancestors who, so we have been told, lived in mud-and-straw hovels and spent any breaks from laboriously maintaining their primitive way of life in crude and earthy merriment. Recent research has diminished a little the uncomfortable simplicity of their homes though, where we can glimpse them, we must still suspect that their domestic arrangements gave few opportunities for the personal niceties we take for granted. But the name of Sapperton suggests at least that the first English were not all unwashed. Unexpectedly it means 'soap-makers' farmstead'. Even if the 'soap' may have been fuller's earth used mainly for wool-cleaning, we can hope that some early Sappertonians, while treading or 'walking' the cloth, glimpsed the hygienic possibilities for themselves.

TWELVE

The Ways to Nan Tow's Tump and Hetty Pegler's

On the ridge a mile southwest of Sapperton is a road junction known as Chapman's Cross. No picnic parties stop to admire the almost level fields spreading out from it, and the traffic has never been sufficient to prompt the building of an inn. The road running east–west, the A 419 from Cirencester to Stroud, is not one of the great highways; the lane crossing it in a northeast–southwest direction serves only by-roads to nearby villages. Chapman's Cross seems hardly to justify a name. That it acquired one suggests that before the days of signposts it had some significance, though history does not tell if it was called after a local landowner named Chapman or whether in the seventeenth and eighteenth centuries it was a recognised stopping-place for pedlars.

Three roads cross there. One, the quiet lane which has followed the curve of the upper Frome for the past ten miles, is on the line of the prehistoric Way. The main road is, perhaps, two or three millennia younger. It starts in Roman Cirencester; as a lane it reaches Minchinhampton which, a thousand years before being acquired by nuns—the 'minchen' of its name—had been protected by late Iron Age earthworks. The third route passes Chapman's Cross a little to the east. An unobtrusive track between thick hedges alive with finches in summer, it makes its way southwards. On Tarlton Down it disappears on the ground, but its line is taken up on the map as the boundary between the parishes of Cherington and Rodmarton. The route re-emerges as first a footpath and then as a lane passing between a long barrow and a tumulus. This apparently unremarkable route is given a significance by the recording in 1340 of a salt path in Rodmarton parish. With the once-great Malmesbury abbey only a few miles to the south it seems more than probable that salt-carriers, having followed the prehistoric Way from above Winchcombe to Chapman's Cross, went across country to provide Malmesbury with its salt supply.

This lane was clearly an off-shoot from the prehistoric Way which after leaving the Cotswold Edge about Birdlip, made a great easterly curve to avoid the deep Frome valley. Now, as the Frome makes westwards, the Way can return to the Edge along the ridge which runs southwest from Chapman's Cross and avoids both the valley in which Tetbury lies and the combes which cut deeply into the escarpment between Stroud and Wotton-under-Edge. The lane making southwest must follow its course, but after a couple of miles, at Lowesmoor Farm, it disappears for a while. The present lane bears away to Cherington. It seems that the original route has for a mile or two been blotted out by farming activities.

Cherington is worth the detour. Set about a diminutive green, many of its trim grey houses, mainly 'Georgian' in appearance, look down into the thickly wooded valley below; indeed the Yew Tree Inn, once surely more than the local, turns its side to the village as if determined to enjoy the view (though by doing so it does not risk losing its more desperate customers to the drinking fountain, small but decorative, on the village green; that has long run dry). The nearby church has a chancel of almost untouched thirteenth-century simplicity, and a fifteenth-century roof supported on corbels with good portraits unidentifiably royal or noble. Opposite, the village school has windows of thirteenth-century pattern as if trying to fit or perhaps, as their style is a little later, trying to go one better.

A mile southeast of Cherington the prehistoric Way reappears as a track heading west and skirting corn fields. After most of a mile it becomes a metalled lane until Chavenage Green, a pair of cottages at the meeting of fine avenues of horse-chestnuts and limes. But to hurry along it is to miss Avening, north of the route. Though at first glance less rural than Cherington—some recent houses attempt a traditional colouring from reconstituted stone but are hardly traditional in design—Avening village looks more prosperous than Cobbett found it in 1827: 'The work and the trade is so flat that in, I should think, much more than a hundred acres of ground which I have seen today covered with rails or racks for the drying of cloth, I do not think that I have seen one single acre where the racks had cloth upon them.'

Even the non-architecturally inclined visitor should find something to interest him in Avening church. There can be few other buildings which can claim to have been the work of the Conqueror's Queen Matilda, and the circumstances in which she undertook the duty suggest that she had more womanly impetuosity than is allowed by the history books where she seems very much in the background of her husband's achievements. The story tells that while the unmarried daughter of the count of Flanders, Matilda had been considered as a bride for the thane Brictric of English royal blood. He, however, had not responded. Later, after the Conquest and becoming Queen Matilda, she 'persuaded her husband to dispossess Brictric of all his lands' including Avening. As the village then had no priest it seems certain that its first church was planned by Matilda who resided at times in the house then on the site of Avening Court. The work she ordered is still substantially Avening's church. Internally it is impressively Norman though not darkly so as its windows were enlarged in the 1200s and the 1500s. The tower, too, is original and of Norman bulk (the battlements, seeming to us appropriate, were added about 1400). There are remarkably fine groined stone roofs to tower and chancel, with much of the intervening stone set oddly vertically; as the original church had a short apsidal chancel which was lengthened in about 1340, there must have been some very skilful matching. By contemporary standards the details are lavish, notably the twisted shafts to the north doorway capped with twining branches and, on one side, a strange beast whose two bodies combine to a single head. Perhaps from the beginning her Norman Royal Highness had decided to give the church (together with nearby Minchinhampton) to L'Abbaye aux Dames, Caen, a newly-founded house for ladies of noble birth whose first abbess was Cecily, daughter of William and Matilda; or was her piety prompted—as the story asserts—by remorse at the fate of the unwelcoming Brictric? Following his dispossession and disgrace, he had died in prison.

How much the villagers of Avening benefited from having such a splendid church is not easy to tell. The surviving records imply that the living was used rather as a reward for other duties while the services were conducted not by the appointed rector but by a salaried vicar. Avening's first recorded incumbent, William de Montfort who was living in 1291, was also chaplain to Pope Alexander IV and held prebends in London, Lichfield and Hereford, plus benefices in nine parishes 'to the amount of 300 marks' (£200 when many a labourer's family lived on less than £3 a year). It seems unlikely that he ever resided in Avening. His successor in 1294, Peter Douche, was granted 'a licence from William Ginsborough, bishop of Winchester ... to study within the Kingdom of England, or without, frôm the present date [March 1304] for three years'. His duties at Avening were to be taken over by 'Peter Doucet, Acolyte' but he 'was not instituted because he was absent and not in Holy Orders', though three years later the bishop of Worcester ordered that he should be 'restored' to Avening church. The appointment of a vicar did not mean that he undertook his duties continuously. In July 1325, William de Leobury was granted 'protection till Christmas' by Edward II in order that he might accompany 'the Bishop of Winchester going beyond the sea on the king's service'. Nor, it seems, was the passing over of the duties to a vicar all that the people of Avening knew about it. Philip Bonvalet, rector of Avening during the 1370s and 'proctor in England of the Abbess of Caen', prompted a series of complaints about interference with the abbey's tenants, the seizure of their lands and so on. The Reformation did not end the absentee rectors. Avening's most distinguished incumbent was Robert Frampton, bishop of Gloucester. No doubt his duties as bishop prevented his living and working in Avening, and they were to lead him briefly to the Tower; Frampton was one of the Seven Bishops who defied James II and thus helped unwittingly to bring about the Glorious Revolution so beloved by Whig historians.

Avening church has gathered several monuments, some good Stuart ones almost hidden by the organ, and in the dark north transept an impressive one of 1615 to Henry Brydges, 'son to John Lord Chandos, Baron of Shewdley'. His effigy kneels in prayer in the contemporary fashion though in his case it might have been an indication that he had in his later years forsaken the life which had once made him notorious. He allegedly acted the highwayman in his youth: 'there are stories of horses shod hind before, and of terror which he created in the whole countryside'. More certain than stories is James I's act of pardon of 1611:

> Whereas Henry Brydges, formerly of Avening in the County of Gloucester ... did arm and supply with gunpowder, picks, darts and other weapons of warlike nature, the ships called the Salamander, of the port of Bristol, and the Mary Grace of Penzance on the coast of Cornwall, and did feloniously send the same to sea, and support, aid and abet John Kirkham and Thomas Maid, the respective captains and others their accomplices and associates,

in perpetrating piracy on the ship the Walefische [a Danish vessel] and its cargo of salt, hemp, and coined metal: Know all men that we by our clemency by this our pardon, remit, relax, and condone and forgive the said Henry Brydges, formerly of Avening, in the county of Gloucester, merchant.

Since the offence had been committed some thirty years earlier, it seems that either the law had been very dilatory or, perhaps in order to live out his remaining years with an easy conscience, Brydges had confessed to his youthful escapade. We must hope that, either way, his accomplices were then unlikely to have to face justice; at that time 'common people' rarely shared in royal pardons.

Near Brydges' monument, a blocked doorway is claimed to be the entrance to a hermit's cell. Such rarities were more usually built as external additions from which a small opening gave a view of the altar. The suggested position of the cell here could not have given such a view; it seems more likely that the doorway gave access to the rood loft. But if the visitor experiences a thrill from assuming he or she is close to where a fifteenth-century fanatic lived in religious seclusion and discomfort, who would deny such a bonus to sight-seeing?

The south transept of Avening church is 'the museum', though one gets the impression that since its few showcases were set up Avening's long past has aroused little interest. There are also in it wall monuments, good ones of the 1700s and 1800s, but so placed as to be difficult to see. More eye-catching are some local bye-gones including a breast plough—such one man-power machines were in use until less than a century ago. There is, too, a collection of bones gathered when New Stone-agers were disturbed by the rector of 1806 who dug up the burial chamber which stood southeast of the village and re-erected its stones behind his garden. The remains will remind the archaeologically inclined that there are several items around Avening: three long barrows to the north, one known as Norn's Tump and another as the Tingle Stone from the block standing at its northern end. There seem to have been no recent investigations, though one barrow (unspecified), opened in 1870, is said to have contained a 'skeleton in a sitting position'. A monolith, the Long Stone, may have been part of a group—a writer early in this century tells that another similar stone near by had been removed several years earlier—but appears never to have been associated with a burial. Of the hole in the stone 'report says that the superstitious mothers were in the habit of passing rickety children through ... with the idea that they would by such means become strong'.

Two miles southwest of Avening, near Chavenage Green approximately on the prehistoric Way, stands Chavenage House, Elizabethan and once visited by Cromwell and his son-in-law, Ireton. It seems the house owner of that time, the Parliamentarian Colonel Nathaniel Stephens, needed persuading to follow the King's defeat in the Civil Wars to its logical conclusion and sign the Bill of Impeachment which would put Charles on trial—and the probable outcome of that must have been uncomfortably clear to Stephens. The story is told at Chavenage of a heated argument in which, contrary to the accepted notions of women's inability to understand politics, Stephens' sister Abigail joined in on the King's behalf. Her efforts apparently did not override Cromwell's and Ireton's arguments ... nor, if legend tells the truth, did they persuade the king to leave Chavenage in peace. It is told that on the day of Colonel Stephens' death in 1660 Charles's ghost appeared, driving the funeral carriage. Later, the ineffectual Abigail became the 'grey lady' still liable to wander the panelled passages. Despite her royalist sympathies, her shade once disturbed the rest of Queen Victoria's granddaughter, Princess Marie Louise, who when staying at Chavenage used a bedroom believed to have been used by Cromwell or one of his officers. A room is still known as Cromwell's and another as Ireton's. Both now have good tapestries befitting the fine interior which the visitor may see if he calls on a summer Tuesday.

At Chavenage Green the line of the ancient Way is taken up by a footpath which some authorities suggest is a Roman straightening of the original route. The walker will find that the path dwindles to rough going alongside field-walls and has all but disappeared before he reaches the A 46. Motorists will have to take the lane going westwards and then turn south along the A 46.

The Way here is avoiding Ozleworth Bottom, one of the many sudden-sided, tree-screened combes that have been carved into the Edge. In it three villages are hidden. All are worth the slight meander, though truly the best way to reach them is on foot beside the Little Avon.

The highest, Newington Bagpath, is a church, a farm and a row of cottages—now a single dwelling—that once housed the village weavers. The mill which improbably drew its power during the 1680s from the minute stream has long disappeared. So, too, has the castle, the cause of the dry moat encircling a platform scarcely higher than the surrounding land east of the church. The choice of site, on the wrong side of the steep valley to have controlled traffic along the tracks then in use, is puzzling; and history tells nothing of the place.

The castle has long gone; the nearby church seems about to follow it. Of Norman origin, remodelled in the 1300s and given an inappropriately elaborate new chancel in 1858, its tower is succumbing to ivy, the gravestones are being submerged in nettles, and a notice on the locked door warns of 'internal and external danger'. Vandals have already broken some windows so that the curious can peer into the simple little nave in which for seven hundred years the villagers met. Now it stands a forlorn reminder not only of departed people but also of their departed hopes and beliefs ... while, as for centuries before church or castle was built, the sheep bleat on the opposite hillside.

Boxwell, a curving mile and a half down the valley, is even more remote; the only road to it is marked 'Private Drive'. Named from the box-trees which grew about it before the Conquest—and many of their descendants still contribute to the greenness of the place—Boxwell is little more than Boxwell Court and the church. Built in about 1450 as an abbot of Gloucester's manorhouse, the Court came into the possession of the Huntleys at the Reformation, and was altered internally in the 1600s when it served briefly as a hiding-place for Prince Charles (later Charles II) after his defeat at Worcester. Additions made early in the last century have given it improbable castellations. The church is good thirteenth-century and, though small, has an original arcade and aisle; 'Perp' windows were inserted about 1490. Externally, in the absence of a tower, its most striking feature is the large, original bellcote. Could its curious resemblance to a head wearing a pointed cap have been intentional?

For the motorist, the third village in the valley, Ozleworth, is most easily reached up the lane from the hamlet of Wortley, a good grouping of farm buildings. Narrow and twisting, the lane becomes increasingly more remote. Below a sudden turn stands a pair of cottages, the only survivors of the village of about 1600 which was 'seated in the depth of a deep valley where the inhabitants may (if usually they did not) cut, make, and cast their billet wood and faggots in at their chimney pots, to save other carriage'. Above, on the hillside, stands the rest of Ozleworth, the Anglo-Saxon's 'blackbird frequented farm': a farmhouse, two more cottages, and Ozleworth Park set finely overlooking the thickly wooded valley. Of Ozleworth's sight, its ancient and rare church, there is no sign until one follows the curving drive past the pillared entrance-front of the House.

The situation in a circular churchyard screened by trees gives this, one of the most fascinating of Cotswold churches, an atmosphere of ancient remoteness. It is, architecturally, of at least three periods of building, and yet the impression is not of usual growth to fit changing needs of those it served, but of wholeness. It is as if the church was built as it now stands, complete, individual, and strangely apart from the very secular world.

Its history, variously interpreted by the experts, suggests that the irregularly hexagonal tower, a rare feature, may not have been intended for a church at all. A note inside draws attention to 'arrow slits', long ago blocked, and considers that the tower may have formed part of a hunting-lodge of the Berkeley lords of the manor soon after the Conquest. About 1130, when Roger de Berkeley gave the advowson to Leonard Stanley priory (from whom it soon passed to St Peter's abbey at Gloucester), the severely plain arch, now leading to the chancel, must have been fashioned and probably the top storey of the tower with its round-headed windows was added to provide some light. The base of the tower must then have served as the nave, a pattern used in some small pre-Conquest churches which has prompted the suggestion that Ozleworth's tower is Saxon. Somewhere about 1250 the chancel was remodelled and given its square end, and another arch cut in the tower to give access to the nave that was added at the same time.

Internally the church is also remarkable—when the visitor has accepted the need for rather heavy-handed lime-washing. The south door, late Norman, and the century-later arch leading to the lancet-lit nave, are carved with amazing skill and rare individuality. The leaf-buds on the capitals are much more deeply undercut than is usual for their time—could those to the doorway have been recut perhaps a half-century after the doorway was built?—while the nave arch is an astonishing piece of work. Verey describes it as 'pierced chevrons across not along the order'; it is, rather, a series of elongated 'broad arrows' following the line of the arch and cut so that they appear to lie one upon another, a restless effect when compared with the earlier plain arch to the chancel. It is all clearly the work of a very original and very skilled mason.

The lane uphill from Ozleworth offers the sight of two more contrasting 'monuments'. Newark House was 'New Work' when built from the stone of Kingswood Abbey shortly after the Reformation; the battlements and the Gothic porch that catch the visitor's eye are additions made by the Clutterbuck gentlemen clothiers before the last decline of the wool-cloth trade. Three of the family are remembered in Ozleworth church, including Lewis, the most distinguished. To the north is the Radio Station tower which may, a century or two ahead, be viewed as our contribution to the Cotswold landscape. It is hard to imagine that visitors then will assert, as modern ones sometimes strive to do, that recent building is coming to blend with the old. The tower is, and will remain, an intrusion from a technological world that knows nothing of a way of life which evolved out of its setting among the limestone hills.

On the ridge southeastwards of the Ozleworth valley the line of the ancient Way is taken up by the A 46. Before reaching Nan Tow's Tump, lanes lead off to Leighterton standing high in a level fieldscape and often cursorily treated by the guide-books: its church was 'severely restored' in 1877, its farmhouses can boast no date before 1784, its cottages are mostly 'Victorian Tudor'; even its long barrow, hidden by a great clump of trees, was opened two centuries ago and left so exposed that the burial chambers 'have completely disintegrated'. Yet Leighterton, set among chestnut-trees, is an honest-looking place of good stone farms, the barns of two of which give shelter to doves—from which we may deduce that landowners as late as 1780 either insisted on their ancient rights or were partial to pigeon pie. Its church may make one regret the loss of what had been before heavy-handed restorers got to work and, later, its reredos painter exercised his skill—though whether his obviously Victorian child-angels will irritate with their sentimentality or bring a nostalgic smile is a personal matter. Perhaps the Hadfields are right when, in their book *The Cotswolds,* they assert that the reredos 'will be a study in contemporary costume in years to come' —though that, surely, was not the artist's intention. Meanwhile, for those keen on medieval work there is at least the font. Good fourteenth-century fonts are not so readily found. Its shields, bordered with flowers, show the symbols of the Passion: the Cross, the Crown of Thorns, the hammer and scourges, the seamless garment, four nails, a ladder, and the spear and sponge, and one left blank.

And for any visitor, whatever his architectural tastes, there is the Royal Oak, more truly a village pub than many on Cotswold.

A mile and a half southwest of Leighterton one of the better known of Cotswold's barrows stands beside the A 46. It must for many centuries have been a guide to travellers along the ancient Way. More recently trees and bushes have obscured it and in summer it has to be looked for. Known as Nan Tow's Tump, it is round and rather high for a Bronze Age barrow—which is what it is usually classified as, though it appears not yet to have been dug and peoples other than Bronze-agers raised round barrows. The height is said to have been necessary in order that Nan Tow, a local witch, could be buried standing ... though why she should have been, legend does not tell. And that, in turn, makes one wonder about the legend of Nan Tow's Tump and legends in general. For, however improbable they sound in our twentieth-century ears, legends always had a beginning, perhaps in some ancient and all-but-forgotten religious ceremony, perhaps in a misinterpretation of an actual discovery. Those tempted to dismiss legends as nonsense should call to mind the story—well over a hundred years old now—of a certain large mound in Flintshire where it was said that at midnight could be seen a knight on a horse furnished with golden armour. The experts of course pooh-poohed the legend with the superiority that always marks their kind ... until, on digging into the tumulus to see what it really did contain, they unearthed a piece of early gold horse-armour so rare that it was sent to the British Museum. We can only guess whether the legend had lasted from the original burial or if someone some time had ventured to look inside. Somewhat similarly, one cannot help wondering if the legend of Nan Tow's burial could have been prompted by some treasure-seekers secretly making enough of a hole in the mound to find a skeleton, not standing perhaps but sufficiently near the upright to alarm peering eyes; and if one among them recalled that once thereabouts had lived an old, uncared-for woman (who would in the past have been suspected of witchcraft) whose burial-place was unrecorded and who had been called Nan Tow ...

The road running east–west at Chapman's Cross and now linking Cirencester with Stroud is not generally assumed to be of Roman origin—which, in view of its eastern terminus, is a little unexpected.

Before its diversion near Chalford into the Frome valley, this road led to Minchinhampton; if Mrs Elsie M. Clifford's deductions about the earthworks on Minchinhampton Common are correct, it would seem more than likely that this hill-top route was trodden, if not by Roman armies, at least by a few probing parties. For in her *Bagendon: a Belgic Oppidum*, Mrs Clifford suggests that Minchinhampton's peninsula formed by the deep valleys of the Frome and the Nailsworth stream was the home of anti-Roman guerrillas during the decade after Bagendon's submission. The ditch cut into the solid rock, and the resulting bank known as 'The Bulwarks', defending Minchinhampton Common from the easy eastern approach, have been dated to the first half of the First Century A.D.

As Mrs Clifford tells, on the death in A.D. 41 of the Belgic 'king' Cunobelinus (who sixteen centuries later posthumously became Shakespeare's Cymbeline), his territory covering much of the Thames valley was divided between two sons. One son accepted Roman rule; the other, Caratacus, though defeated in A.D. 43, reappeared fighting in alliance with the warlike Silures of the Welsh borderland in A.D. 47. In the intervening four years, Mrs Clifford suggests, the major earthworks on Minchinhampton Common were raised to defend the base from which Caratacus carried on his anti-Roman activities. Not until the Romans had outflanked Minchinhampton —probably using the ancient Way to reach the Edge about Birdlip and then following an Iron Age track to the ford at Kingsholm north of Gloucester—did Caratacus withdraw to Wales from where he is known to have continued his fight. It was not until A.D. 75 that his allies, the Silures, were subdued. By then the Roman military base had moved to Gloucester, and Cirencester was becoming the administrative and market centre for Cotswold.

Caratacus' defensive efforts (if they are his) were not the first earthworks on Minchinhampton Common, or the last. There is a Neolithic barrow, long ago crudely opened, known as Whitfield's Tump since the early Methodist preached there. Nearby are the remains of a round barrow, probably Bronze Age. There are two camps, Amberley and Pinfarthing, though whether their lowly banks are traces of Iron Age works or merely medieval field boundaries the experts have yet to determine. There are also dozens of other swellings and hollows, some of which are possibly prehistoric, some probably medieval (artificial rabbit warrens perhaps), and some certainly twentieth-century bunkers for the benefit (if that is the right word) of those for whom Minchinhampton Common is the golf course.

The little town, having grown up about a hollow midway between the Frome and the Nailsworth valleys whose waters drove the woollen mills, was naturally a centre for the trade. Many of its streets are narrow, tilting and lined with houses of the Stuart and Georgian centuries; the observant will catch embellishments from four-centre-arched doorways of lingering Tudor fashion, through a shell-hood or two and finials of a century or so later, to Regency details and Victorian Gothic. More recent houses, many of them pleasant, are on the outskirts. Alongside the little market place stands the Market House, built in 1698 by Philip Sheppard, lord of the manor and an early member of the family of clothiers that was to dominate the local trade for a century. A local story tells that Mrs Siddons once acted in the Market House; it is known that she performed at Bath in 1778 and 1782 and visited Stroud and Cheltenham. A half-century later the upper floor of the Market House was being used as the local school. By that time, too, Minchinhampton was feeling the decline of the wool trade. There was 'a great strike of the hand-loom weavers in 1825, for an increase of wages and for equalising prices for their work.... It was enforced by the leaders of the movement on their fellows by strong parties visiting the weavers in their homes and demanding the surrender of their shuttles, thus rendering them perforce idle'. Already mills were being closed or adapted to other uses. Only Longford Mill, owned by the Playne family, was able to survive by foresight, the damming of its stream to form a lake ensuring adequate water-power and, later, by installing up-to-date machinery. It is still making the famous cloth.

Across the Market Place from the Market Hall stands the church, with its curious truncated and crowned spire, presenting its finest feature—its south transept—to the town. The building suffered a very thorough restoration in 1842–3. The town suffered from it, too, for when the lowering of the level of the nave and the churchyard was in progress 'gruesome and horrible sights were to be seen when a grave was dug in the old and crowded part.... Soil thrown up by excavation ... was spread on pasture land or taken away and used as garden manure'. Three years later the Medical Officer was writing: 'I have practised as a surgeon here for sixteen years and, until the last two years, I have no recollection of having had a single case of typhus fever.... Within the last two months we have had upwards of 150.' Disputes about the cause of the epidemic were sharpened by the feelings of those townspeople whose ancestors' remains had been disturbed. The visitation of the disease and the feelings, reported in the press, became a matter of national concern. According to the *History of the Parishes of Minchinhampton and Avening*, by A. T. Playne (of the Longford Mill owning family), the epidemic was spread through the local water supply. Minchinhampton then relied in part on springs issuing from where the layer of fuller's earth checked the natural seepage through the upper layer of limestone; but through the limestone vertical fissures, known locally as 'lizens', had not provided any natural filtering of the contaminated water.

The restoration of the church which had brought such misfortune to Minchinhampton has not improved the building. It is a rather gaunt place, its surviving items of interest—mainly monuments—either tucked away in corners or stuck up high above the Victorian arcade. It was apparently by chance that the south transept did not go the way of the rest of the building. Built about 1300 by the knight and lady whose effigies lie in the gracefully arched tomb recess—probably Sir Peter and Lady Matilda de la Mere—it is perhaps the most complete and beautiful example of the 'Decorated' on all Cotswold.

Clinging to the steep slopes of the plateau on which Minchinhampton stands are many hamlets and some noteworthy houses. The local great house is Gatcombe, a mile to the southeast, built about 1770 for the Shepherds ... and, when the family fortunes dwindled with the decline of the cloth trade, bought by the 'eminent writer on Political Economy', David Ricardo. There seems something modern about the sequence of ownership: when the businessman fails the economist takes his place. East of Minchinhampton is Amberley, the 'Enderley' of *John Halifax, Gentleman.* Mrs Craik lived in Rose Cottage while she was writing the novel and below, beside the valley-following road from Nailsworth to Stroud, stands Dunkirk Mill which she made John Halifax's. Now otherwise occupied, it is perhaps the finest of the mills of the neighbourhood, long, tall, stone-chimneyed and mostly stone-roofed. Since Mrs Craik wrote her 'very noble presentation of the highest ideal of English middle-class life', it has acquired a background of aspens and silver birches.

From Minchinhampton in any direction but eastwards the motorist will find himself zigzagging down through hamlets of cottages clinging to the sharp hillslopes. Like those about Chalford, they were built for the wool-workers and sited on what were pack-horse paths. Across the valley is Woodchester, but whether the traveller will think that straggling village worth a visit may depend not so much on its rows of cottages built when its up-and-down street was the main road along the valley, but on the year. For Wood chester's masterpiece only becomes visible once a decade.

It is situated in—or, rather, under—the yard of the original church now but a few fragments of wall along a 'No Through Road' at the north end of the village. The church's builders, around 1100, used as a firm, level foundation 'one of the finest examples of Roman mosaic work north of the Alps'. Part of it may have been damaged when the church was built; later investigations have not always been beneficial, though in a memorable one in 1797, Samuel Lysons, the leading local antiquary of the day, made coloured sketches of much that he found. It has long been considered that, in the absence of a large building to protect it, the work is safer left earth-covered. Not until 1983 will it again be on view.

What has been revealed shows that about A.D. 300 Woodchester had possessed a villa of at least sixty rooms, many of them floored with fine mosaics, the one in the main hall depicting the Orpheus legend. The workmanship as well as the size imply that Woodchester villa was larger and more imposing than the better known one at Chedworth; it may have been unequalled in Britain, and has been suggested as the country house of the Roman governor of Gloucester.

Those who do not insist on seeing the real thing may not have to wait until 1983. Two local experts in such matters, Bob Woodward and Brian Bull, are presently creating as exact a copy as possible of the Orpheus mosaic in disused Rowland Hill's Tabernacle in Wotton-under-Edge, aided by four months' on-the-spot research, careful colour photography, and the fact that much of the variously coloured stone used in the original came from local sources. A lot of work will have been done before the projected opening day in spring 1976; the pieces of stone have to be matched and shaped exactly, all one and a half million of them.

Visitors to Woodchester might also like to glance at one of the best of the surviving round houses—it is at the southern end of the village—that were built in the wool areas from about 1600. Though much has been written about the famous trade, there seems some uncertainty about the original purpose of these round houses. Some authorities suggest that they were for drying either the spun wool or the finished cloth, others that teasels, used to raise the nap on the cloth before shearing, were dried in them preparatory to use. It is not improbable that they were used for varied purposes, for they were built with slatted floors to allow easy draught and had smoke vents for when heating was needed. Woodchester's example is a pleasantly plump, round-capped building with a medieval look about it.

From Woodchester a lane leads up to Selsley Common and the B 4066 from Stroud to Dursley. For much of its route it keeps close to the rim of the ridge and so suggests an early origin; it could have been the Welsh Way recorded hereabouts in the eighth century. Three long barrows are poised above the drop to the Vale. That on Selsley Common had its central portion investigated so carelessly that it looks more like two round barrows (and is locally known as 'The Toots', the Anglo-Saxon word for a look-out place). Next comes Nympsfield Long Barrow, just where the ridge bulges into a lofty spur with an almost precipitous drop to it. Then one of Cotswold's best known of Neolithic masterpieces, Hetty Pegler's Tump, a mile to the south. Even to the least archaeologically-inclined passer-by each is worth a pause—if only for the view. The Edge here is at its steepest and through the tree tops can be seen the lowland reaching out to the Severn estuary looking like an elongated, sinuous lake under the Forest of Dean. Nympsfield's barrow is currently being attended to by experts. The forlorn double row of large stones is being supplemented by dry-stone walling on the ancient pattern to return the burial chambers to their original completeness. With a few decades' weathering the barrow may begin to look a little nearer its appearance when the Anglo-Saxons named it 'shrine-field', and they were so impressed by its antiquity that they borrowed the first syllable from the Celtic.

Nympsfield village, only just below the crest, is an open little place. The thirsty will speedily notice its Rose and Crown, a good-looking house of Stuart age which, if built as an inn, suggests that there was once considerable traffic through the village. Otherwise Nympsfield looks so quiet that one would guess little has happened there since Sir George Huntley, the lord of the manor in 1620, forced his ideas of enclosure upon his tenants in order to make of the village land a park stocked with 'deer, conies, hog, sheep and horses', after which the locals, 'out of a rurall reluctation against such enclosures', judged it fitting that Huntley died shortly afterwards from a fall from his horse.

In the past it was accepted that ownership of land gave very considerable rights. Our more egalitarian age might think it excessive that the wife of an owner of a portion of Cotswold Edge near Uley should thereby be remembered in perpetuity. But, beyond naming her 'tump', Hetty Pegler's claim to fame is unrecorded. The visitor, it seems, can indulge his fancies, making Hetty a local beauty who graced her Tump on innocent al fresco parties, or a harassed wife-and-mother who sought quiet there when the children and/or the servants were too much for her, or a cuckolding hussy who defiantly met her lover on the elevated spot.

The visitor will probably find it harder to indulge his imagination when entering Hetty Pegler's Tump (key at the cottage a half-mile southwest, and torches recommended). Though first investigated in 1821 and again in 1854, it remains far more nearly complete than most Cotswold long barrows. (In fact two of the five burial chambers have been sealed off and there has been some repair work to the walls.) All told, the remains of some twenty-five New Stone-agers have been discovered, only one, as is usual, having 'retained very much its original position—the sitting or rather squatting—the head having fallen forward in decay'. Also discovered were 'some pieces of coarse earthenware and charcoal ... and a small vessel which cannot now be found'—how tantalising nineteenth-century investigators can be! An additional, later burial accompanied by three Roman coins was also discovered in the earth covering; the barrow had, it seems, remained a hallowed place through three millennia.

For today's visitor it is still impressive. The great slabs of stone inter-packed with dry-stone walling to form the internal walls tell of considerable collective effort. The bulk of the mound, even after 5,000 years of weathering, adds to that impression. But beyond the vaguest outline we can only guess how its builders fared, what they made of life, what they believed in. We may glance around, merely curious about a place that was for them wrapped in secrecy and sacredness, or shudder at the thought of what has been discovered there, or feel uneasily intruding. We can know nothing.

Where, a half-mile to the south, the road curves to find a way down to Uley village, we may repeat something of that experience, though in a more open situation. For the road is avoiding the ramparts of Uley Bury fort. Still impressive they frame the flat and roughly rectangular end of the ridge, adding on three sides to the protection of the sharp fall of the hillside which looks even sharper when seen through the tall, slim trunks of the quiet beeches. The massive banks and the siting—the fort would even now prove awkward to attack on foot—tell that the Iron-agers lived in an uneasy world ... though whether tribes-people or captured slaves undertook the immense toil of fashioning the two-mile-long double defences, we cannot be sure. We can, however, hazard that at times some of the occupants glanced beyond their immediate surroundings and noticed the view: to the east the Edge, here with its combes and spurs thick with trees, curving round the hollow in which Uley lies; to the south the Edge sweeping on through more woods to the great thrust of Stinchcombe Hill; to the west, beyond the sudden lump of Cam Long Down—the devil's handiwork, legend says—the lowland reaching out to the Severn. The Iron-agers would not have known the field pattern; but the hills were theirs, too.

Uley Bury fort must end a route used in the Iron Age if not earlier. It is probable that a Neolithic route led from about Nympsfield Long Barrow in a curve through southeast to southwest, approximately the line taken by the ridge-following lane that, a mile south of Uley village, becomes the B 4058 and part of an 'RAC Scenic Route' to Wotton-under-Edge. Wotton is certainly worth a visit, but to keep rigidly to prehistory hereabouts would be to miss two other places of more than usual interest.

Uley, once famous for its blue cloth, is a long street of varied houses; it is not everywhere that has its Post Office in a Stuart setting. At its upper end, about a small green, stand several prim, flat-fronted houses of the 1700s, and the Old Crown Inn which is older. Here a lane, narrow and secretive, which leads eastwards is worth following, particularly on a Friday in June or July. It leads to Owlpen.

The setting is unforgettable. The Edge, thickly wooded, curves round a small combe, seeming almost to shut it off from the twentieth-century world. A manorhouse of about 1470 forms the main part of the present building; an east wing was added in 1616, and some windows enlarged in 1720, very early Georgian. And during its life Owlpen manorhouse has acquired the necessary outbuildings: a barn perhaps as old as the original house, a corn mill of about 1700 and, a half-century or so older, what is called the Court House but also probably served as a summer-house in which Stuart ladies and gentlemen sat and chatted and admired the view without the risk that strong sunlight or a sudden shower might damage their fine and costly silks. But the actual dates are of little moment at Owlpen. All—manorhouse, outbuildings, and the church (truly Victorian imitating medieval but that is indiscernible through the evergreens), against a backdrop of more woods—all are in stone and so of a piece. There is nowhere quite like Owlpen in the Cotswolds or, indeed, anywhere else.

If the visitor has chosen one of the few Fridays when the house is opened to the public, he will see with pleasure that internally Owlpen is also delightful. The Great Chamber—the core of the house in Tudor and earlier times—still has its fireplace of about 1540, and its ceiling, too, and even the door and the door-hinges; it has, also, a rarity in the painted cloth wall-hanging of Charles II's time. Much of the rest of the house is as its Stuart and early Georgian owners made it . . . but it does not look like a show-place arranged for visitors. Owlpen gives the impression of being still what it has been for over four centuries, a setting for living.

However one travels, from Uley to Wotton is an up-and-down business, the lanes so climb and dive about a landscape cut with hidden combes. A slightly indirect route may appeal to those who recall the significance of North Nibley. It once belonged to the Berkeleys and so much of its story is included in that classic of five centuries of family history, John Smyth's *Lives of the Berkeleys*—and if that title suggests that during his stewardship of the 'hundred and liberty of Berkeley' from 1597 to 1640, Smyth was a sycophantic recorder of noble doings, the reader will find that he had few illusions about his master's ancestors and so has left to us a work of exceptional historical interest and unusual perception. North Nibley—or, to be precise, Nibley Green a half-mile beyond the church—came into history during that nasty period known euphemistically as the Wars of the Roses. North Nibley's contribution turned out to be 'the last private battle fought in England'.

Those wishing for details will find them in Smyth's book or more readily in E. S. Lindley's *Wotton-under-Edge*. For the present it is enough to recall that the trouble arose, as so often happened, from a marriage settlement: a Berkeley heiress had married a Beauchamp earl of Warwick and in the absence abroad of the Berkeley heir-male, her husband determined to seize the entire Berkeley possessions. Not unnaturally, Berkeley on his return opposed such an idea . . . and through the next half-dozen generations and one hundred and fifty years the struggle persisted, one side or the other seizing lands and establishments and demonstrating their 'rights' over their tenants by 'collecting rents by force, and destroying villages and devastating the countryside'. When, during the York–Lancaster struggle for the crown, the central government's attention was diverted elsewhere, open fighting broke out. By 1469 the second generation to the dispute, in the persons of Lord Lisle and Lord William Berkeley, could command forces at over a thousand apiece—according to Smyth who had his information from elderly grandsons of eye-witnesses. Their meeting at North Nibley was brief. Lord Berkeley, says Smyth, 'sent up ... the first shower of his arrows, that one Black Will (so called) shot the Lord Lisle as his beaver [visor] was up'. With the opposing leader so speedily dealt with, the Berkeleys celebrated by regaining nearby Wotton manor-house so vigorously that Lady Lisle, in residence and expecting, had a miscarriage, thereby 'extinguishing all hope of continuance of the [rival] male line' ... until within a few years relations by marriage took over the quarrel and kept it going into the 1600s when it was at last settled by compensation valued, Smyth reckoned, at more than a quarter of the value of the Berkeley possessions.

North Nibley appears to have long forgotten its unhappy story. It is a quiet place with some good houses along its street, several of them with plastering over the stone as is customary in this part of Cotswold. In the church there is only one link with North Nibley's moment in history: the kneeling, black-dressed effigy of Grace Smyth 'for the space of Twelve Yeares and 35 Dayes the wife of John Smyth, Gent'. Such meticulous recording of the length of her married life suggests that she may have found being wife to the author of the *Lives of the Berkeleys* a tedious business; and one wonders what to make of the inscription's final phrase about 'her voluntary leavinge this life the IXth Day of Nov. 1609'.

North Nibley has no monument to another of its former residents, Mary Heath, whose story chance has preserved. It is not untypical of the early seventeenth century when each village had to provide for its own poor. Mary was born in nearby Stinchcombe but when about twenty she was living with her mother in North Nibley. She had also become pregnant and, being unmarried, threatened to burden the village with an extra, unwanted inhabitant. Therefore she left either 'of her own accord or by the means of the Nibley men'. A few weeks later she had returned although her mother had been 'forewarned by Nibley men before and since her coming again not to receive her any more'. After staying with her mother 'guestwise for some short time', she left for Alkington 'where she was whipped for begging and sent from thence by warrant to her place of birth, being Stinchcombe'. There a few weeks later her baby was born ... to become immediately the cause of a wrangle about which parish—Nibley, Stinchcombe or Alkington—had to support mother and child. Legal uncertainties provided opportunities for passing on responsibility. The warrant by which Alkington had deported the girl had not been signed by the local clergyman and was therefore questionable; the law was unsure 'whether a woman within a month of her delivery may be sent to her place of birth as a rogue'. As the birthplace of both Mary and her child—but not presumably of the father—Stinchcombe tried to avoid responsibility by petitioning the quarter sessions, but the three J.P.s there ordered to settle the matter could find nowhere else to burden. A not uncommon story in those days ... and perhaps the people of North Nibley had other worries. Not long before, the villagers had themselves built a row of almshouses, providing the stone, timber, thatch, and the wagons to cart them. The 'six distinct habitations with chimnies in them' they produced had, however, given rise to another legal dispute. The almshouses had been built on church land; but the jury decided to let the houses stand 'in regard to the great numbers of poor people there, destitute of habitation, living for the most part from relief and alms of the inhabitants'. At about the same time the churchwardens, no doubt anxious over the declining wool-cloth trade and the diminishing opportunities for work for the young, took a census of the children who 'are fit to be bound apprentice to other men, and that now live pilfering and stealing in every corner'. The churchwardens found fifty-three such 'poor children'. A glance about North Nibley now suggests that that figure must have been something like half the child population of the time. All told, it is not surprising that when, a few years later, Charles I's government required a 'forced loan' of £8 6s. od. of the Nibley householders, they only paid up, under protest, on the fifth demand.

If North Nibley can show nothing of its battle or its almshouses, it has its monument; indeed the visitor can hardly miss the ponderous tower standing high on the Edge immediately above the village. But, again, North Nibley seems unlucky. The tower was 'Erected A.D. 1866 in grateful remembrance of William Tyndale, translator of the English Bible ... He suffered martyrdom at Vilvorde in Flanders on 6th October, 1536'; but someone, somewhere, has slipped up. According to J. F. Mozley's careful biography,

William Tyndale, the martyr's namesake who lived in North Nibley about 1500 was unrelated to the 'translator of the English Bible' of whose birth-place we know only that it was 'on the borders of Wales'.

A winding road skirting the spurs of the escarpment leads to Wotton-under-Edge. Woods cling to the slopes; they must have reached out across the lowland when, at least a century and a half before the Conquest, the Saxons established their 'farmstead in the wood', Wood-ton. Though the setting is more dramatic than Burford's and its church-tower is as fine as Campden's, visitors who expect every Cotswold town to resemble those photogenic gems may be disappointed in Wotton. The local custom of plastering the stone-built houses and of colouring the plaster in varying creams and greys and buffs—and of picking out door-surrounds and dripstones in black, too—detracts from the unity which unplastered stone gives to many a Cotswold town. And it must be added, the church has not benefited from the architectural convictions of two Victorian vicars, the first of whom remodelled the thirteenth-century nave according to his notions of Gothic Revival, and the second of whom determined to improve on such an improvement. The result is a large but unappealing building, and even its collection of monuments, mainly eighteenth-century and many featuring urns, are stuck up on the walls like items in an inefficient museum (and many are now dusty, chipped and faded while the most human of them is hidden by the organ). The main interest for visitors is the fine brass to Thomas, Lord Berkeley and his wife Margaret, the couple who by being so inept as to produce only a daughter—the Elizabeth Berkeley who married into the Beauchamps—unwittingly started the prolonged and often violent dispute which gave North Nibley its claim to fame.

Such first impressions are, however, unjust to Wotton. It is a town to get to know. If the visitor hesitates to walk around holding Verey's summary of all the noteworthy buildings—and he lists over thirty of them varying from the ancient Ram Inn to Lady Berkeley's Grammar School, founded in 1384, rebuilt in 1726—he should before arrival get hold of E. S. Lindley's *Wotton-under-Edge: Men and Affairs of a Cotswold Town.* The product of much research and understanding, it tells of all that has gone into the making of one of the most interesting of little towns from the struggles of the Berkeleys and the Beauchamps to the struggles of the leading townspeople, circa 1860, to replace with an adequate drainage system the 'vast number of the privies [which] empty themselves into open channels in the streets' and so put an end to the visitations of cholera. It tells of the weavers' rioting in the 1820s as the cloth trade began to leave the neighbourhood and of how the organ on which Handel played comes to be in the church. It tells of Stephen Hopkins who sailed with the Pilgrim Fathers on the *Mayflower*, and of Moore Adey who befriended Oscar Wilde, spent years searching for imaginary treasure in his Under-the-Hill House, and died in a mental hospital in 1945, the last descendant of one of the clothier families who had in the 1600s and 1700s brought prosperity to the town. Mr Lindley tells the fascinating and very human story that lies within the town the visitors see.

THIRTEEN

Towards another Beginning

The fate of Roman roads is a puzzling matter. One would have expected that even during the period of Anglo-Saxon colonisation such efficient routes would have remained in sufficient use to have ensured their survival. Recent historical research has shed quite a lot of light on what were formerly dismissed as the Dark Ages. We now know that within a few generations the Angles and Saxons and Jutes were outgrowing the self-sufficiency of the settlements they had won from Briton, marsh and forest, and had established markets and business on a comparatively wide scale by contemporary standards. Overseas trade was being developed, too, and English churchmen were taking a large part in Christianising the occupants of their ancestral German lands, while Anglo-Saxon books, embroidery and jewellery were prized even in more civilised southern Europe. Such developments entailed considerable travelling and would have ensured that the Roman roads survived in usable condition ... at least, so one would suppose. That some stretches did survive—and are still in use—emphasises the oddity that other stretches, though they must even after a generation or so of neglect have made for easier going than unpaved tracks, became so little used that they have disappeared—as was noticed earlier in connexion with the Cotswold-crossing Ryknild Street.

The great Foss Way is another case in point. After nearly 2,000 years it still carves its line across the easterly slopes of Cotswold linking Moreton-in-Marsh, Stow, Northleach and Cirencester ... and then, though Bath became a place of some importance to the Anglo-Saxons, the Foss Way, the obvious route to it, became side-tracked. (It is from southwest of Cirencester still a dozen miles of wide green track, quiet and easy-going for the walker after Kemble airfield has been avoided. On the way the observant may catch sight of the Roman *agger*, the raised portions crossing low-lying stretches, and investigation has shown that much of the original underlies the earth and the shaggy growth of the past fifteen hundred years.) The modern route, the A 433, goes wandering off through Tetbury, an important place in early medieval times, before reaching the Jurassic Way a couple of miles south of Nan Tow's Tump.

Curiously, a very minor route of supposed Roman usage and in part duplicating the Foss Way seems to have fared better; at least, its course has remained in constant use. It is the lane which branches off the A 419 rather more than two miles west of Cirencester to go through the villages of Coates, Tarlton and Rodmarton, before climbing gently to reach the prehistoric Way as it curves to avoid the combe in which Avening lies.

In his authoritative *Roman Roads in Britain,* I. D. Margary includes this route though he confesses that it is 'not convincing in directness, continuity, or appearance', and on the outskirts of Rodmarton it passes the site of a Roman villa. Though querying Margary is scarcely to be thought of, one cannot help wondering if the Romans did not again take over an earlier route; after all, with the Foss Way less than two miles away there would seem little point in deliberately making a very secondary road hereabouts and the original builder of the villa was unlikely to have chosen an almost inaccessible site.

Whatever we may assume about this way's origin, it leads through an undramatic country of cornfields and woods, and passes two villages which are in different ways as telling as many that are more featured in the books. Coates, the more northerly, attracts visitors knowledgeable in canals and railways; both the Thames–Severn canal and the Brunel-built railway which put it out of business enter noteworthy tunnels in Coates parish. The canal tunnel is also visited by picnic parties, for the now-dry canal, a deep cleft filled with beeches, is an ideal playground for the children while their parents call at the Tunnel House, a surprisingly large and boldly bayed inn to have been built for the bargees. Below it, the tunnel entrance, once an architectural feature, has a notice on its decaying dignity: 'Danger: Falling Masonry'. A mile to the southeast, near the Iron Age camp in Trewsbury Park, was until recently another attraction; but the statue of Old Father Thames—or was he Neptune reclining at ease?—which probably graced the original Crystal Palace and was placed at Trewsbury to mark the first infant trickle of the Thames, has been so damaged that it has been moved to St John's lock, Lechlade. It is unlikely that the replacing and vandal-proof mass of granite will acquire the same appeal. The visitor to Coates, however, need not leave without contemplating another piece of sculpture far older than Old Father Thames and in a far stranger context.

It is to be found on the tower of Coates church. The church itself, more gracefully proportioned and internally more restful than many reckoned tourists' 'musts', was built mainly during the century in which the inspired Early English was developing into the graceful 'Decorated'. The tower was added about 1360—that is, within a decade or so of the first hideous visitation of the Black Death, and at a time when there can have been little thought of church-building. And, as a Latin inscription on the tower tells, it was built as a memorial; in English translation the inscription asks that prayers should be said 'for the souls of John Wiat, formerly Rector of Coates, and of Richard his brother, Rector of Rodmartin, and for the souls of their parents'. Yet even on a work built for such a purpose we meet another of those disturbing juxtapositions that we have noticed at Elkstone and Winchcombe and elsewhere. For only a yard or so away from the inscription is the carved and contemporary figure of the most hideous being imagined by the medieval mind: an anthropophagus, a cannibalistic creature here shown as little more than a face and a huge mouth into which it is stuffing a human victim clutched by greedy hands. Surely something more than vague chat about 'quaint medieval customs' or 'probable religious significance' is needed to explain such a monstrous piece of work in such a context. And is it coincidence that it was fashioned when the horrors of the Black Death were still fresh in everyone's mind?

Near Tarlton, a place of dark grey stone and dark thatch, is one of the Round Houses built about 1790 as dwellings for the canal maintenance men. Rodmarton is more distinguished. Most of its houses are work of the last century but carefully in the Cotswold tradition, befitting the village whose large, many-gabled manor-house was designed by Ernest Barnsley of the Cotswold revival group and fitted and furnished down to the last detail by his associates, Waals, Sidney Barnsley and Gimson. It is their most complete collective masterpiece, 'the final and perfect flowering of the Cotswold vernacular style,' Miss Edith Brill calls it, and adds that 'one cannot imagine that circumstances, architect, craftsmen, the desire and the means will ever come together again'. The house is rarely opened to the public; as in their lifetime, it seems that much of these fine craftsmen's work is not for most of us.

A mile west of Rodmarton and hidden by a great clump of trees stands Windmill Tump, a Neolithic long barrow far older than any windmill. Like Belas Knap it has a false entrance blocked by slabs at its eastern end; two burial chambers were entered from the north and south sides of the barrow. The entrances to these each had a lesser hole—a 'port-hole' to the archaeologists—cut into it just large enough to allow the passage of a body after the chamber had been all but sealed up. The actual chambers had been cut into the rock so that three steps down had been constructed; and the chambers were walled partly with stone slabs standing vertically, partly with layers of horizontal walling. It is probable that the roofs had been corbelled. The barrow, now closed, was excavated in 1863 and again in 1939. The remains of thirteen bodies 'apparently of both sexes and all ages ... in great confusion' were found in the north chamber. Bafflingly some bone fragments showed evidence of burning, but not sufficient to assert cremation. Also found were tools of flint and greenstone which had originated far from Rodmarton.

Near the long barrow the lane makes a sudden S-bend before continuing to reach the ancient Way above Cherington ... which would be unremarkable if a little over a mile to the north another parallel lane linking Tarlton with the prehistoric Way did not make a similar S-bend. Both lanes are crossing the line of the track which bypassed Chapman's Cross on the Cirencester–Minchinhampton road and which, as has been suggested, may have been used by the salt-carriers en route for Malmesbury. From the S-bend near Rodmarton long barrow the line of this minor but ancient route becomes both a lane and a parish boundary, an indication of its existence in Norman times. To turn aside from the lane up to the prehistoric Way will, therefore, be to follow another old route, perhaps not quite so ancient; and it will call at Tetbury. On the way there is the Trouble House, long, orange-painted and claiming seventeenth-century origin. Once the Wagon and Horses, it is said to owe its change of name to two successive innkeepers who decided to refurbish the place, then derelict, each of whom, becoming depressed at the cost, killed himself—the first by hanging, the second by drowning. Within a few years the house witnessed trouble of another kind: the local agricultural labourers, angered at the risk to their employment by the arrival of new farming machinery, destroyed an example outside the inn. Rioting resulted, the military were called in, there were several arrests, and some of the labourers were transported. All this is shown pictorially on the sign-board, and in more detail in the bar. Though on a main road, the Trouble House has remained a 'local' in atmosphere rather than acquire questionable charms for the benefit of motoring passers-by.

Formerly books on the Cotswolds rarely accorded to Tetbury the space lavished on Campden or Bibury, while its photographically-inclined visitors tended to direct their lenses only on its chubby-columned Market House or on The Chipping, a street leading from the former market-place so steep that it breaks into steps and so provides a touch of olde worlde quaintness. More recently Tetbury has been more than glanced at. Indeed it is reported as determinedly becoming a tourist attraction ... which means that its inns from the days when Tetbury was a recognised stopping-place for the stage-coaches have been modernised internally, cafés have taken over the ground floors of some former houses, and the Antiques signs have gone up (making some of us wonder, again, at the foresight which enabled our furniture-making, potting, and knick-knack-devising ancestors to produce such quantities of their handiwork as to keep up with today's increasing demand). Tetbury is still, however, not overdone. Its centre, mainly a mixture of seventeenth-century gabled and eighteenth-century flat-fronted—and mostly in the local creamy-grey stone—is still largely that of a town which had thrived on marketing wool and cloth. Business declined early in the 1800s when, despite quite a lot of local unemployment, it contrived to keep up appearances until rather belatedly (and, as it happened, briefly) the railway reached it and still more recently it attracted some not obtrusive light industries.

The town seems to be doing quite well as a tourist centre. It has an attractive openness from the little greens which are dotted about the place, but if, recalling Fairford or Campden, some hints of the medieval are expected ...

Tetbury once had a castle but little more than the traces of its earthen banks are to be seen. It also had an early priory but any portions that remain are hidden in private gardens. And Tetbury church is an architect's production of 1791. In some ways it is more than remarkable. The huge windows, owing much to the Gothic, are amazing in their size, and the columns reaching to the lofty, vaulted roof are incredibly slim (and are made of wood and iron). There are, it must be admitted, dignity and spaciousness. And yet much is lacking. A few monuments from the earlier church are set high on the wall so that they are difficult to read, two effigies, of local workmanship and Elizabethan date, are tucked away in a side passage as if Tetbury is ashamed of them. And, above all, the baffling entry by which the visitor is met not by a comprehensive view of the building as a whole but by a blank wall through which doors give on to the individual pews, and the pews themselves so high walled that only heads are visible when the audience sits.... And the word 'audience' is not inappropriate. This is, one feels, not a church where the local people congregated to worship, but where they were expected to sit and listen—and in the 1780s probably to hour-long sermons. It has no hint of a place which has grown with the changing needs of its parishioners. It has, rather, been imposed on them by its architect.

And yet all that is of its time and place. If the visitor to Tetbury thinks in terms of the more celebrated and photogenic Cotswold tourist attractions, he may be disappointed. Tetbury is, like Wotton-under-Edge and Blockley, a genuine place, the product more of its people and its history than, as yet, of restorers, preservers, and antiquators.

Which is perhaps why that forthright travelling critic, old Cobbett, liked Tetbury and on a 'Rural Ride' of 1826 considered it 'a very pretty town' with 'a beautiful ancient church'. (The church was the present one, then not forty years old, but even now one hesitates to argue with Cobbett.) His appreciation, however, may have arisen in part from his delight in the 'large flocks of goldfinches feeding on the thistle-seed on the roadside' or from self-satisfaction at the outcome of an incident on the way:

> Just before I got into Tutbury [sic] I was met by a good many people, some running and some walking fast, one of the first of whom asked me if I had met an 'old man' some distance back. I asked what sort of a man: 'A poor man.' 'I don't recollect, indeed; but what are you all pursuing him for?' 'He has been *stealing*.' 'What has he been stealing?' 'Cabbages.' 'Where?' 'Out of Mr Glover, the hatter's, garden.' 'What! Do you call that *stealing*: and would you punish a man, a poor man, and, therefore, in all likelihood, a hungry man too, and moreover an old man? Do you set up a hue-and-cry after, and would you punish, such a man for taking a few cabbages, when the Holy Bible, which, I dare say, you profess to believe in....

How old Cobbett, ever the champion of the under-dog, must have enjoyed his own indignation, and how satisfied he must have been when, after leaving the gathering, he looked back and saw that 'the pursuers went more slowly'.

Before continuing southwestwards, a glance at Beverstone west along the A 4135 and the only castle remaining on Cotswold. It seems a little odd that an area so economically important for so long should not have attracted more permanent castles than those which occupied the now vacant mottes at Brimpsfield and Miserden; it seems even odder that the only surviving castle of note should have been sited at Beverstone. The fieldscape spreads about it level, quiet and almost featureless; one would have thought that one of Cotswold's sharper hills would have offered a more defensible site. Perhaps the clue to the choice is to be found in the stronghold thereabouts which was held during the decades before the Conquest by the powerful Godwin family, one of whose sons was to become King Harold. It was the Godwins' base during their quarrel with Edward the Confessor over his liking for Norman advisers; when fortune went briefly against them and Godwin and three of his four sons were outlawed, Beverstone was seized by the king. No record survives of the appearance of the Godwin stronghold, or what structure was raised by Roger de Berkeley to whom the Conqueror granted the manor, for his creation was destroyed by Stephen. The present building, standing in pleasant gardens and not opened to the public, was begun in 1225. It appears to have consisted of a rectangular courtyard protected by a tower at each corner; most of two of the towers and part of the wall linking them are visible through the trees. It was enlarged and a gatehouse added—the remains of which can be seen from the lane to the church—about 1360 when, as Leland tells, 'after Poyters Lord Berkele buildid the Castell of Beverstane thoroughly, a Pile at that time very preaty', another reminder that ransoms could make feudal warfare a profitable business. His lordship apparently built more comfortable accommodation in the courtyard, much of which remains, though it must have suffered when in 1644 the castle was besieged by the Parliamentarians (it had by then been sold to Sir Michael Hicks who added some further rooms). The castle surrendered easily, however, because its Royalist commander, Colonel Oglethorpe, happened at the time to be away visiting a young lady at a nearby farm.

In Beverstone church, round behind the castle, is work older than any in the castle: a piece of sculpture showing the Resurrection and probably of Saxon workmanship on the south wall of the tower. Even through nine centuries of weathering and some deliberate damage, the graceful pose shows that the first English produced artists in stone. Inside the church there are hints of the same feeling though of later date in the arcade of about 1220, perhaps from a rebuilding by the Berkeley builder of the castle. The capitals are not of the usual Norman shapes, often somewhat rigid, but have gentle looping motifs. This church has other things to show, including a fifteenth-century screen which once acted as a support for a Victorian rector's climbing roses; a stone pulpit, nicely carved, of about 1500; and, externally, in the wall of the Berkeley chapel four stone coffin covers, probably of the thirteenth century. It seems that when the Lord Berkeley who refashioned the castle out of his winnings at Poitiers added a family chapel to the nearby church, he did not scruple to use whatever suitable stone was at hand. Perhaps it is just that no Berkeley monument now remains there.

Southwestwards from Tetbury the road leads through a quiet countryside. Off the road to the south lies Westonbirt village, a little place of gabled and precise cottages built in the 1860s, along a lane for the owner of the great house a 'nineteenth-century Elizabethan-style palace' and long a girls' school. Visitors hereabouts are more attracted to the famous Arboretum on the other side of the main road. Now in the care of the Forestry Commission, it has been claimed as one of the finest collections of trees in Europe. A visit at any season of the year is amazing and colourful, even in winter—for there are many, many evergreens. Every imaginable variation on the idea of a tree is there, in every shade of foliage, every pattern of branch and twig, every shape of leaf and fashioning of bark and trunk.

Didmarton, the last village before reaching the main road that has taken over the ancient Way, groups its houses, many of them colour-washed, along the curving road and down side streets. It looks too innocent a place to have a name that remembers a boundary between rival kingdoms. In the guide-books it is credited with three churches. One, Victorian in Early English style, stands off the road; another, truly that of the village of Oldbury-on-the-Hill now reduced to a single farm of Stuart date, rises across the cornfields all but forgotten; the third, at the east end of the village, was until recently an attraction for the ecclesiologist. Only five years ago, Verey in his *Buildings of Gloucestershire* could describe it as 'a remarkable example of a medieval church in its eighteenth-century condition', and praise the survival of its two-decker pulpit, from under the sounding board of which the Georgian vicar thundered or remonstrated for an hour or so each Sunday morning and evening, and the trim, contemporary box-pews in which the congregation listened or dozed, and the wainscoting, all painted in delicate green. They are still there—just. Some of the wood has been pulled from the damp and blotched walls, the pulpit leans away from the wall, and the wooden stairs to the little bell-turret cum-clock-tower have a notice warning of danger overhead. It seems Didmarton is uncertain whether or not to try to preserve it and, since the church has not the obvious appeal of the truly ancient nor the village much likelihood of becoming a 'must' for tourists, few of the thousands who daily pass along the road are inclined to help. Now, neither a survival nor a ruin, the church is in that stage of disintegration which is most truly pathetic. It looks too dejected to appeal, but it is not yet sufficiently ruined to attract those who might sentimentalise it.

Southwest of Didmarton the road picks up the A 46, there taking the ancient Way through the hamlet of Dunkirk with, at Petty France, opportunity for Jane Austen fans to renew acquaintance with Catherine Morland, surely the most appealingly naïve of heroines. Callers at the present hotel can look across the road to the house which was the hotel of 1798 (then only ten years old) where she found 'nothing to be done but to eat without being hungry'—but Catherine was hardly in the mood to judge fairly. She was impetuously longing for the imagined horrors of Northanger Abbey, preparatory to finding—so Miss Austen assures us—a more restful satisfaction in the arms of Henry Tilney.

From hereabouts until Bath, the Way was improved by the Romans; I. D. Margary in his *Roman Roads in Britain* points to stretches of embankment and lengths of *agger* of Roman origin, helping the road to take easily the gentle rises and falls while an expansive fieldscape reaches out eastwards and the rim of the escarpment hides the fall to the west. Even the M 4 hardly intrudes. It is here in a cutting and not until the driver is actually negotiating the roundabout can the traffic below be seen, as ever streaming from somewhere to somewhere else as if the land through which it is passing is of no account. How aggressively purposeful a motorway looks when viewed from above and when we have time to wander;

and how quickly we shed our detachment and resume our very twentieth-century habits when we, too, need a quick route. And, whether the cutting was necessary to avoid too steep a gradient or intended to prevent too much intrusion into the landscape, we may be grateful that, on Cotswold at least, the planners restrained themselves ... which is, perhaps, some slight compensation for the mixed effects the car has had upon Cotswold and England generally. It has, of course, brought many visitors who would otherwise have known little or nothing of what Cotswold has to show; indeed, without tourism and its allies, the retired and the locally commuting, much of what we now admire would have fallen into sorry ruin or gone altogether. It has brought, too, irreversible changes to the ways of living of many a Cotsaller, as those whose memories reach back sixty or more years can recall and those who are younger will find in Edith Brill's delightful, sympathetic but slightly wistful *Life and Traditions on the Cotswolds*. And, latterly, it has brought increasing awareness of the need to keep as much as possible of all that has gone into the making of the present.

The sight of the motorway brings thoughts of leaving. For those who still have a little longer there is, south of the motorway, the last stretch of the much older Way over Lansdown Hill to Bath. For the walker there are a few more miles of path of ancient origin, keeping close to the Edge and so visiting Edward IV's pre-Tewkesbury camping-place, the fine Iron Age fort above Little Sodbury. Or there is the lane below the Edge, as ever a twisting, up-and-down village-linking route. It leads to Dyrham, a fitting place to end at.

Hawkesbury should be included, but not only rather workaday and high-standing Hawkesbury Upton. A lane twists down through woods and past old quarries to reveal suddenly what is left of the earlier Hawkesbury. In one of the quietest of combes stands the medieval church between the Old Rectory and the decaying remains of a farmhouse, a row of once-dependent cottages and the once-necessary farm-buildings. Architecturally the church spans from the thirteenth century to the early sixteenth; but more striking in the lonely situation is its dignity—there are few churches, even on Cotswold, to rival it. Elsewhere, in a photogenic village perhaps or gracing the streets of a little town, tourists would be sure not to pass it by. But in that out-of-the-way combe it is possible to sit on the little fragment of green where still the former village's water-supply bubbles, or on the churchyard wall, for a summer half-hour without any company other than the cattle in the adjoining fields, the finches fluttering about the may bushes and the swallows sweeping in and out of the vacant farm windows.

Horton a mile and a half to the south attracts more visitors. Horton Court, opened to the public on summer Wednesdays and Saturdays, is architecturally the most unexpected of mixtures. To one side is a Norman hall—Norman work outside a church or castle is a rarity anywhere—which seems to have served as a priest's house, was divided into an upper chapel and a lower living room early in the eighteenth century, became for a while a school, and in 1884 was returned as nearly as possible to its original condition. The main House was built in 1521 for William Knight, bishop of Bath and Wells in Henry VIII's time who among his other duties went in 1527 to Rome in an attempt to speed up the annulment of Henry's marriage to Catherine of Aragon. The trip was unwittingly to hasten the Reformation in England and to add to Horton House. Rome had just suffered a sack from the unpaid and mutinous troops of the Emperor Charles V, nephew to Queen Catherine; and the Pope, Clement VII, was virtually a prisoner. On his way across France Knight contacted Wolsey, who was trying to enlist French support against the Emperor and also, knowing something of Henry's wish to set aside Catherine, was sounding out the possibilities for a politically advantageous match between Henry and a sister of Francis of France. Knight told Wolsey, however, of Henry's real desires, and as the Boleyns were among Wolsey's enemies the news cannot have pleased him. Wolsey tried to keep some control of a very tricky situation by calling for a council of cardinals to act in the Pope's name while His Holiness was imprisoned, but only four cardinals responded. Meanwhile, shortly after reaching Rome, Knight learnt that the Emperor had astutely released the Pope—and with the decision-making again nominally in papal hands, Wolsey's scheming dissolved. Knight was, at least initially, more successful. A considerable bribe to an influential papal adviser helped the Pope to agree to a commission being set up to consider Henry's case against Catherine . . . but as the Emperor was hostile to any move that could result in the annulment of his aunt's marriage and the Imperial troops were to remain uncomfortably close to Rome, the agreement proved worthless. Despite the ultimate futility of his mission, Knight seems to have retained an appreciation of Roman architectural fashions. The Ambulatory at Horton House, a kind of loggia built for Knight, hints of Italian inspiration; it is a more tangible outcome of his trip to Rome than he could bring back to his royal master.

Nearby Horton church looks much as it must have done in Knight's time. It had been remodelled in about 1520, from which time dates the good porch with its vaulted roof and its unusually jolly carved figures. The nave windows are of the same date though the arcade is older, as may be the corbel showing a man sticking out his tongue—not, we may hope, in disrespect for his surroundings. Near the door is an odd-looking tablet to Baron Carlo de Tuyll—odd-looking, that is, until one remembers the Art Nouveau movement of the early years of this century.

On through Little Sodbury below its Iron Age fort and Old Sodbury with some good houses, a church standing finely high, and a toll-house (now a restaurant) on what was the stage-coach route from Bristol to London. Then comes Dodington Park as rebuilt between 1796 and 1816, very impressively porticoed (though the purist may find hints of mixing the Roman and Greek versions of the Classical). Beside it stands the also-rebuilt church; both are in the park laid out a little earlier by the best-remembered creator of landscapes, 'Capability' Brown. Those who drop in on a summer afternoon may wonder how that master designer of 'natural' vistas as a setting for leisurely-living Georgian ladies and gentlemen would react to his achievement at Dodington becoming, at least for today's younger visitors, an adjunct to 'Adventureland' and 'the Carriage Museum' and the 'Narrow Gauge Railway'. Or would 'Capability' be more surprised to see that the children of even the humblest of us are far healthier and better-clothed than those of the poor of his day?

At Dyrham, our last stopping place, there are again the traditional neighbours: church and great house. They are older than Dodington's and in their quiet combe below the Edge feel more withdrawn from today's world. The visitor can wander and look more leisurely.

The house, Dyrham Park, is William-and-Mary, built in two goes by William Blathwayt. He must, one feels, have been an adaptable politician for he held office under the varying demands of Charles II, James II, William III, and Queen Anne. He was Secretary for War during William's struggles with France but, even so, found time to build Dyrham. In 1686 he had married Mary Wynter, heiress of Dyrham manor, and in 1692 he built a long, shallow building—what are now in effect the rooms looking on the garden. As political advancement brought opportunity and wealth, he added a few years later the front half of the house, designed carefully in keeping by William Talman, considered second only to Wren in contemporary architectural circles. The house has scarcely been touched since. Outside and in it is still essentially Blathwayt's house, even much of the internal decoration, for it has remained in the family until recently. The visitor on a summer Wednesday, Thursday or Friday can wander round the major rooms and, if his imagination is up to it, feel something of the grace and ease which, at least to us, seems to surround eighteenth-century living.

Near by, the church recalls earlier owners of Dyrham. Though originally built about 1260, it is now mainly a remodelling of a century and a half later, probably undertaken by Sir Maurice Russel and his lady whose brass is on the church floor, but not always as noticeable as no doubt they would have wished. Good brasses have to be preserved these days and often a portion of the floor hides the monument to the last of the Russels from the casual visitor. Sir Maurice left only daughters, through one of whom the manor passed to the Dennis family who are remembered in the church only by a broken stone, discovered in a later restoration, ignominiously serving upside-down as paving and now given a place of slight note near the 'family' pew. The Dennises appear not to have prospered and in 1571 the manor was sold to Sir George Wynter. He must have been of a family that benefited from the wealth that could be won by the forceful opportunist in Tudor times, and his tomb in the church is one of the most elaborate on Cotswold—though when one looks into the workmanship one suspects that Wynter (assuming he ordered the tomb himself) was concerned more with making a striking first impression than with creating a work of art. Or perhaps at the time he was somewhat troubled by what his son John was up to. In 1571 John had sailed with Drake on the Spanish-America raid that was to be completed with the famous round trip—though John Wynter, commanding the little *Elizabeth,* became separated from the other vessels in the violent weather about the Horn and turned back. His return did not, however, exclude him from Philip of Spain's subsequent displeasure and, until Queen Elizabeth made up her mind about her policy towards Spain, John's position appears to have remained uncertain. When Sir George died, his property, including Dyrham, was held in trust for Sir John 'till he should have cleared himself of the charge of piracy'. It seems the charge was eventually dropped, for the Wynters remained in possession of Dyrham until the last of the line, the heiress Mary, married William Blathwayt. Mary's parents are remembered in a large tablet on the south wall of the church but, except for three younger sons who became rectors of Dyrham, the Blathwayts are unnoted there.

Much in all this is not untypical: the sequence of owners, the occasions when one here and there contributed to national matters and so earned a mention in history, the younger sons becoming rectors of the family living, the patchy traces they have left in the church. Dyrham House is now in the care and the possession of the National Trust—and that, too, is not untypical. Though a link with the wool that has made so much of Cotswold is missing, the rest of what is to be seen at Dyrham sums up in miniature much of what has happened in many a small village in England. It seems the right place to end at. It seems even more so when the visitor makes his way up to the main road that rests on the Roman improvement to the prehistoric Way. He will be passing close to where, fourteen hundred years ago, the West Saxon leaders 'Cuthine and Ceawlin fought against the Britons and killed three kings, Conmail, Condidan and Farinmail' and so made Cotswold part of their and our England.

For Further Reading

Those books to which special reference has been made have been mentioned in the appropriate places in the text. For those readers who would like to study in more detail some aspects of Cotswold, a few additional books may be helpful.

On prehistory, Glyn Daniel's *Prehistoric Chamber Tombs of England and Wales* (Cambridge University Press, 1950) covers the subject comprehensively, while *Gloucestershire Barrows* by H. O'Neill and L. V. Grinsell (Bristol and Gloucester Archaeological Society, 1960) is a more localised study. Both should be supplemented by reference to the more recent publications of the local Archaeological Society. For Roman sites, such as Chedworth and Cirencester, informative pamphlets are available for visitors.

For architecture generally, the most complete recent record is David Verey's *Gloucestershire: The Cotswolds* in the 'Buildings of England' series (Penguin, 1970). For churches, the earlier *Gloucestershire* by J. C. Cox (Methuen, 1949) is still of value.

For details about individual places and for local history it is necessary to refer to local books. These, having mostly been written several decades ago, vary considerably and particularly with the earlier (and sometimes more sentimental) ones the reader has to go warily. Some are classics of local history such as A. T. Playne's *Minchinhampton and Avening* (Gloucester, 1915), Mary Sturge Gretton's *Burford Past and Present* (Faber, reprinted 1945), and E. S. Lindley's *Wotton-under-Edge* (Museum Press, 1962). Others are more personal like Arthur Gibbs's *A Cotteswold Village* (Travellers' Library, 1929) and W. St Clair Baddeley's *A Cotteswold Shrine* (K. Paul, 1908). Most of these, long out of print, can be studied at local libraries (Stroud has a very good selection).

To these should be added the many pamphlets available in local churches and village shops. Though often slight in appearance, many are thoughtful, informative works—Taynton's and Painswick's are notable examples. The modest sheets in churches are often these days very good within their compass and draw visitors' attention to details that may be overlooked (though some noteworthy churches —e.g. Winchcombe and Buckland—have still to urge a knowledgeable resident to make up deficiencies). Also the local magazine *Cotswold Life* often includes much that outsiders will find interesting: residents' recollections, studies of individual places, and up-to-date accounts of discoveries and happenings.

Other items of local history have to be gathered from many sources. Place-names often give clues, sometimes unexpected, to ancient customs and land-uses, and A. H. Smith's four-volume *Place-Names of Gloucestershire* (Cambridge University Press, 1964) is a work of amazing and fascinating detail. As interesting though very different are two books containing much detailed matter not readily available to the general reader: *Gloucestershire Studies*, edited by H. P. R. Finberg (Leicester University Press, 1957) and W. B. Willcox's *Gloucestershire, a Study in Local Government* (Yale University Press, 1940). The former includes many transcripts and discussions of documents ranging from the early medieval to the eighteenth century; Willcox's book, concentrating mainly on the Stuart century, contains many illuminating accounts of local happenings.

On the special subject of the Wool Trade are Eileen Power's *The Wool Trade in English Mediaeval History* (Oxford University Press, 1941), providing the clearest general impression, while Peter J. Bowden's *The Wool Trade in Tudor and Stuart England* (Macmillan, 1962) and K. G. Ponting's *The Wool Trade Past and Present* (Columbine Press, 1961) bring the subject more up to date. For records of individual Cotswold mills, there is Jennifer Tann's *Gloucestershire Woollen Mills* (David and Charles, 1967) with a gazetteer of most mills surviving or departed.

For those interested in such matters as the geology of the region, its wild flowers, and the plans for its future, there are chapters in *The Cotswolds: a New Study*, edited by Charles and Alice Mary Hadfield (David and Charles, 1973), while readers inclining towards the rural ways of living of fifty and more years ago will find absorbing reading in Edith Brill's *Life and Traditions on the Cotswolds* (Dent, 1973).

Finally, it is pleasant to report that the early classic among county histories—and a book to which all writers on the region are at least in part indebted—Sir Robert Atkyns' *Ancient and Present State of*

Glostershire—which has been for two and a half centuries a rarity owing to the destruction by fire of nearly all the original copies, has been recently reprinted by E. P. Publishing Ltd., of Wakefield.

Index

Index